for George Vaill

who adds to Yale's
staying power every day —
with affectionate regard

George W. Pierson

Feb, 1973

THE MOVING AMERICAN

THE MOVING

I am a part of all that I have met;
Yet all experience is an arch wherethro'
Gleams that untravell'd world whose margin fades
Forever and forever when I move.

—TENNYSON, *Ulysses*

AMERICAN

George W. Pierson

ALFRED A. KNOPF
New York   1973

THIS IS A BORZOI BOOK
PUBLISHED BY ALFRED A. KNOPF, INC.

*Credit or acknowledgment for material reprinted by
permission will be found in the Notes section in the back
of the book.*

Library of Congress Cataloging in Publication Data
Pierson, George Wilson
The moving American.
Includes bibliographical references.
1. National characteristics, American.
2. Migration, Internal—United States. I. Title.
E169.1.P555   301.32'6'0973   72–2259
ISBN 0–394–47934–3

Manufactured in the United States of America
FIRST EDITION

for

L.V.P.

Contents

Contents

Foreword

To live is to move. We cannot live without moving. Some forms of life seems almost motionless, but with man movement has become essential and habitual. We take motion for granted.

On reflection, movement seems a good deal like breathing: another necessary, commonplace act. Who thinks about breathing? The air is all about us, odorless, tasteless, invisible yet indispensable. Awake or asleep, at play or at work, we inhale and exhale continuously, automatically. It is true we can feel the air, hear the wind, smell the smog, see the dust flying or the cloud-borne moisture. But most of us only start worrying when overexertion leaves us gasping, or emphysema sets in, or the hurricane warnings are up, or the air becomes almost too polluted to breathe. Ordinarily we give the complex, life-sustaining process of breathing hardly a thought. All we know is that we cannot stop.

And so in a way it is with moving. Movement is the precondition to action, the breath of social animation, the quite visible yet rarely noticed act that makes possible most of the performances of man. Though we can sometimes do something about it, we can't do without it. We take it for granted but can't stop. There seem to be almost as many reasons for moving as for living, including the penalty: if this spatial respiration is arrested, we begin to suffocate. A society without movement is like a man without breath: soon dead.

Moving has, and has had, it seems to me, some neglected and deeper meanings for modern society, and especially for us Americans. For if all men have the ability to move, and many the opportunity, not all have developed the proclivity—the desire and habit of movement—and few if any societies have absorbed spatial mobility as profoundly into their way of life as we have done in this country.

What movement has meant in the creation of American civilization, and in the formation of our national character, will be the theme of this book.

Acknowledgments

If movement seems to a degree inevitable, and a commonplace of human existence, it has not gone entirely unnoticed. In fact, many of the causes and consequences and characteristics of spatial mobility have been identified and described (some of them over and over again) by thoughtful observers ever since the record of human experiences was first captured in folklore and writing. Yet not until recently have scholars given systematic attention to the subject. It follows that most of the ideas here expressed have been anticipated—they may even seem commonplaces—yet perhaps never have they been brought together into a coherent and meaningful whole.

My debts, inevitably, are more than can possibly be acknowledged. Yet I should like to pay tribute to some seminal thinkers. First of all, I owe my interest in the subject, and much of the deeper illumination, to Alexis de Tocqueville and his masterful study of American democracy in the 1830's. Next, a fascination with Frederick Jackson Turner's "frontier hypothesis" but a growing dissatisfaction with his materialism—particularly with his concentration on "free land" as the explanation or causal factor in Americanization—drove me to try to disentangle the discordant bundle of his ideas and shift the focus toward the factor of spatial mobility instead. Meanwhile, the broad cultural-anthropological approach of Ralph H. Gabriel, as he propounded it in the Yale Graduate School, opened wider horizons. And a small and too little noticed book of essays by Dixon Ryan Fox on *Ideas in Motion* (1935) confirmed and strengthened my interest.

Since 1940 my readings have been diverse and miscellaneous. But I should like to acknowledge particularly my debts to the pertinent writings of E. G. Ravenstein, Pitirim Sorokin, Rudolf Heberle, André Maurois, and John Steinbeck—and to the discourse as well as the writings of Ellsworth Huntington, Frank Thistlethwaite, Franklin D. Scott, and Everett S. Lee—each to be quoted and cited repeatedly in this study.*

During three decades of preoccupation with other historical concerns and publications, my sideline monomania about motion has inevitably come to the attention of colleagues and friends; and the number who have aided me with comments and suggestions, books, articles, and illustrative clippings, is almost past counting. If I mention here only the great help of C. Vann Woodward, Guy S. Métraux, Bernard N. Schilling, and the members of my family, I trust I will not be misunderstood. My thanks go to all.

Finally, I should like to thank the editors and publishers of the *Yale Review*, the *Virginia Quarterly*, the *South Atlantic Quarterly*, the *American Historical Review*, and the *American Quarterly* for first giving light to some of the splinters or fragments of my theme, and now for granting me permission to re-use materials they first published. Each such use will be acknowledged in its proper place.

* This book was finished and in galleys before the announcement of the publication of Vance Packard's *Nation of Strangers*. Neither Mr. Packard nor I was aware of our common concerns, and I regret not being able to refer readers to appropriate passages in his striking interpretation.

THE MOVING AMERICAN

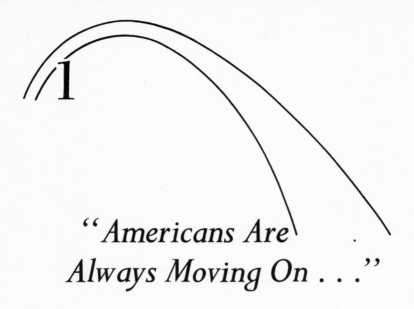

1

"Americans Are Always Moving On . . ."

A key to some peculiarities in our national character?

Each people has its secrets, and its figures of mystery. In recent years I have been led to think more and more about one of the most ubiquitous but enigmatic characters of American history. I call him "The Moving American." And the better one gets to know him the more secrets he seems to confide, the more answers to the great riddle of our national character.

What are Americans? Europeans at one remove? For almost four centuries those Old World peoples have been colonizing our shores, sending us their sons and daughters, their arts and sciences, their ideas and their prejudices. Yet for Europeans from the beginning, even as for the nonwestern world today, we remain the unknown quantity, the number one puzzle. The power of our economy is no longer a secret, but to our cousins of Europe it has seemed power in the hands of children. Where we boast a practical know-how, they have seen us as dollar-chasers, materialistic, money-crazy. We have taken pride in our democracy, but they notice chiefly its shortcomings —our color prejudices, our spectacular divorce rates, our lurid crimes of violence. To a Frenchman all Americans are wealthy; yet culturally we strike him as discouragingly middle-class, crude, and vulgar. In particular, we are said to lack the attributes of the highest civilization, for com-pared to the parent societies of Europe ours is and has been an unartistic, anti-intellectual, and astonishingly herd-minded nation. The optimism of America has been unmistakable, and our idealism and generosity are freely acknowledged. Yet in the absence of an appreciation of older cultures our very humanitarianism often seems too naïve, too aggressive. Most of all they find us volatile, ex-citable, unstable, and contradictory. It troubles the world to contemplate a society so mass-minded and conformist in thought yet so undisciplined in action—at the same time so practical but so visionary—so conservative in many ways yet so unpredictable in foreign policy. How deal with such a tangle of contradictions? The images have been sharp enough: Uncle Shylock and the Presbyterian preacher, Babbitt of Main Street and the Hollywood Goddess of Love, Chicago gangsters, Yankee uplifters, or bespectacled engineers; but how make of such types a family or a na-tional character? I suggest that the American character would be clearer if they would add to this rogues' gallery still another portrait: the portrait of The Moving American.

Think of the *Mayflower* or a prairie schooner, a pad-dlewheeler or a Stratocruiser. It doesn't matter. For we began as explorers, empire builders, pilgrims, and ref-ugees, and we have been moving, moving ever since. In fact we have been and are still today the most mobile people on the face of the earth. Foreign travelers have sensed it. Our census takers have proved it. Our poets have made it their song.

The first great tide flowed West. "Westward the Course of Empire takes its way," prophesied Bishop Berkeley. "Westward the Star of Empire takes its way," agreed John Quincy Adams. "They play at leap-frog with their lands," confessed a startled colonial observer.[1] The settlers, reported Governor Dunmore, "acquire no attachment to Place: But wandering about Seems engrafted in their Nature; and it is a weakness incident to it, that they should for ever imagine the Lands further off, are Still better than those upon which they have already Settled."[2] "Americans are the Western Pilgrims," wrote the perceiving Crèvecoeur—and from the Revolution to the Civil War all our pocket compasses continued to point West. "Go West, young man, and grow up with the country," advised Horace Greeley. "Ioway—that's where the tall corn grows." We are "a bivouac rather than a nation," trumpeted an observer in the 1860's, "a grand army moving from the Atlantic to the Pacific, and pitching tents by the way."[3] Still into the twentieth century—"America is west and the wind blowing," sings Archibald MacLeish.

But if you would really like to remind a European, read him the opening lines of the epic that Stephen Vincent Benét began but unfortunately did not live to finish. Symbolically he called it "Western Star":

> Americans are always moving on.
> It's an old Spanish custom gone astray,
> A sort of English fever, I believe,
> Or just a mere desire to take French leave,
> I couldn't say. I couldn't really say.
> But, when the whistle blows, they go away.
> Sometimes there never was a whistle blown,

But they don't care, for they can blow their own
Whistles of willow-stick and rabbit-bone,
Quail-calling through the rain
A dozen tunes but only one refrain,
"We don't know where we're going, but we're on our
way."

. . .

Americans, what are Americans?
I went downtown as I had done before.
I took my girl to town
To buy a calico gown,
I traded in my pelts at Offut's store.
And then, when I came back, the folks were gone,
Warm ashes on the hearth, but nothing more.
And, if you ask me just what made them go,
And what they thought they'd get by going there,
Why, you can ask the horses, or the Ford,
Hauling its gypsy children through the mud
With the wry klaxon croaking "Going on!"
And the tame rooster on the running-board.
But I don't know—I do not really know.
I think it must be something in the blood.
Perhaps it's only something in the air.

Oh, paint your wagons with "Pike's Peak or Bust!"
Pack up the fiddle, rosin up the bow,
Vamoose, skedaddle, mosey, hit the grit!
(We pick our words, like nuggets, for the shine,
And, where they didn't fit, we make them fit,
Whittling a language out of birch and pine.)
We're off for Californ-iay,
We're off down the wild O-hi-o!
And every girl on Natchez Bluff
Will cry as we go by-o!
So when the gospel train pulls out
And God calls "All Aboard!"
Will you be there with the Lord, brother,
Will you be there with the Lord?

Yes, I'll be there,
Oh, I'll be there,
I'll have crossed that rolling river in the morning! [4]

How many Americans actually crossed the Mississippi? We cannot count them exactly, for some who were later found in that land "where seldom is heard a discouraging word" *must* have been born there. Still, as late as 1930 the census figures indicated that three times as many persons who had been born east of the Mississippi were living west of it as had been born west and were then living east: a net drain from the East of five million souls. Remembering such figures, one is inclined to agree with the historian who declared that "the most persistent theme in American history is the westward march of the American people."

But notice also a second and rival movement: townward, city-ward, to the great centers. Competing with the great open spaces were the great closed places, those new magnets called New York, Pittsburgh, Cincinnati, St. Louis, Chicago. As far back as 1790, the little seaboard towns had started to grow at a faster rate than the rest of the country. By 1870, the nation's 150 cities were actually attracting a larger number of newcomers than the rural regions. Before 1930, our population had become predominantly urban. *Going to town* became the new American definition of success. And today four out of every five Americans live in a city.

But there has also been a third and even greater movement than these two. Without ever reaching the frontier, or landing in Detroit, San Francisco, or New Orleans, Americans have moved and have kept moving from farm to farm, from state to state, from town to town, back and forth, from job to job, around and around. There is a fever in our blood. We have itching feet. Here today

7

and gone tomorrow. Let's go. 'Scuse our dust. Fill 'er up. Freewheeling. Howdy, stranger.

As early as 1831, Alexis de Tocqueville was stunned by the sheer restlessness of Jacksonian America. After moving to America, the German Francis Lieber declared he felt all the time as if tied to the wing of a windmill. He deduced that there were stationary nations and moving nations, and that movement had become the American "historical task." Said the South American statesman Sarmiento: "If God were suddenly to call the world to judgment He would surprise two-thirds of the American population on the road like ants." [5] Giant hotels became an American phenomenon. Steamboats were floating hotels. After the Civil War came the parlor car and the sleeper. Next, the automobile "restated the national principle"— and soon there wasn't anything Americans wouldn't do on wheels: eat, drink, sleep, or propagate the race. The Americans, cried startled Frenchmen, even "make the love in the automobile." Also a bank deposit. In due course we developed drive-in banks, drive-in restaurants, drive-in theaters, and park-and-pray churches,[6] to say nothing of some chapels on wheels, and three times as many motels as we had hotels before.

Can this fever be registered on a thermometer? It can. For example, economists tell us that transportation and communications form and have formed a larger fraction of the economy with us than with any other people except nomads and camel drivers. Again, it is the testimony of the census takers that, after the peak of the westward movement, some 20 per cent or one out of every five people were found in states where they had not been born; but today—with the frontier closed and the cities already fairly occupied, that is, at a time when we ought to have been settling down—the proportion of out-of-state origins has risen to about one in three, and this takes no account of those who went home the year before, or who have removed more than once, or who have moved around in the same state.[7]

Some people have moved so much they have lost all touch. "I Wish I Could Remember," sang Stephen Leacock . . .

> I wish I could remember
> The house where I was born
> And the little window where perhaps
> The sun peeped in at morn.
>
> But father can't remember
> And mother can't recall
> Where they lived in that December—
> If it was a house at all.
>
> It may have been a boarding house
> Or family hotel,
> A flat or else a tenement,
> It's very hard to tell.
>
> There is only one thing certain from
>   my questioning as yet,
> Wherever I was born it was a matter of regret.[8]

Remember when October 1 was moving day? Today all the days of the year hardly suffice for the moves we wish to make. Three hundred and fifty years ago we took to the woods. Today we knock around the world. The habit of moving is in our blood.

But why?

The answer has seemed simple, in fact of negligible importance. For migration, after all, has been merely a means, a neutral connecting link, the empty corridor down which the pilgrim has passed to his goal. I agree that migration did begin as a method—a device—not as an end in itself but as a means to other ends. Yet these ends deserve examination. So, too, does the connecting link. Let me try here to make just a beginning.

What ends has migration served, beside the grand conquest of the continent? First, whether we like it or not, we must face the fact that to a certain degree the New World has served as the dumping ground for the Old. No sooner had the beachheads been established than England began shipping out her misfits and her undesirables: such undesirables as her heretics and her rebels, such misfits as her criminals and unemployed. Nor did this flow cease with the Revolution. For the backwoods and the whole West then served as refuse dumps for the East. Thus, on every frontier were to be found not only gamblers and adventurers but also a shiftless and criminal scum: murderers, highwaymen, and river toughs—what Crèvecoeur called "the most hideous parts of our society." He who had once, as they said, "skipped to America," was soon in the new lingo "gone to Texas"—and presently the vigilantes would be urging him on again. Having been escorted out of town once or twice more, he might land up in the Los Angeles underworld. Migration was a convenient purge— and brought many undesirables.

Migration, in the second place, meant freedom: a voluntary movement of escape. As we all know, for a great variety of individuals and groups it offered escape from some kind of tyranny: from religious persecution, or military service, or political oppression, or economic discrimination—all of which made such colonies as Pennsylvania, and the great West afterwards, the land of the free and the asylum of the downtrodden. To the oppressed of Europe, America has offered one long series of Emancipation Proclamations.

Still a third army of immigrants was motivated by an ambiguous mixture of moralities. For this lesser but still considerable number, the flight to America was inspired rather by the desire to escape from one's own errors and failures, from debts one couldn't pay, from a reputation too bad to live down, from an atmosphere that seemed poisoned and hopeless, from obligations one was unwilling to meet. By crossing the Atlantic one might escape one's neighbors—and even oneself. In Virginia, past mistakes would be forgiven—and with a second move, even a New England Puritan might be able to leave behind his sense of original sin. So America became also the hope of failures, a hiding place, or the land of the second chance. In Ohio one could start over, in California find a new faith. Even today not a little interstate migration seems inspired by the state tax collectors, or an unhappy marriage, or a failure in business, or emotional frustration, or the metropolitan police.

Still another powerful motive for flight was dissatisfaction with the progress of Europe. Because that progress was too slow—or because it was too fast. America appealed to radicals and missionaries and utopians and reformers of all stripes, for here one might build a new and better society, and shake off the dead hand of the past. The dead hand of the past but its very live grasp, too. For in some ways and to some people old Europe was entirely too lively, too demanding in its intellectual standards, too powerfully full of improvement or change. On the frontiers a man might be allowed to stay what he was. The peasants of the Continent, in an industrializing century, could go either to the new cities of Europe or to farms in the New World—and the short walk in to town often seemed the harder journey. Occupationally considered, the westward movement was in part a conservative drift: I confess that it was not until I had been teaching American history for years that I realized that the settlement of the Mississippi Valley was to a considerable extent manned by those who were so set in their habits, or so afraid of the new factory way of life just being introduced from England, that they preferred to move and move again, rather than give up their old and backward profession of farming. We Americans have fled the present as well as the past.

But it is as the road to a better future that migration has served its greatest use. In our lexicon, movement means improvement. Some of our immigrants may have been the rejects and the fugitives of Europe, but the vast majority came to our shores, and then leapfrogged West, and then went to town, and after that moved from city to city in order to reach a place where the resources were not all pre-empted, where the competition was more open, where promotion was easier, where one could *rise* in society and better oneself. In other words, lateral movement implied vertical movement, too. On the margins of empire, in the frontier areas, in the sprawling new cities, class barriers broke down, society became atomic, the enterprising and the aggressive could rise. Especially if you got there first, for the latecomers would have to pay you for your land, work in your shop, push you upstairs. Horace Greeley, remember, gave two pieces of advice, not one: "Go West, young man, *and grow up with the country.*" Thus it was: onward and *upward* with the West! The West was a kind of elevator. One moved sideways in order to reach the elevator, then pressed the button for some higher floor. So in the end American mobility had to be vertical as well as lateral if it was to be judged a success. If I may enlarge this metaphor, our society has been filled with escalators, East as well as West, and if enough of them failed at once there was trouble. What was it made the despair of the 1930's? The fact that suddenly all the escalators stopped at once, and for the first time in our history, for "Okie" and factory hand alike, there was no place to go. Mobility has been the lubricant in our society: our fluid drive.

THROUGH HISTORY WITH J. WESLEY SMITH
"But Mr. Greeley—I like it here in the East!"
—*The Saturday Review*, September 28, 1946
By Burr Shafer.
Copyright 1946 by The Saturday Review Associates, Inc.

It remains to notice one more important cause of movement. To a degree we have always moved but today perhaps more than ever for sheer excitement and pleasure. Driving has become "the country's favorite outdoor recreation." In these United States the honeymoon is a natural. Travel is packaged. Tourists support a multi-billion-dollar industry. In Eisenhower's first year in the presidency, it was estimated that 72 million Americans (one-half our total population) were spending at least part of their vacation on trips or on the road. By 1966, just in automobiles alone, we covered the equivalent of some 2 million round trips to the moon, or 39 million trips around the world. And in 1971, by A.A.A. calculations, a total of 110 million people would roll up 280 billion U.S. highway miles just in holiday travel.[9]

We began by asserting our rights to Life, Liberty, and the Pursuit of Happiness—but as one of our leading historians once remarked, the pursuit of happiness has changed to the happiness of pursuit. From outcasts to joyriders! As the saying goes: "We've come a long way."

But has it all been a joy-ride? Pascal would not have thought so. Pascal, you will recall, had an aphorism to the effect that a large part of man's troubles come from his inability to stay in one room. Now whether or not we Americans have gone out of our way to find trouble, it must be admitted that since time immemorial migration has been a dangerous, costly, desperately difficult business. It has been the great eliminator as well as the great promoter.[10] Sociologists call it "selective." The drive has to be unusually strong or the attachments to the old society very weak for individuals to be able to leave. So not all elements move. The migration is only partial. And there results the onesided or unbalanced society. Indeed, one may go so far as to assert that the transatlantic and transcontinental migrations not only limited American society but twisted the American temperament and gave shape to our whole national character.

Socially, the most obvious thing about the English colonizing process was the fact that it brought us a decapitated society. No royalty, no aristocracy, no leisure class. Practically no bishops or judges or scientists or great statesmen made the journey. With insignificant exceptions the highest ranks, the highest professions, the men of highest learning and highest crafts and skills all stayed at home. And so did their arts and way of life: their leisure-class culture. Why? Well, the upper classes were already successful at home and could hardly hope to better themselves in a wilderness. And who came instead? A small army of Puritans, to whom their austere faith was more important than all the arts and refinements of life. Also a vast swarm out of the lower middle classes, to whom the arts of leisure were suspect, and the chance to better themselves economically meant everything. So if American society started and remained materialistic, it was not just because of the wealth of this continent but because for three hundred years we drew far less than our share of cultivated folk and far more than our share of materialists out of Europe. The unbalanced society.

If Americans proved themselves astonishingly anti-intellectual, and unmusical and unartistic, it wasn't just because they had to lead a hand-to-mouth existence and didn't have time, but because, with certain honorable exceptions, our forefathers were people who even before they took ship had paid no attention to the things of the mind and had given mighty small time to the arts. There were exceptions, but I think this generalization will stand. As the generations passed, of course, the new societies struggled to replace the missing elements with the aid of a home-grown trading and planter aristocracy, which in the eighteenth century did begin to patronize the arts. But first the Revolution drove out the Tories, and then the Louisiana Purchase and the Jacksonian revolution pulled the rug of authority out from under the feet of the cultured classes of the seaboard. In effect, it has been the ease

15

of escape, the wealth of new occupations, and the rapidity of change which have again and again postponed the establishment of an American aristocracy. Lacking a settled élite with an organic tradition, yet a little uneasy on that account, we have accordingly been driven to borrow; and in the nineteenth century we distinguished ourselves as the greatest style thieves of modern times. Even in the field of building, where we ought to have excelled, we abandoned our Georgian inheritance to rush into one revival movement after another, to keep up with the Joneses. In the field of literature, I believe it was the Bostonians who most effectively exploited the discovery that to borrow books and ideas from Europe was not only elevating in itself but a sure way to get ahead of the Joneses. Unfortunately, most of the Joneses had gone West. So if the American tree has been slow to bear fruit, the fault may be in its having too often been topped and transplanted.

Still another great imbalance produced by migration has been in the emotions. As Hansen quoted a German commentator of 1816: "Emigration is a form of suicide because it separates a person from all that life gives except the material wants of simple animal existence." There are those who dispute the point. But, in the face of such risks or possibilities, who was most likely to go and to make a go of the venture? The pessimists? Hardly. The timid? Not likely, for it became a proverb that "the cowards never started and the weaklings died on the way." The old, the well-balanced, or the skeptical? No. Rather, the young and enthusiastic and the congenitally optimistic. It was above all the suggestible and wishful thinkers who caught the America Fever. Migration was no more rational than man himself. Pioneering, says Lewis Mumford, was the romantic movement in action.[11] And the new land rewarded and perpetuated the type.

Not to be overlooked, also, are certain psychological effects of the moving process.* These exiles had to ship light, and on their rough journeys, like as not, they lost still more baggage overboard. The result, intentionally or not, was a tremendous destruction of culture. Yet they could not bring themselves to part with everything they had known. Even the most careless clung to one or two shreds of their past, and the purposeful clung with such purpose that they achieved an intenser faith. On these empty coasts, what they had struggled so hard to save came to seem still more important than it had at home. It expanded into the vacuum of their lives. They would never give it up. Thus our New World communities, so scornful of their inheritance in many ways, became in some particulars quite astonishingly conservative. Watching how the New England saints tried to build a whole civilization on the Bible, or how the Pennsylvania Germans struggled to preserve their farming and their arts, one suddenly grasps a secret, a key to one of the contradictions that so puzzle our friends in Europe. From their experience, Americans cannot help being in some things completely experimental, in others just exactly the opposite.

Again the repetition of movement, and especially the forming of new communities out of strangers and chance arrivals, without prior knowledge of each other, credentials of status, or established reputations, operated to make these communities a good deal more egalitarian than they might otherwise have been. As a friend of mine

* The psychological causes and consequences of mobility provide a haunting theme, which will be pursued in the folklore and slang of the western tradition (ch. 3), in discussions of nomadism and of mobile homes (chs. 4 and 5), in my analysis of the institutional and social consequences of our restlessness (chs. 6 and 7), and in the concluding explanations and theoretical interpretations (chs. 8, 9, and 10).

once observed, our frontier democracy was a democracy of circumstance and mixture as well as of conviction. It followed that after these conglomerations had a chance to sort themselves out a little, things no longer looked quite the same; and out of the democratic wilderness came monopolists, ruling families, and company towns. Perhaps this will help us to understand the later Middle West, in its vagaries and deviations from the egalitarian ideal.

Finally, we should begin to pay attention to the psychological, almost neurotic aftereffects of having to journey so much on one's own. Certain aspects of this phenomenon have been remarked and brilliantly interpreted. But it will bear repeating that Americans have been a lonely crowd, restless, detached, and craving of company. Hence we became a nation of joiners. With the old family and village units falling apart in our hands, we had to call on our churches and schools, our Elks and Masons and Odd Fellows and Rotary, to take up the slack. (A. M. Schlesinger, Sr., once quoted Will Rogers as saying that "Americans will join anything in town but their own family.")[12] Perhaps this throws light, too, on our penchant for legislating people into morality—for with the restraints of tradition and custom no longer authoritative, didn't we have to try to do a good deal of our governing, perhaps even too much, by statute law? Or again one might ask, with personal backgrounds at such a discount, why would Americans not be aggressive? And with moral insecurity universal and inescapable, why should anyone be surprised at the almost religious terror with which even the best of us sometimes regard public opinion? Having repudiated the old gods we must somewhere find an authority that is firm.

Europeans should be told that if Americans are the hardest-working people on earth, and play with the same frenzy, and whip through a museum with almost highway speed, it is not only because there is so much more of Calvinism than of humanism, of the working class than of the leisure class, in our blood, but because there is something stifling to us about a museum. In all our history we have never learned to sit still. Similarly, if there are fewer regional differences in the whole United States than in any small country in Europe, the explanation is that we have been the most restless people of whom there is reliable record. The American moves with a fine abandon, but the abandoning leaves its mark: on our churches, on our government, on our schools. How better sum up the perennial dilemma of our liberal arts colleges than by recognizing that they have been trying to teach the great classical-Christian tradition to people in flight from Europe and the whole past? Certainly, if strangers find us optimistic to the point of wishful thinking, the answer must be that America started as an escape toward the future and it was the young and the hopeful and the romantic who kept coming and were rewarded. Finally, if European statesmen find public opinion in this country unstable, excitable, impatient, and dogmatic, we could tell them why. A hundred years ago Dickens made the same charge. "Your inconstancy," said he, "your inconstancy has passed into a proverb." [13]

Yet one has the feeling that our inconstancy can be overestimated. For underneath all the turbulence runs a curious consistency. We may be restless but we have got used to change. Expecting the unexpected, we have learned to live with it, too. Startled visitors ask why the detachment from place has not destroyed all ties, or the ease of self-improvement all classes. Yet status, code, and way of life: all these The Moving American has been learning to carry with him. His telephone line to the past may seem frayed, but his lateral communications have been developed into a fantastic network of intelligence. No society in history has been so stitched together with information. And no citizens have ever been so assaulted by words. To the European, our advertising inevitably comes as a shock. But let him watch a typical commuter as he drives swiftly home at night—past a succession of giant billboards, only half-listening to the insinuating, insistent voice of some high-pressure radio commercial—and it may dawn on the visitor that for a people who have seen so many strange sights and encountered so many miracles, nothing but the exaggeration of advertising will catch the attention. At all events, through this torrent of persuasion the American moves almost unheeding. Before going to bed he may even out of curiosity turn on the news. And on the morrow, after a breakfast of packaged promises, he drives cheerfully back to his work. Like the nomads or the Plains Indians of yesterday we have become stabilized in our instability?

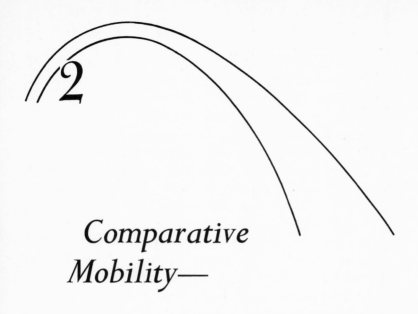

Comparative Mobility—

Some Old World customs,
gone American

Americans are unstable? Obviously. But not alone. Wandering is no American monopoly, no New World novelty. Immemorially, man has been an outcast and a wanderer. Since the Garden of Eden the descendants of Adam and Eve have found themselves repeatedly on the road. Abraham and Moses, King David and the Old Testament prophets learned about exile. The Greeks had their Argonauts; Homer sang the wanderings of the ever-restless Odysseus. And even the soil-bound medieval peasantry would not be without experience of pilgrims or Viking rovers or tales of the Wandering Jew.

The first focus of our inquiry will therefore be on lateral or spatial movement as it has been known by western man since the Cro-Magnon dawn. How does American mobility look against the horizons of human experience?

Let me begin with a fable for our time.

One day, not too long ago, a single-engine airplane flying from New Haven to Rhode Island ran out of power, came down safely on Expressway 95, and was promptly hit by a mobile home.

About the same time, a team of youth researchers discovered that, out of more than a thousand boys and girls whom they had been studying, 70 per cent remembered their families having moved once, twice, even three or four times, and 18 per cent remembered their families having moved five or more times. Eighty per cent did admit to having lived in the same house for one year, but only 50 per cent for as long as five.[1]

Does this folk music begin to sound familiar? In the same year of 1964, the American Petroleum Institute announced that we Americans, using 55 million oil credit cards, drove 86 million motor vehicles some 838 billion miles, and lost some 43,000 lives on the road. Meanwhile, at a single oil company it was taking 650 trained employees to keep track of the credit transactions—and on a routine day they had to handle 4,000 changes of address: which figured out to a residential mobility of 30 per cent in a single year.[2]

With our automotive civilization, we live in a state of "perpetual transportation"—and as a not surprising coincidence it appears that almost one-fifth of all the revenues of all these fifty United States now derives from the automobile.

But let us not suppose that we are the only highway nomads, the only people on the move. Englishmen have been notorious world wanderers. And even the French have been learning about auto-mobility. In 1964, for example, the Paris automobile show generated such traffic that the Parisians had to be advised to go by subway: *"Pour aller au Salon de l'Auto, prenez le Métro."* *

So Europe, too, has this restlessness, this mobility fever? Indeed Europe has long had it, much longer than we. Europe has known mobility in all its forms, for hundreds, even thousands of years. But we've had this motion sickness worse. We've been the footloose folk—and the scars of the experience show on our people and our land. It has even warped our national psychology.

So there I have restated my theme. My theme is that mobility, as a cultural triumph or failure, is a human achievement—not strictly American. In all its varieties and consequences mobility was known to, or invented by, Europeans long before this country was settled. Yet nowhere has free movement been so unrestrained or gener-

---

* A few years earlier:

"Paris est vide, Paris est triste . . .

"Paris, jusqu'à dimanche dernier, était plein comme un oeuf . . .

"C'est fini. Pourquoi? Parce que le Grand Palais a fermé ses portes: 'Un seul salon nous quitte et tout est dépeuplé!' . . . un seul? Pardon: le seul, le salon de l'Auto. 'Le Salon,' quoi!"

". . . L'automobilisme, c'est l'instrument des grands, le plaisir des gros, le besoin des moyens et le désir des petits. C'est aussi l'érudition des pauvres. C'est en tout cas la religion de toute la France: Voilà pourquoi le Salon a eu un million cent soixante mille visiteurs en dix jours"—Frank Bridel, "L'Automobilisme, religion française," *Gazette de Lausanne,* 22, 23 octobre 1955.

A few years later, in reporting on the yearly Salon de l'Auto, U.P.I. quoted one French women's magazine as saying that all French households were now families of three: "the husband, the wife—and the automobile" ("Cherchez la femme—she's got wheels," New Haven *Register,* Oct. 29, 1962). And two years after that, the great sit-in strike was finally broken, in part apparently because the strikers made the mistake of stopping the distribution of gasoline. There followed a wild parade of honking cars careening through the boulevards—"La kermesse aux klaxons," *Le Monde,* 2–3 juin 1964.

I am indebted for these and other tell-tale omens to Guy S. Métraux, editor of the *Journal of World History.* The reader may be entertained also by Gloria Emerson, "French and Cars: It has to be love," *The New York Times,* May 21, 1967.

ated such drastic consequences as with us. So it is here that it can best be studied, here that we can perhaps begin to understand what has been happening to us and what may in some degree happen to our friends in the wider world tomorrow.

Let us scrutinize the two halves of this proposition.

Mobility, we ventured to suggest, is an ancient tradition, and has appeared in many guises. Indeed, it has been an extraordinarily complex phenomenon, varied in its forms, confused in its motivations, and often contradictory in its results. On many of man's migrations in the past we have no statistics at all, and only the most general recorded observations; while mobility as a psychological phenomenon or even as a social act is only just beginning to be studied systematically. Yet perhaps we do know enough to distinguish certain major categories and identify the most important kinds of human movement.

There was first the gradual, unplanned, prehistoric migration now known as *Dispersion*—the slow outward drift into empty or sparsely occupied country (what Franklin D. Scott calls the "Creeping Expansion").[3] The earliest occupation of Europe by primitive man, or the invasion of North America by the Indian aborigines, were examples of this creeping expansion. Perhaps also the peaceful infiltration of the Roman Empire by the tribal Germans in their *Völkerwanderung*, or, in modern times, the massive percolation of the Chinese into Southeast Asia and Manchuria, have partaken in some degree of this primitive mobility we call dispersion.

There came next the more rapid, organized, and hostile migrations which we call *Conquest*. Conquest is deliberate armed migration, and may result in empire building or in empire collapse. It may take the form of a massive military movement, as with the Roman Empire or the

Moslem conquests or the Golden Horde, or it may be mounted in what Scott calls the "sharp thin thrust," as with the Vikings, or the Spaniards in Mexico. Conquest appeals to soldiers and adventurers, but also to priests. The Crusaders belong to this class.

Resembling such armed migrations, but often with a friendlier, more peaceful and beneficent intent, is *Colonization*. America was created by colonization from Europe. But the Europeans have practiced it elsewhere, and have had it practiced on themselves, or have practiced it on each other.

A fourth and rather different kind of international migration has been deportation or *Forced Migration:* [4] the driving out of the heretics, the expulsion of the aristocrats in the French Revolution (the persecution of the Tories in ours), the exchange of minority groups between two sovereign powers, and in more recent times the repatriation of the Greeks or the pogroms against the Jews. The slave trade was a particularly flagrant species of forced migration, in which both sides of the Atlantic shared. And the men and women who were pushed out or carried off or bought and sold can hardly have seen this transport of human livestock in just the same light as did the ambitious conquerors or the hopeful colonists.

One might mention next what we call *Nomadism,* or the practice of perpetual motion, the constitutional inability to settle down. The imprisonment of small clusters of people within a never-ending cycle of movement—as with the desert folk driving their flocks from oasis to oasis, or the mysterious comings and goings of the Gypsies, or the seasonal circuit of the Mexican fruit pickers up and down our West Coast—have been variations on this theme.

But there has been still a sixth major category of international mobility, and for modern times far more important. This is *Immigration and Emigration:* the free, voluntary, private transfer of individuals, families, congregations, even villages or whole countrysides from one country to another. Here the sending and receiving states are largely passive, and the initiatives rest in private hands. But these same initiatives derive from a kaleidoscope of experiences and spring from the widest range of human designs. Thus we know that a man may take ship for the New World, or leave Italy for France, or even move about within the United Kingdom, because he is looking for adventure or change or something new—or because he is a student with something important to learn—or because he is an expert with a professional skill to impart—or because his health forces him to seek a better climate, or his doctor prescribes the waters, or he wants to rest his nerves and recharge his emotional batteries—or he may move because he has just married a stranger, or must get his first job, or has been retired from active work. Moreover, the move may not satisfy, so that he moves again and in so doing joins that large company of emigrants and immigrants who are "birds of passage," who may return home or instead may try moving again.

Among all the motivations for migration, of course, the economic has often seemed the most influential: the search for a job, the hope of bettering oneself. Yet here, too, the variety of incentives is almost beyond counting. A man may be looking for El Dorado, for gold in the streets; or he may be a speculator on the prowl for more land. He may be a young apprentice looking for work, an old hired hand turned adrift, or a day laborer suddenly unemployed. Again, he may be an inventor seeking ears that are more open, or a fugitive craftsman with industrial secrets to sell, or a skilled operative looking for still better pay; or he may follow a trade from country to country, or take advantage of an industry his fellow countrymen have already organized and pre-empted and migrate with the Cornish miners to Pennsylvania, or become an Italian bootblack in New York, or sell flowers with his fellow Greeks. But let us not forget that such occupational systems of movement had already been organized and long practiced in Europe. As the distinguished English historian Frank Thistlethwaite has pointed out,[5] the *padroni* system was already shipping workers about the Mediterranean before it attracted and organized its immigrants over here.

And there are many other things about European emigration that are worth American notice. The "push" factors were European and were often stronger than the "pulls." With the decline of feudal localism, people were freed for moving. With the agricultural revolution, the peasant was forced off the land. With the industrialization of Europe, many farm folk simply had to move in to the factories or seek a free farm in the New World north or south. So once again we are driven to recognize the priorities of Europe. For essentially it was the modernization of the Continent (not the discovery of America) that freed men from their bondage to place and invited or even forced them to move: from the soil to the city, from province to province, from country to country, from the Old World to the New. It was the breakup of the old order again that incited men to move up in society, to climb the social ladder, by changing occupations, and locations too. As Lewis Mumford long since so cogently observed: the romantic pioneer and the businessman, these were types that appeared in old Europe long before they made their conquest of America. We may almost all seem to be middle class in the United States, but we hardly invented the breed. Nor even did the marginal man, the hobo and the wobbly, the alienated personalities or the beatnik temperaments, originate over here. The cities of Europe have long known these furtive folk. For drifters the *quais* and old *quartiers* of Paris have perennially served as resort.

All of which should remind us of still a seventh most important category, the *Internal Migration* which each of our nations has known.

Internal migration, let us recognize, is very like emigration and immigration. It is largely private and voluntary. It is caused by the same hardships, energized by the same emotions, respondent to the same occupational opportunities, economic drives, social impulses, or frictions of change. A peasant may cross the Atlantic or simply move to Marseille. A miner is offered opportunities in Colorado but also closer by. For the ailing or melancholic, there will be continental spas and health resorts more accessible than the Fountain of Youth. Tourists can make a pilgrimage to the natural wonders of their own country. Men of enterprise can resort to the nearer centers of capital. Indeed, for two centuries the modernization of Europe has been setting its populations into internal migrations more thoroughly, more massively even, than into emigration abroad.

So I think we must recognize that the great transatlantic migration has not been unique either in its motivations or in its personnel. Indeed, it has not even been the largest fraction of Europe's modern restlessness. For every man who moved out of Europe, many stayed and moved or are moving at home. As Thistlethwaite so perceptively argues, we should regard the great transatlantic dispersion "not as the dominant demographic factor of the nineteenth century, but as a subordinate feature of demographic trends within Europe."

The students of population do tell us that Europe and

Africa between them sent in the neighborhood of some 75 million persons across the Atlantic, of whom more than half came to settle in the U.S.A. And only about one-third of these North American settlers later returned home. So the 25 million net migration to our shores did constitute the single largest, most spectacular, and most successful folk movement of the nineteenth century. But it was not a new human experience. It was not unique. It did not equal in volume the cumulative movements going on elsewhere. Let me say again: all the kinds of mobility our immigrants practiced had long been known in Europe. And I think it can or will be shown that most of the causes of their crossing the Atlantic were European, not American.

So if we would inquire into human mobility, its ninety-nine varieties and its group secrets, and if we become curious about the psychological or social incitements to restlessness and their spatial cures, it is to the Old World we may turn. And it is in Europe that there is surely much to learn.

And yet . . .

And yet it is here, in America, that free mobility can best be studied. For not only was the whole American movement carried on within the horizon of visibility and the time span of the written record, but it is here that mobility has been most widely practiced, carried to its furthest extremes, even, as it were, housebroken and domesticated. We Americans have taken what I shall call the "M-Factor" into our lives, into our public institutions, into our private and social psychology to such an extent that mobility has become an essential ingredient in the American way of life. Mobility has been and is something special here, something so different in degree as to approach a difference in kind. Our comparisons with Europe must therefore be in part contrasts as well as likenesses.

Can it really be proved that ours has been the mobile society par excellence? I believe it can. Or it will be, when we unearth and assess what can be known. Let me here just posit some possibilities. I believe the mobility of our people was and is greater per man, and proportionately a much more important element, not only in the fabric of our expectations but in the structure and balance of our society. And I argue this on the following grounds.

First, we all began as immigrants. Whether our first American ancestors arrived in 1607, 1848, 1907, or since World War II, our origins were unanimously immigrant and have been these 360 years—whereas of the awakening masses who stayed in Europe only some left their village or province or patrimony behind.

In the second place, once the settlers had landed, it proved difficult to settle down. Their sons and their sons' sons spread out from the seaport towns, moved along the coast or up river, and filled in the vacant back country from colony to colony. Thereafter came the assault on the mountain barriers, and the drive West. The conquest of the continent became the obsession of our successful nationalists, and of many nineteenth-century immigrants too. It came to be expected that the young folks would strike out on their own. In a word, we found ourselves committed to movement. The trip across the Atlantic had been but the first stage of our journey. And if in Europe more people were beginning to move about than had ever left for America, in America the movements westward surpassed in frequency, distances, and varieties of participants anything that had yet been seen.

Frederick Jackson Turner caught the vision of what had been going on, but in a limited and partial way. The frontier meant movement, he said, movement over and over again. What he failed to notice was that as early as

1830, perhaps even as early as 1790, the elements of our society who actually saw the wilderness, or participated in the frontier experience, formed a declining percentage of our total population. From as far back as 1830, at least, more Americans moved to other destinations than to wilderness frontiers. And when those frontiers were gone they kept on moving, more regularly, more feverishly, more miscellaneously than ever before. So where the census figures of 1850 and 1870 had caught some 24 per cent of the population living in states where they had not been born, and by 1900 that figure had dropped to 20.6 per cent, by 1930 it was back to 24 per cent, by 1950 to 26.5 per cent, and by 1960 to 29.6 per cent.* Turner's "frontier" was the spectacular cutting edge of our westward movement. It created a myth. It confirmed the expectation and the habit of moving. But so did our cities. Then as now,

---

* The estimates of current mobility vary slightly, but agree in emphasis. Thus it is reiterated that 18–21% (or one out of every five persons over one year old—or one out of every five families) seem to move every year. The 1960 Census indicated that, out of 159 million persons five years of age or older, 75 million had changed residence since 1955 (an annual rate of 10% per year not counting repeaters). Of these 75 million, some 14 million (or 8.8%) had moved to another county and a second 14 million had moved to another state. If such were the returns for just five years, it staggers the imagination to contemplate how many will ultimately abandon the state of their birth before they die. At the moment of writing, all the returns from the 1970 Census were not in. The "Current Population Reports" of the Bureau of the Census (1971) showed that, between March 1969 and March 1970, out of a total population of 199 million persons one year old and over in the United States, 36.5 million (or 18.4%) had moved, of whom 13.3 million had moved at least a county away (this in a single year). The annual *Statistical Abstract of the United States* shows that between 3 and 4% of the total population one year or older have been moving across state lines every year, and F. D. Scott has noted that 40% of all Americans over the age of fifty now live in states other than that of their birth.

For the census figures and other sample estimates, the reader may consult recent issues of *Statistical Abstract of the United States;* also *Population Bulletin,* May 1964, and *The Economist,* Jan. 18, 1964.

the interstate migrations were but a small fraction of the internal movement actually taking place. Statistical samplings of the most variegated character illustrate and confirm these facts. And today our demographers assert without fear of contradiction that, residentially speaking, ours is the most mobile population of which we have reliable knowledge.

But there are other witnesses, and have been since our national beginnings, to testify to this strange propensity, even peculiarity, of our nation. In the 1830's Michael Chevalier thought that America's "most suitable emblem would be [not Andrew Jackson but] a locomotive engine or a steamboat." [6] And, as we shall have opportunities to notice, foreign visitor after foreign visitor was struck, not only by the restlessness or mobile tendency of the Americans, but by the way it was reflected in or was affecting our character, and by the way it was aided by or giving shape to our institutions. From Crèvecoeur to Chevalier to André Siegfried and other observant Frenchmen of our day, from Francis Lieber to Rudolf Heberle (both German scholar-expatriates, but a century apart), from Francis J. Grund to Charles Dickens to the peripatetic British journalists and commentators of our own experience, the interest or the puzzlement have been perennial. We don't seem anchored to place. Our families are all scattered about. Our loyalties are to abstractions and constitutions, not to birthplace or homestead or inherited associations. We share an extraordinary freedom to move again and again. No locality need claim us long. In 1847 the South American Sarmiento was astonished by our railroading, our caravanserai hotels, and the sheer numbers out on the roads. Today we are on the road still. Indeed, more than ever. We have "a love affair" with the motorcar. The automobile, they observe, is our chief status symbol.

True, the American people have known few persecutions or deportations, and almost no flights from famine.*
But in the planting of new territories and colonies, in the cross-country pursuit of economic opportunity, in travel for curiosity or health or recreation, or in most of the kinds of free movement that Europe pioneered and has long known, we have had and still have no equals. Small wonder that the spatial pursuit of happiness in this headlong and disorderly way has generated some astonishing effects.

But before venturing anything on the far-reaching consequences, let us ask: WHY? How did it happen that we became so footloose and fancy-free? What freed us to keep wandering? Here it seems to me we are on more difficult ground. But perhaps a few tentative answers can be hazarded.

A first answer is surely that, for a number of reasons (as noted elsewhere), we attracted the mobile temperaments. Out of Europe came settlers who, by and large, were more willing to move.

A second answer may be that the transatlantic passage represented such a drastic cutting of ties—such a catastrophic abandonment and so difficult a return (psychologically as well as physically)—that the New World Europeans became, as it were, permanently uprooted, with-

---

* Yet one is tempted to recall the Dust Bowl "Okies" of the 1930's, and the incredulous hoots of the European cinema-goers when *The Grapes of Wrath* showed the "destitute" Joad family migrating westward *in a car!*—as recalled by Frank Donovan in his entertaining *Wheels for a Nation* (New York, 1965, p. 187). Donovan quoted the statement that "an automobile is a mobile status symbol and a mobile status symbol comes as close as you can to defining the American dream." He also cited the remark that if some new Gulliver were to land on our shores today he would find, not Lilliputians, but centaurs riding on four wheels: "In the land of the Carboys, Gulliver would have said, the ultimate disgrace is not to be moving"—(pp. 236, 261).

out immemorial and instinctive attachments to any particular company or spot.

To these exiles came then the invitation of the great open spaces. The rich free lands and resources of the continent beckoned. So in America there was not only more space, there were not only more places to go, but more opportunities and more wealth to be got by the going.

Still a fourth powerful push came from an accident: the accident that during the 360 years of our history, and most particularly during the nineteenth century, the whole structure of western society on both sides of the Atlantic was undergoing a series of tremendous transformations. What we call the political, commercial, agricultural, and industrial revolutions not only destroyed the static rigidities which had held men in their places so long, but provided the means of escape and offered rewards for those who would step out and seize them. Our national development, it hardly need be repeated, owed much to the new democratic participation, but much also to the new capital and the Industrial Revolution. Without the new means of transport and communication, without steam engines and steamboats and better roads, and without the habits that these new facilities generated, we would hardly have been so ready to take advantage of the discovery of oil, and the European invention of the automobile or "gasoline buggy."

Yet Europe, it will quickly be observed, had these new tools and opportunities too. Why did not the people of the Continent also cut loose from their fixed abodes?

To this question there must be a whole catalogue of answers. But many of them, I think, can be summed up in one word: barrier. In Europe there were too many difficulties. The old structures of Church and State, the old authorities of family and class, the old commitments to field or shop, the old attachments to village and countryside: these were all being eroded, but they could not melt away over night. Nowhere were the military frontiers far distant, and these frontiers remained hard to cross. Everywhere the inherited prejudice of province and language still obstructed the way.

Whereas over here there soon came to be one language and one limitless expanse. Nowhere in our freer society were there the same high fences. No states could imprison their citizens, or keep them from wandering. No systems of authority had survived the Atlantic passage still strong enough to keep men in their place. And no government could be made strong enough afterward to prevent the hunters and the pioneers, the squatters and the speculators, the traders and the lawyers, the missionaries and the politicians from seeping West.

To sum up this argument or explanation: We have been more mobile because we attracted out of Europe the mobile temperaments, because these wanderers found themselves uprooted and unattached, because there were so many places to go, because there were so many means of going and rewards to be had for the venture, because the transformation of the old agrarian order now freed us for going, and because there were not and are not today the traditional social barriers to fence us in.

The results? Surely if we have been so mobile, that mobility must have had some rather obvious and visible effects on our society and on what we please to call the American character? I am convinced this is true. I think the effects of our playing so fast and loose with locality can be seen everywhere. For good and for ill the moving has put its marks on us. In fact, both the gains for personal freedom and the scars from our spatial exposures can be detected in so many American attitudes, value judgments, social customs, and institutional structures that not even the most obvious can be quick-listed here.

Instead, let me simply fix on one point, one peculiar feature of our historical development, that might be especially illuminating to our brothers in Europe. It has been remarked again and again, and often with no little astonishment, that our young republic is now one of the oldest governments in the world. For some reason or reasons, in three hundred years we have experienced only one revolution, and one civil war, and the first was less drastic than the great revolutions in Europe. How could such things be? How it is that our younger generations, or our disadvantaged groups, or our disappointed political schemers, or our regional interests have not raised the flag of rebellion, not once, but over and over again?

A common answer is that we left feudalism behind, and so did not have to destroy before we could build anew. Another has always been that ours has been a country of such rich opportunities and such vast free spaces that rebellion was almost irrelevant. Still a third has been that democratic participation made rebellion unnecessary. And in all these explanations there is the power of truth. But how was it that new privileges did not harden? That social and economic interests did not mobilize for class warfare? That demagogues and rabblerousers have enjoyed such fleeting moments of success? And how was it we could so easily take advantage of our opportunities and our open spaces, whether East or West, whether of frontier or of town?

Was it not perhaps because ours has been a most mixed and pluralistic society (abetted by immigration, and migrations and countermigrations over the years)? Was it not also because ours has been an exceedingly fluid and open society (made possible by mobilities of many

sorts)? Was it not that somehow the desperation was missing—that the dissatisfied and dissenter temperaments
could almost always pack up and go—that failures could
get a fresh start—that dreamers could found a colony in
California, desperados take off for Texas? The steam built
up less often and less high, I am suggesting, because we
had an almost universal safety valve which operated at
even very low social pressures.*

Which brings one to a still more significant aspect of
this question. Proverbially, ours has been the land of
equality, but of liberty and free opportunity, too. Yet how
have we been able to reconcile equality with an individualism which gave opportunity for quite unequal achieve-
ments or rewards? In the corporate sphere, the sphere of
large economic organizations, it is clear that we have
striven to counter the grosser evils of inequality by regulation of trade, by interstate commerce legislation, by anti-
trust and anti-monopoly laws, by a public redistribution of
wealth through income and inheritance taxes. But for the
individual American, unless racial prejudice prevented,
has it not been the freedom to move which has made pos-

* The similarity of this proposition to Turner's frontier as safety
valve should be noted, but not exaggerated. Turner said it was (empty)
space or "free land" that promoted freedom and democracy. I am suggesting that all kinds of space, settled as well as unsettled, urban as well
as rural, were made available by our expectation and practice of moving;
and I am further suggesting that the expectation and practice of moving
increased when there was no more free land or empty space. Hence mobility has continued to serve as safety valve. See Everett S. Lee, "The
Turner Thesis Re-examined," *American Quarterly* (Spring 1961); and
compare Thistlethwaite, *The Great Experiment*, pp. xii and 26; and
P. Sorokin, *Social Mobility* (1927), p. 381. It may be noted that Kulischer in the *Encyclopaedia Britannica* finds that migrants, both in peace
and in war, have tended to generate further migrations either by themselves or by others. Oscar Handlin sees a kind of American multiplication or reciprocation: "The fluidity of American society, the diversity of
its population, and the looseness of its institutional forms interacted upon
and stimulated one another." *Daedalus* (Spring 1961), p. 223.

sible the symbiosis of equality and individual initiative in our effervescent society? If our young men, or our less successful, had had to sit still and watch the hopeless piling up of the inequalities of power and wealth, either revolution or a crushing state socialism could hardly have been avoided. Whereas, as things have been, an ambitious man could generally get away from the "big shot" at home and perhaps even become a "big shot" himself in some other place. Quite average characters, too, had the feeling that they could start over: even when all the empty spaces had long since been in part occupied, a man still had a second or even a fifth chance. In consequence, happily, a man didn't always have to go. The mere conviction of such possibilities gave him comfort, self-confidence, and no little bargaining power. Moreover, in a society as mobile as ours, no boss's empire was apt to sit quiet under him. Given provocation, his own lieutenants would walk out and start building rival railroads or automobiles. As witness what happened to Henry Ford.

The mobility factor, I conclude, has been *our great American permit to be both more free and more equal* than our contemporaries could manage to become in the more static societies of Europe.

No doubt the effects of mobility, both good and bad, can be exaggerated. Mobility has been but one factor among many, one powerful stimulant among others no less powerful. But I am persuaded we should not take it for granted, as perhaps we have done. And when we discover in how many different ways it has facilitated change, and has helped give shape to our world of the twentieth century, it may be that we will agree that the apparently neutral act of moving is itself not without a broad social significance.

America has been the *locus classicus,* perhaps I may

be forgiven for calling it the *dislocus classicus,* of mobility. So a comparative study of human movement here and abroad will help us to understand what Americans are to-day. Possibly it will even give us some hints of the direction in which the peoples of Europe are now turning, and an inkling of what they might be like in the years to come.

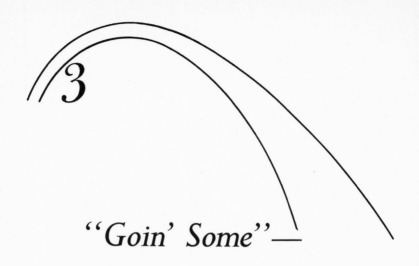

"Goin' Some"—

On intuitions of language
and the metaphors of motion

The causes of our New World fever must have varied—but the fever has been with us from the beginning. Here today and gone tomorrow. Planters by destiny, we refused to stay planted: settlers forever, we have never settled down. Was it hope? Was it just curiosity? Was it rather some nameless anxiety? Whatever lay behind this mysterious, pervasive uneasiness, the spectacular mobility of the pioneers has only intensified with the years. Willing and unwilling, aimless or purposeful, feverish or out of habit, we Americans have moved and moved and kept moving.

But how is one to glimpse the deeper meanings—how grasp this quicksilver *mobility*, and squeeze out its psychic implications?

One day, after a disappointing and even faintly ludicrous encounter with some encyclopedias,[1] it occurred to me to wonder if there must not be some lore, some wisdom of the race, locked away in our proverbs. The English, especially, have they not been world wanderers? What did they learn, or what have others had to tell us about wandering? Taking *Bartlett's Familiar Quotations* off the shelf, I found my way to two half-forgotten sayings:

> "The rolling stone never gathereth mosse."
> "Three removes are (is) as bad as a fire."

The first of these, from John Heywood's *Proverbes,* appeared to derive from the ancients; the second (with the singular verb) was coined by Benjamin Franklin in *Poor Richard's Almanac* for 1758, presumably from the materials in some earlier maxim. So the origins of these sayings might be lost, but their substance had withstood the tooth of time and earned them modern translations: "A rolling stone gathers no moss," [2] and "Three moves are as good as a fire." Evidently the carelessness and destructiveness of constant movement have seemed so obvious in our western world as to warrant preservation by vivid metaphor. The truths thus epitomized, are they not also suggestive of certain happy-go-lucky temperaments in our American society, to say nothing of the regrettable process of cultural elimination or abandonment that attended the first settlements and the leapfrogging movement West? To get virgin land many pioneers left society and literature and the higher arts and skills behind? The culture of the frontier tended to be limited and meager in the extreme? Three removes . . . ?

Yet two proverbs, alone, could hardly frame a broad portrait of the moving Americans. And for a time I had trouble finding more. In fact, it was not until I had supplemented Bartlett with E. Fuller's *Thesaurus of Quotations,* and this in turn with Stevenson's *Home Books of Quota-*

tions and of Proverbs, and pursued in these and other collections the thought of movement right through the alphabet of cues—from absence to distance to emigrant, nomad, trail, and way; from abroad to change to exile, home, travel, wanderer, and where; from ancestors to pilgrims and vagrants—that the mother lode of western maxims and proverbs began to yield its ore.

It is in the Book of Genesis (XLIX: 4) that one may perhaps find the first progenitor of that legendary Yankee: the jack-of-all-trades who was master of none. His name was Reuben: "Unstable as water, thou shalt not excel."

"Absence makes the heart grow fonder," at first supposed to be of nineteenth-century composition, has now been traced back some 360 years. Yet its message seems timeless. The love of the absent—with the suggestion also of the mystic distortion caused by feeling—must have been familiar to the ancients. Certainly, many of our immigrants in moments of pain illustrated this proverb by the way they idealized their fatherland, to their own disillusionment if they ever went back. Whereas others obviously preferred to practice instead the old Homeric saying: "Out of sight, out of mind."

Then through all the literatures of our tradition one begins to hear the cries of the exiles, the uprooted. "Exile is death," wrote Ovid; and death is exile: "He shall return no more to his house, neither shall his place know him any more," we read in the Book of Job (VII: 10). "My punishment is greater than I can bear," cried Cain, when the Lord condemned him to be "a fugitive and a vagabond in the earth. And the Lord set a mark upon Cain." Is there no mark on us?

"Eating the bitter bread of banishment" we find in Shakespeare. "I know how men in exile feed on dreams," wrote Aeschylus with Greek sensitivity in his *Agamem-*

non. By contrast, Horace was full of Roman stoicism and determination: They change their sky but not their minds, who cross the sea—"Caelum non animum mutant qui trans mare currunt." And again: "What exile from his country ever escaped himself?"

The Roman courage and superiority emerge again strongly in Cicero's "Exile is terrible to those who have, as it were, a circumscribed habitation, but not to those who look upon the whole world as one city." By comparison the children of Israel, of Christ, and of Mohammed spoke out of a fierce religious determination. They would endure forty years in a wilderness—for a promised land. "Since they would not listen to you at home," wrote Arnold Zweig, ". . . happy he that goes into exile. For banishment is often the only means of saving the nobler possessions of the world." And from the Koran: "Whosoever fleeth from his country for the sake of God's true religion, shall find in the earth many forced to do the same, and plenty of provision." The reader may ask himself which of these prophecies has not found its American illustration and fulfillment. The longing, the regret, the bitterness of exile, the fierce determination, and the stoic pride—one senses that these emotions were experienced somewhat unequally by the peoples and faiths of the past. But to the varieties of the American experience each has contributed.

When the consideration of Europe's thinkers swung away from exile to free movement, Montaigne recognized that in a certain sense motion is implicit in civilization: "Stability itself is nothing else than a more sluggish motion." Pascal, however, declared, ". . . que tout le malheur des hommes vient d'une seule chose, qui est de ne savoir pas demeurer au repos dans une chambre." [3] And so we discover that from classic times to the twentieth century Europeans have never wearied of discussing the virtues and (especially) the vices of travel. "Voyage, travel, and change of place impart vigor," had been the surprisingly modern suggestion in Seneca. "He who never leaves his country is full of prejudices," wrote Goldoni; and "Travel teaches toleration," thought Disraeli. But generally the verdict was much less favorable, or at best divided. "Fools are aye fond o' flittin', wise men o' sittin'," declared a Scottish proverb. "Blessed is he that continueth where he is," said Carlyle, and ". . . from all packers and carpenters, and flittings by night and by day, good Lord deliver us." [4] Others subscribed to the verdict that "Travel makes a wise man better, but a fool worse." When Cowper suggested, "How much a dunce that has been set to roam, Excels a dunce that has been left at home," the majority was clearly against him. Most seem to have been convinced that "if an ass goes travelling, he'll not come home a horse"—which was also epitomized in the German: "If a goose flies across the sea, there comes back a quack-quack."

> He travelled here, he travelled there;—
> But not the value of a hair
> Was head or heart the better.
>
> WORDSWORTH

This brings us to recognize that almost overwhelmingly (if one may trust the maxims and proverbs) the sages seem not to have approved the kinds of mobility in which we Americans have been indulging. "Than roaming nothing is more evil for mortals," is from the *Odyssey*. "He dwells nowhere that dwells everywhere," is quoted from Martial. "Un sort errant ne conduit qu'a l'erreur," sang Gresset (*Vert-Vert*, Chant I): "for a wandering life only leads us astray." The French "Un peuple sans feu ni lieu" carries its own unmistakable flavor. "Show me a man who cares no more for one place than for another," wrote

Southey, "and I will show you a man who loves nothing but himself. Beware of those who are homeless by choice." Almost 1800 years before, Seneca had expressed the same feeling: "Everywhere is nowhere. When a person spends all his time in foreign travel, he ends by having many acquaintances and no friends." In such judgments are there not foreshadowed and rejected some of the very traits and attitudes for which Americans have often been criticized: the restlessness which gets us into so much trouble, the craving for something or some place else, the loneliness and rootlessness of our wanderers, the selfishness of our acquisitive code, the superficiality of many human relations, the ruthlessness of the confirmed vagrant? Beware of those who are homeless by choice!

"Oublier, c'est mourir," wrote Alfred de Musset to Lamartine, and in one moment of feeling implicitly indicted still another of our basic beliefs and practices. For to move is so often to turn one's back: that is, deliberately to forget. By emigrating a man could even shut the door on his own ancestors, and by that act bury his past. Our inveterate preference for the new, our disrespect for elders, our careless disregard of traditions, may not these traits derive as much from the acceptance and habit of mobility as from any other aspect of the American condition? Irresistibly, the suggestion comes to us from these old proverbs that movement may appeal to certain special types; also that there may be a range of rather particular reasons for going and some rather impressive psychological and social consequences for the goer. The stay-at-homes at least seem to have thought so.

When one turns to the English writers and poets, a change of mood becomes evident. By contrast to the Continentals, what seems particularly to have struck the English literary imagination about mobility and foreign travel

were the irresistible delights of adventure, with the inevitable longing for peace and for home. "Whan that Aprille
. . .", wrote Chaucer, "than longen folk to goon on pilgrimages." But "Oh, to be in England, now that April's
there," sighed Robert Browning. Tennyson saw in Ulysses
a soldier-adventurer "for always roaming with a hungry
heart," an explorer who could not rest from travel, who
would "drink life to the lees," a seeker who would "follow
knowledge like a sinking star."

> Yet all experience is an arch wherethro'
> Gleams that untravell'd world whose margin fades
> For ever and for ever when I move.

Robert Louis Stevenson knew the same insatiable
hunger, the same unappeasable longing to lie still. "To
travel hopefully is a better thing than to arrive," he once
wrote; yet he dreamed of the hills of home.

> This be the verse you grave for me:
> "Here he lies where he longed to be;
> Home is the sailor, home from sea,
> And the hunter home from the hill."

Later, Masefield would immortalize Englishmen's sea
fever: "I must go down to the seas again, to the lonely sea
and the sky."

It was Kipling, however, more than any of his countrymen, who would feel the pull of the unknown: "Pull
out, pull out, on the Long Trail—the trail that is always
new!" Kipling knew the sharp spur that venturing forth on
one's own can give to ambition: "High hopes faint on the
warm hearthstone; he travels the fastest who travels alone."
But perhaps he most memorably voiced the uneasy, whispering conscience of man the explorer:

> Something hidden. Go and find it.
> Go and look behind the Ranges—

> Something lost behind the Ranges
> Lost and waiting for you. Go!

To Kipling, as to so many eminent Victorians, the world
was the Lord's, under English management, to be explored, to be conquered, to be civilized. And ranging the
ends of the earth, dwelling in strange places, coming to
know the mysterious and unfathomable, dying far from
home: these were a part of the White Man's Burden. So it
is almost as if Englishmen saw in travel what they themselves were putting into it: discovery, adventure, ambition, pride, idealism, and self-sacrifice. Almost as if for
them the words of movement were the expression of half-
realized desires. Unlike the French, they were not afraid
to go abroad. By the waters of Babylon they neither
wailed nor wept. Like the sturdy Romans, an Englishman
needed only the cloak of his citizenship to go anywhere. In
moving he did not have to change.

But now in the same language I began to stumble on
other sayings—or, rather, not quite in the same language.
"Home was never like this," is an American saying. "Absence makes the heart grow fonder—of somebody else":
that is anonymous but surely unmistakable. "The great
thing in this world is not so much where we are, but in
what direction we are moving," insisted Oliver Wendell
Holmes. "Drop anchor anywhere and the anchor will drag
—that is, if your soul is a limitless, fathomless sea and not
a dog pond," barked Elbert Hubbard. Again one encounters: "A man cannot very well make a place for himself in
the sun if he keeps continually taking refuge under the
family tree."

The American activism and engagement with speed
seem very clear in such aphorisms as: "The world is moving so fast these days that the man who says it can't be
done is generally interrupted by someone doing it" (El-

bert Hubbard). Or again: "Stand still and watch the world go by—and it will."

In the seventeenth century, William Penn was of the opinion that "A man, like a watch, is to be valued for his going." In the twentieth century, George Santayana noted that "All his life he [the American] jumps into the train after it has started and jumps out before it has stopped; and he never once gets left behind or breaks a leg." As a small boy, taking the ferry to Staten Island, I can remember my father pointing out how, even though we were not due to leave for five minutes, the moment the embarking passengers caught sight of the ferry in the slip, they started to run. More than most, the American fears to be left behind? Generally, he moves with confidence. "This generation has a rendezvous with destiny," proclaimed Franklin Delano Roosevelt. "The American people never carry an umbrella. They prepare to walk in eternal sunshine," declared Alfred E. Smith. Sometimes the boasting has been a little wry. "America is a nation that conceives many odd inventions for getting somewhere but can think of nothing to do when it gets there," quipped Will Rogers. "Methods of locomotion have improved greatly in recent years," said Don Herold, "but places to go remain about the same."

From the beginning there's been "a long, long trail a-winding into the land of my dreams." And it's been a lonely trail, however crowded with fellow pilgrims. Thoreau once defined city life as "millions of people being lonely together." Oddly enough it was an English poet, Wordsworth, who wrote that ". . . stepping westward seemed to be a kind of heavenly destiny," while from the American poet Longfellow came: "Stay, stay at home, my heart, and rest; Home-keeping hearts are happiest." Yet, does one not have the feeling that the Englishman could be a little remote and serene because he was not going, whereas the American poet counseled rest, but knew in his heart it was hopeless to think of staying? Listen to Edna St. Vincent Millay:

> My heart is warm with the friends I make
> And better friends I'll not be knowing;
> But there isn't a train I wouldn't take
> No matter where it's going.

Years ago, Walt Whitman sang of the open road. It seems just yesterday that my great-aunt Harriet, *aet.* 87, whimsically sent word:

> I know my life is nearly spent
> Because my want to go is went.

Slang! What about the American vernacular? They say things are *touch-and-go.* We are told so-and-so is always *on the go,* or maybe *going to the dogs,* or *gone to blazes.* Our preachers speak of the *ongoing work.* We *go for* somebody or something, and with feelings either pro or con. Taking my courage in both hands, one day I shut my Bartlett and opened Partridge's *Dictionary of Slang and Unconventional English*—and found no end of "go-words." Partridge listed *go down with* and *go off the deep end* as English, but *go-getter, go-to-meeting* clothes, to *go places,* and *the going's good* as American. *That goes with me,* he identified as English in origin, American also by adoption. *Go-ahead,* as an adjective, was born in America and borrowed by England. So were: *to go back on, go behind,* and *go over big.* However, there seemed to be more Australian slang usages of "go" than either English or American (especially in vol. 2), and gradually it began to appear that Partridge was much stronger on the Cockney, criminal, Australian, or Canadian vernacular than he was on what Mencken used to call the American slanguage.

This was immediately made unmistakable by the *American Thesaurus of Slang*, edited by L. V. Berry and M. V. D. Bark. There the slang words expressing movement just pour across the pages, with no less than thirteen columns in the index just for the word *go*. Americans can go: *all out, all the way, to pieces*, or *around in circles; bughouse, hay-wire* or *nuts; bad, blooey, boom*, or *broke; hogwild, head over heels, great guns, lickety-split*, or *like a bat out of hell*. They can go *steady, straight, sour*, or *wrong*. They can go *their own sweet way*, and tell others to go *fly a kite, jump in the lake, peddle their papers*, or (more insultingly) go *way back and sit down*. We will go *down the line* for a friend; go for *six* or a *sleighride*; go it *alone* or *one better*; go off *the rail* or *one's rocker*; go on *the loose, a bender, the rocks*, or *the wagon*; go out *of circulation*; go the *distance, works*, or *whole hog*; go to *bat for, beat the band, the races, the mat*, or *the wall*; go up *the spout* or *the river*.

There are also a number of "gone-words," which (because the action is finished? the journey is done? the thing is past?) stand mostly for some kind of failure. Thus gone *bad*, gone *gosling*, gone *in the upper story*. We say either go to or gone to *grass, pot, seed, smash*, or *sleep on the job*. Characteristically, of a man who's finished or dying, we say: he's a *goner*. We have other verbs of motion, too, to express human failure: thus, he *ran out of steam*, he *went downhill*, or he was *on his last legs, with one foot in the grave (and the other on a banana peel)*. A man who has no chance is *out of the running*. A man who comes out second best is an *also-ran*. As Mencken long ago pointed out, an Englishman *stands* for a seat in Parliament but an American *runs* for election. "Let's get this country moving again," was John F. Kennedy's slogan. "Get a wiggle on," we say to our children. And to a friend: "Shake a leg," "Keep a-goin'," "Don't let anything stop you."

On the thought of motion, itself, we have let our imaginations run riot. In lieu of "travel" we may *bat about, thumb a ride, fly light, leg it, jump across lots, hit town,* or *pound the pavement.* Especially we like to travel fast: *to step on it, give 'er the gas, open 'er up, pour it on, hop it, barrel it, hot-foot it,* and *tear-ass around.* The act of going fast may become *scoot, spin,* or *skedaddle.* And speed, itself, as noun or verb, may be *bat, dust, zip, rip, flash, highball, bum, blue streak, lickety-split, greased lightning, ripsnorter, a shot out of hell.* (At the moment, one will be reminded, we are manufacturing a new slanguage for the air and space age, and the needs of the jet set.)

Instead of leaving, or departing in a dignified way, Americans may *blow, clear out, fade, beat it, scram, pull up stakes, get going,* or *take off in a cloud of dust.* Our words for flight and escape are, to say the least, eloquent of long practice and also considerable ingenuity in the arts of evasion. Thus we *duck out on, walk out on, run out on;* we give someone the *go-by* or the *run-around;* we *skip, slide out, take it on the lam, make a break* or *a get-away, show our heels, take the air,* or *break for the tall timber.* And of course we hope to *get away with it,* to *get beyond reach,* and to *quit while still ahead.*

What is even more interesting than the varieties of abandon, however, is the way we apply thoughts of movement to processes or action of a rather different order. Thus, we seem given to defining success in terms of motion, failure in its opposite. So-and-so, we say, is a *comer,* a *go-getter;* or he's a *hot shot,* he's *going places.* By and by he's running a *going concern,* and, if he's wise, he *never lets any grass grow under his feet.* After a short *stretch,* or sometimes it seems *in less than no time,* he's *arrived.*

By contrast, to *get left behind* or to *get caught in a rut* is to fail. He *missed the bus,* we tell each other (or *missed the boat*). A corporation that's not doing well is *not going anywhere.* Its president, perhaps, *got bogged down* in administration. Its business is *at a standstill.* Don't be a *stick-in-the-mud,* we urge a friend. Why not try a *comeback?* You don't want to be a *flat tire.*

As with success, so with life and death, we seem instinctively to think in terms of forward motion. A man who is growing old is *slowing up.* Younger men regard him as a *back number,* a *has-been.* By and by he reaches the *end of the trail* or *passes away.* And death itself used to be spoken of as *turning up one's toes, going west,* or *crossing the divide.* For like reasons a progressive-minded individual is *up-and-coming,* or he has *get-up-and-git;* whereas a conservative is called *slow-coach, moss-back, old-timer, dodo,* or *stand-patter.* In our vocabulary, slow is not a flattering appellation. If you're slow, you're both anti-social and *getting no place fast,* or you're *glue-footed* or *slower than death.* If you are free, on the other hand, you have *leeway* (naut.) and can *go your own sweet way.* Independence enables you to *go it alone* or *paddle your own canoe.*

What about marriage and the family? Here I have found fewer metaphors of motion, possibly because when a man *gets hitched,* he is supposed to settle down and stay put. It's true that originally he asked a girl to *go with him.* If he has a roving eye, he may *step out* on her now and again. But if he *chases* women too much, he may *trip himself up,* because his wife may sue him for divorce, which will mean the *end of their road together.* And the alimony she will insist on will be *all the traffic will bear.* Happily, with a little love and forbearance, most of us avoid any such *dead-end street.**

Are Americans unique in such jargon? Surely, all cultures know motion or change, and most languages must make a good deal of the word GO. *Comment ça va?* says the Frenchman, also *Allons,* and *Va-t-en!* and *Ce chapeau vous va bien.* Again, a word like *mouvement* may be used in a number of senses. Yet the word *arriviste* hardly conveys the approval of the American *arrived.* Ultimately, the engagement of the French with images of mobility will have to be tested by the students of the language; meanwhile, to an amateur of things French, their enthusiasm for either the idea or the actuality of motion has until recent years seemed decidedly limited.

The Germans, for their part, have given us *wanderlust, wandervögel,* and *wanderjahre,* as well as *wie geht's,* and a wide assortment of combinations and meanings for the words *gehen, kommen,* and *fahren* (probably much wider than for the like words in French). After all, Americans didn't invent locomotion. And the Germans have been no *slow-pokes* on the road westward. From the Thirty Years' War to World War II, from the days of the Palatines and Moravians and Dunkards to those of Albert Einstein and the professors, the Germans have been the most numerous and determined of our immigrant populations out of Europe. Yet in German, one will find, the vocabulary of motion hardly approaches American dimensions.

The English? Since Drake and the Elizabethan sea-

* No enumeration of slang metaphors can hope to be complete. Recently, I have stumbled (!) across: "I want out"; "That paint-brush has a lot of mileage in it yet"; "A good stopping-off spot"; "Coffee . . . to go"; "He doesn't know whether he's coming or going"; and the even more disquieting "Where did you go? Out. What did you do? Nothing."

dogs, the English (and the Scots and Irish, too) have been adventurers and world conquerors, explorers and colonizers, ubiquitous wanderers and the tourists par excellence. For them, more than for others, was the Continental civilization of spas and hotels created—and in the nineteenth-century emigration, "Nul peuple plus disponible dans toutes ses couches." [5] So in many aspects of mobility the English preceded, we perhaps merely exaggerated— what they invented, we practiced—and their words we spoke just with a special accent.

At the same time it is fair to ask about the differences. For example, have the two peoples the same notions about place? Have the English, and especially their ruling classes, ever lost their feeling for the land? Is it they or we who have abandoned the ancestral homesteads? Which of our two societies is uprooted and is even quite cheerful about it? Which likes the idea of escape? When we both say *off to the races*, do we and they mean the same thing? Do *speed* and *fast* carry quite the same messages both sides of the water? And, generally, have the two peoples looked at movement through quite the same lenses of expectation and acceptance?

Let us concede that, however far we have traveled, the words *Let's go!* must first have been uttered in Europe. Let us also face the fact that a full and comparative study of the emotive messages in the four languages—French, German, English, and American—has yet to be made. All the same, even an innocent amateur may wonder whether any society before ours has ever taken the images of activity and motion so warmly into its heart and speech.

Does this word hunt through the dictionaries suggest any profound conclusions about American character and culture? Possibly not. It may simply be that Americans have been more inventive and colorful in their vocabulary than their European cousins—and have been so because they are both democratic and vulgar. As Mencken clearly pointed out, here any man has been good enough to vote or coin a word or expression, with no barriers of good taste and no aristocrats to stand in the way. Yet does it not remain curious that Americans should have chosen to put so many of their thoughts into terms suggesting mobility? To an astonishing degree, our word pictures have been vivid motion pictures, our metaphors the metaphors of movement.

How may one come to know a people? Some of us prefer to judge the ethos of a society by its politics or its political economy. Others will single out its art and great literature. Still others will draw illumination from a study of the folklore and traditions of a people, or from their buildings and public monuments. Might not even our most inveterate institutional historians get cues from common speech?

Anthropologists have sometimes defined culture as the man-made and learned part of the environment, resulting from man's abilities in language and in toolmaking. Which is to suggest that by language man has learned to master ideas (and communicate); and by the tools of engineering and science to conquer the physical environment, space, and time. But these relations will vary from people to people. And, from their colonial beginnings, Americans seem to have been unusually good at annihilating distance, shortening time, and moving at ease among their fellows. So it should not surprise us that their language reflects a love of speed and the confidence with which they have used and abused space. Having experienced so much change and mobility, they naturally took its images into their speech.

Did their language and vocabulary in turn perhaps

make Americans still more mobile? May not our metaphors of movement—themselves learned and handed on and now part of our culture—have helped give us the confidence to leave home, helped teach us the pleasures of mobility, and helped create for us the assumption, the priceless heritage, of feeling free to come and go? May not a language which reflects a stimulant help perpetuate the stimulus, and itself finally play a stimulating role? To this observer the acceptance and recirculation of ideas in common speech might well have a powerful, even cumulative effect.

However such propositions may be decided, or however far the students of our national psychology may see fit to explore the glints in our slang and the many hints in our ancestral baggage of proverbs, this much is clear: If we knew nothing at all about our colonial origins or our westward movement or our feverish twentieth-century restlessness, if all our history were shrouded in darkness, it would still be obvious, even inescapable, that we had been a people much given to movement. Also that we have liked and still like to move more than most. Finally, it would be evident that movement has appealed for special reasons, and to particular psychological types. So those forms of flight or varieties of ambition, that paradoxical mixture of motives which we call American, would become somehow a little easier to understand.

In sober fact, the history that we do have confirms our ways of speech and is illuminated by them. To yoke these two oxen of recorded experience and verbal fancy to one statement: We Americans got out of the European rut of localism, left behind the feudal traditions of man-land relation, and escaped from the immemorial submission to authority rather early. We also challenged the slow pace of time and used our space for a wide variety of purposes, some of them rather disreputable, as has been memorialized in our slang. Americans, so to speak, got started with the modernization of Europe, then got out while the going was good, and have been *goin' some* ever since.

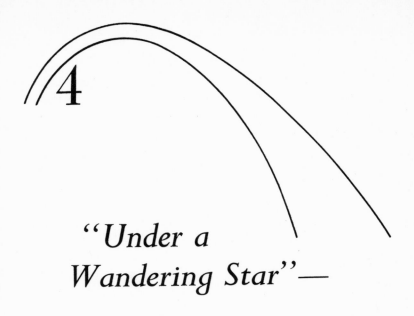

"Under a
Wandering Star"—

Three major brands of movement
today, with some variations and
incidental statistics

"Why, hello! Thought you were abroad. Aren't you on sabbatical?"

Professor P——— nodded, a bit sheepishly. It must have been the fourth time within the week that some colleague had demanded to know what on earth he was "doing in town." Without much conviction, he mumbled something about trying to get ahead on his book by some quiet research in the library. But it seemed to help much more when he confessed that he and his wife would be taking off for Greece in the spring. TRAVEL? That made sense. His friend's face lighted up. Perhaps, after all, P——— wasn't such a hopeless stick-in-the-mud.

Professor P———, in turn, was once again forced to recognize that in our culture a man who does not move

when he can is completely out of step.* His friends re-
proach him. His neighbors are troubled. Even casual acquaintances with quite different professional or business
concerns seem to be waiting for him to take off. And each
day the travel messages in the media, the resort-oriented
shop windows, the four-color ads for golden beaches and
tropical liquors and swimming pools in the sun, the very
airline commercials over his car radio keep reminding him
of what he is missing. "Put your trip in our hands. See how
great the going can be." "Get into this world." "Up, up and
away!" "Sign and fly."

Tourists and Vacationers: The World of Travel

For some years, in a rather casual way, I have been col-
lecting news items about travel, with their quantitative
statistical revelations. Thus on December 27, 1962, and
without any special emphasis, the *Wall Street Journal* reported that more than 2 million United States citizens

* Even if, or perhaps especially if, he's a professor. In a single
week, his mail may bring him a teasing postcard from a colleague at-
tending a scholars' conference in Bermuda, another from a favorite dean
presiding at a foundation-sponsored colloquium on Lake Como, still a third
greeting from a Fulbright lecturer in Japan, not to mention a gay note
from a former secretary now on a dig in Asia Minor with her husband.
Which will remind him that he must write some letters of introduction
for a graduate student pursuing his dissertation in Paris, and say goodbye to
a junior colleague about to shepherd a student tour through the Mediterranean. Thinking about the incessant wanderings of our far-flung academic
tribe brings to mind that West Coast saying: at any given moment one-
third of the Berkeley faculty are in the air.

Compare the sober study of our academic merry-go-round by David G. Brown, *The Mobile Professors*, American Council on Education,
1967: "A man may move three or four times before settling down to live
out his career. Some never do settle down. Job-switching, mostly voluntary, is the rule." Here and there, it seems, the rates of turnover are so
high as to endanger continuity of instruction and administration. Generally, only about 56% stay in or return to the region where they were
themselves educated (pp. 25–6, 32, 89).

were traveling abroad that year, at an estimated expenditure of $2.8 billion. Even so, according to the American Express Company's estimates, this foreign tourism wasn't a circumstance on the volume of domestic travel, on which we were spending about $23 billion, with the Seattle World's Fair alone attracting some 9 million visitors from near and far. Five years later, of course, Expo '67 would draw 50 million entrants, most of whom had to cross at least one international boundary to get there. And by 1971 we would be spending some $40 billion just on domestic vacation and pleasure travel.[1]

In man's long history he has known much wandering but rarely such individual freedom to come and go, or such a high incidence of personal mobility. Once, as we know, going abroad had been dangerous, or forbidden. Then in old Europe foreign travel, especially to distant places and strange climes, had become almost a monopoly of the powerful, the well-born, and the well-to-do. But now, even on the Continent, the upper middle classes are having to share their privileged pleasures of peregrination.[2] And in the United States all roads are open; sightseeing is for everyone; travel is *the* holiday diversion. The unoccupied American has become a tourist and tourism has become organized, rationalized, and packaged.

When congressmen "fly the coop," they are apt to go on a junket. When an appliance dealer wants to reward his best salesmen, he may send them all off to some Miami hotel. Office workers band together for all-expense bus tours of Europe. Garden clubs lure their ladies to the annual meetings by visits to Hawaii or the Virginia plantations. Congregations revive faithful ministers with a prepaid pilgrimage to Jerusalem, a little holiday in Scotland, or a visit to Rome. And "whether it's a short hop or a long, wide sweep around the world," your travel agents are on hand to help. "Use our family plan."

By 1964 our tourist trade had grown almost too large to measure, for the knowledgeable magazines were talking about 64 million tourists (or 130 million), planning to spend $13 million (or $30 billion), "getting away from the rigors and routine of life around the house," or "seeking sun and fun away from home." Tourism, some experts thought, had replaced wheat as the world's largest business. And nine out of ten families, it was claimed, now took their holidays on the road,[3] with some even jetting to Jamaica or the Virgin Islands for the weekend. *

Not everyone could go that far, of course, yet most apparently traveled a considerable distance. In 1959–60, a commission reported that only 9 per cent of U.S. vacationers were moving 50 miles or less, while 44 per cent were traveling between 100 and 500 miles, and another 44 per cent between 500 and 2000. Not all of this was in their own cars; but where, fifty years earlier, almost three-fourths of all travel had been by train, by 1962 less than 3 per cent of it was by rail, perhaps 7 per cent by bus and plane, and the automobile was king (by 1970 less than 1% would be by rail, 9.7% by air, and 89% by motor). In 1966 it was estimated that three out of four families owned their own automobile (by 1970, 82%), and one out of four had a second car in the garage. In the single year

---

* With the introduction into the calendar of the long three-day holiday weekends, American Express noted an increase in the "quick-demand, quick-satisfaction travel phenomena," and began offering special Mini-Holiday accommodations at resort hotels as "off-the-shelf" packages at reduced prices. American Express also introduced Holiday-of-the-Month programs and for several years their reservations service has been offering a "Space Bank" of accommodations and car rentals in more than fifty countries, advertised as giving the prospective traveler access to more than 600,000 rooms by a single telephone call.

1967 the Bureau of Public Roads would clock the total U.S. traffic at close to 1000 billion vehicle miles, or enough to allow each of the nation's almost 100 million motor vehicles to drive from New York to San Francisco, back to New York, and then back to San Francisco again. "Americans now take a total of 257 million trips a year," Hal Boyle solemnly reported, "and spend 2 billion nights away from home." [4] Meanwhile, the federal government had estimated the annual deficit from tourist expenditures abroad at $2 billion, and President Johnson would try to tax our air fares and *per diem* expenses so as to cut down on the dollar drain—which proposals were hardly popular or successful, as we all remember. Perhaps one final figure from the *Population Bulletin* will put a temporary stop light on our statistics: "On August 22, 1962, an unknown but significant American was recorded as the one-*billionth* visitor to the National Parks. It had taken fifty-eight years to accomplish this record, but the second billionth visitor is expected in 1973—only eleven years later!" [5]

Some of these visitors will of course be repeaters. But why go back? Or why go there in the first place?

Such questions can seem simpleminded to an American. A hundred years ago we knew the answers. "Americans have a special call to travel," announced the *North American Review* (1856). "No people on earth have such vagabond habits as ours," observed Nathaniel Hawthorne. "Strong and content I travel the open road," sang patriotic Walt Whitman. Others (as Foster Rhea Dulles has reminded us in his illuminating *Americans Abroad*)[6] looked rather to Europe, and with a pilgrim awe. "To my youthful imagination," he quotes Longfellow, "The Old World was a kind of Holy Land." "None but those who have experienced it" (Washington Irving in his *Sketch Book*) "can form an idea of the delicious throng of sensations which rush into an American's bosom when he first comes in sight of Europe. . . . It is a land of promise, teeming with everything of which his childhood has heard, or on which his studious years have pondered." Europe meant a "romantic return" to the past. Europe meant castles and gothic cathedrals, music and the arts, literature and more civilized living. To cultivated Americans,* "against the background of the leveling influences of Jacksonian democracy . . . Europe appeared bright and glowing"— nor has that glow even yet disappeared.

There sailed to Europe also (as Dulles and many others have regretfully reported) the toadies and the social climbers, the vulgar rich and the crude braggarts, the refugee artist and what Margaret Fuller once called the "booby truant"—our left-bank bohemians and beatniks would perpetuate the species.

So Europe has proved irresistible to a variety of individuals, but for a great diversity of reasons? The same will be found true for our own roads and parks, our mountains and seashores, and great open spaces. We go there to relax and enjoy ourselves; to get out of doors and admire the scenery; to go fishing, or hunting; to play golf, tennis, swim and sail. Or the reasons for going may lie behind us: we take a trip to get away from the office, to get out of the city, to forget our cares, to experience once again the thrill of being free. In a heat wave we make for the beaches, and in winter blizzards dream of some island in the sun. Travel can be instead for health; it rests the nerves, tones up the body's chemistry—as wise doctors know, a change of air can do wonders for the sickly.[7] Travel may also help one

---

* But not to all of them. Especially not to Emerson. For understandable reasons (was he not a patriot and a transcendentalist who lectured a good deal around the country?), he decided that "the soul is no traveller; the wise man stays at home. . . . Travelling is fool's paradise." *Essays*, first series: "Self-Reliance."

to forget. Indeed, travel offers an astonishing range of psychic therapies. In the excitement of new places and encounters, depressions will evaporate and disappointments fade. Travel can mean adventure, new sights and new sounds, encounters with the marvelous or the unexpected. It exercises our sense of wonder. Above all, it appeals to our insatiable curiosity. As James Whitcomb Riley put it: "Around the corner of the street / Who can say what waits for us?" To Americans, travel offers the welcome gift of surprise and that even more elusive delight: romance. To travel is almost always to hope. In the United States no small part of the pursuit of happiness is from place to place.*

Are there other travelers and other reasons to go? There must be a hundred. But perhaps in a preliminary way it will be enough to note that all the conscious motives seem to fall into three major categories: we set out, first, in order to find or to reach something; second, in order to escape and to get away from something; or third, just to enjoy the trip. *So far as we are aware of what we are doing,* most of us emphasize one or the other, or mix all three.

Yet there is obviously also a fourth element: something unconscious and not quite rational in this business. It serves our psychic restlessness and our instinct for

* I once knew a lawyer with a photographic memory who made a systematic recreation out of reliving—in his mind's eye—his European travels and American journeys, step by step and scene by scene. Between vacations the rest of us will try to enjoy travel vicariously, show last summer's movies, give the *National Geographic* to our kids, or ourselves subscribe to *Holiday,* which knows how to appeal [capitalization added]:

"FOOTLOOSE AND FANCY FREE!"
At last you're on that GLORIOUS trip you've always wanted to take!

There's the color and GAIETY of vacation time . . . the THRILL of being FREE from clocks and calendars . . . the dazzling GLAMOUR of FAR-AWAY PLACES . . . and it's all like a wonderful DREAM come true! . . .

change. It promises us things we cannot name yet somehow hanker for. In the hope of what it may bring, we will spend monies we have not got and tolerate discomforts no sane man would endure. We will even afterwards pretend the trip was all fun. Travel somehow feeds deep needs; it reconciles us to ourselves. So, to mix metaphors, going away or going abroad has become an indispensable component in the gear train of our expectations: an identifiable element in the pattern of the American dream.

The consequences? Of course even the most lighthearted holidays, on the scale we indulge in them, are not without social implications—and some of the most obvious by-products are economic. It has long been a commonplace that Americans own more cars, power boats, and planes than all the rest of the world, and that General Motors can be used as a barometer of the United States economy. Even in the Great Depression, we were reported as traveling hundreds of billions of passenger miles a year—and since 1946 that mileage has doubled or tripled—which has done no little to nourish our network of transport by rail, car, bus, boat, and plane, not to mention Hertz and Avis and U-Haul, or the seaside and mountain resorts, or the ranches of Montana and the pleasure palaces of Miami, or all the motels and motor courts and trailer camps and gas pumps and hot dog or ice cream stands that mushroom beside the highways. In 1952, according to *Holiday,* one-fifth of our investments and one-tenth of our consumer expenditures were going toward mobility:[8] a profitable mobility as well as a happy one. In these United States, it would appear, no small part of our capitalistic enterprise has been betting on motion.

In these United States many of the states themselves have become dependent on travel: on its taxes, its indirect revenues, its prestige. The Department of Commerce estimated the total take for the fifty states in fiscal 1967 at 22 per cent of their tax revenues. Americans were now said to be paying federal and state fuel levies at the rate of 47 per cent of the retail price of regular grade gasoline, or almost $1 million an hour: transportation, like the habit-forming pleasures we call alcohol and tobacco, can be taxed pretty steeply. Moreover, as our automobile clubs have discovered to their indignation, the state levies on gas sales, car licenses, and turnpike tolls now support all sorts of things besides roads.[9]

Travel can also have considerable political implications. Abroad, these are likely to range from the ludicrous to the extremely serious: as witness the costume and conduct of some of our more vulgar tourists—or the image of premature wealth that Europeans can hardly help but form—or the dangers of subversion the State Department seems to fear if our citizens take off for Havana or Hanoi. At home, the political possibilities can be humorous and substantial, too. If it hadn't been for Waikiki and our tourists, one may seriously ask, would Hawaii ever have been able to join the Union? Closer by, if New Hampshire had not long since become a glorified boardinghouse, how could its huge legislature have survived? As a certain sardonic friend of mine insists, only the weekend skiers and the summer folk have saved Vermont from going back to the Indians. In sober certainty the ski lifts of our Green Mountain State have been lifting something more than our expectant posteriors.

In season and out we travel, and day after day. So our eating habits are affected along the way. Perhaps we will pack a picnic; more likely, pause at a "diner" or grab a bite at a drive-in or quick-lunch counter. Alternatively, for those whose digestions will not stand such abuse, there are always the Howard Johnson or Holiday or Harvey restau-

rants. We know what *they're like,* for we've met them on
other routes and other holiday trips over the years. First
and last we travel so much that the roadside services have
become almost standardized to meet the recurring expectations.* It would almost seem as if our social organism
has reacted to the travel virus by inventing an antidote.
Surprise is to be neutralized by repetitions?

Abroad, our tourist hordes—commanding no foreign
languages, and nervous about the food, the water, and the
tipping—have shown themselves only too willing to pay
for the comfort and reassurance of the familiar. So American enterprise has produced American-style hotels in almost every Old World capital; and if some wandering
westerner feels homesick there is always a Hilton close by,
each, in the words of its founder, a "little America." As
Daniel J. Boorstin has remarked, "the traveler used to go
about the world to encounter the natives. A function of
the travel agencies now is to prevent this encounter." In
this kind of travel, nothing much changes but the names of
the city and country: we can circle the globe without leaving home. As Boorstin puts it, "the more we move about the
more difficult it becomes not to remain in the same place." [10]

Travel at home can likewise isolate from experience.
We have democratized movement to such a degree that
Main Street is everywhere. With greater speed, we have
also had to enclose our cars. Encapsulation is the price—
and "the great expressways are a guarantee that you can
now drive thousands of miles without seeing anything."
Having taken all sorts of precautions against adventure,

---

* Steinbeck found the food "in the eating places along the roads
. . . clean, tasteless, colorless, and of a complete sameness . . . strong,
pungent, exotic flavors arouse suspicion and dislike and so are eliminated." *Travels with Charley* (New York, 1962), pp. 126–7. The general
blandness of democratic recipes (whether gastronomic or social) has
been noted by Boorstin and many others.

we find that "everywhere turns out to be much the same as everywhere else." [11]

So we put radios and telephones and stereophonic tapes and television and bars in our cars, movies and organs and bar lounges in our planes, Muzak in the little vertical capsules we call elevators.* Having set out, some of us find the journey intolerable unless we can use the time for something else, too. Because of the sameness of the roads and the sameness of the surroundings, we have even been known to doze off. All too many Americans go to sleep at the wheel.

Such mobility can be lethal, and here the record seems shocking. What civilized nation commits the motorized slaughter of which we are guilty? Our accident tolls stagger the European imagination. By 1962, they exceeded 41,000 killed and 1.5 million injured every year (and they have been rising almost irresistibly: a count for 1970 showed some 55,000 killed, 5 million injured). Still and all, our casualty rate per mile traveled if not per person is undoubtedly well below Europe's.[12] To the returning traveler, who has seen something of the fretful malice of the French drivers, the recklessness of the Italians, or the casual irregularity of the English, our ordinary manner of driving will seem astonishingly sedate. It is true that too

---

* Rugged individualists (or humorists) may just rebel. *Stay At Home For A Change,* once advised Hal Boyle. "Why not be different this year . . . ?" "If you go to a mountain or beach resort your wife will want to buy a bunch of fancy new dress-up feathers, and you'll probably both return mosquito-chawed, saddle sore from horseback riding, or burned the color of old leather from too many siestas in the sun. . . . Ideally, a vacation should provide a restful change from the ordinary and enable one to recharge his depleted energy batteries. Where else can this be done better than at home?" (The Associated Press) Almost equally unbelievable was a U.P.I. photo of a Yale sophomore conducting a "sitathon" in his room. His thesis: "It takes far more will power and concentration to stay in one place than dash off in all directions."

Mauldin Draws Another War
—From The Travelers Insurance Companies'
"1970 Book of Street, Highway, and Interstate Accident Facts"
Reproduced by courtesy of Bill Mauldin; copyright © 1970 by
Bill Mauldin.

much horsepower, when combined with alcohol or youthful irresponsibility, can make a shambles of our expressways, especially at holiday seasons or on summer weekends. Yet the same occasions see also the greatest press of travelers on the road; and one has the impression that the steady accumulation of accidents, day by day, owes no little to the sheer unexampled volume of our traffic. After all, don't we spend more of our mortal moments on the road?

Let me epitomize all this tantalizing, captivating, ambiguous, and even frustrating activity we call travel by a symbol. I live in Connecticut. And rising above the skyline of Hartford has for years stood a tower built by one of the insurance companies which have made the prosperity of that city. Appropriately it is called the Travelers Insurance Company—and a greenish light shines from the top. I like to see in this soaring landmark, with its beacon, an emblem of all the romance, adventure, indigestion, health, wealth, freedom, taxes, and mortality brought to us by our roads.

Here Today and Gone Tomorrow: The Business of Moving

The cross-country motorist returns, if he is lucky, with only a dent or two in his fender. The skier rides back to college in his car or on a stretcher. The summer camper decamps with his trophies. The tourist whispers *au revoir* to Paris and flies home. Yet not always to the same house: instead often to a new domicile, on another street, perhaps even in a different town or state. Not all our tickets are round-trip, for we are engaged also in a second and more fundamental kind of movement: THE CHANGING OF OUR PLACE OF RESIDENCE.

This second kind of motion also goes on all the time and affects every one of us. We go to see new places, but to live in them, too. We hear of new jobs or opportunities, and hardly pause to put on our hats. If you or I began by leaving home to go to college, then transferred to a major university for business or professional training, then entered a firm or company in a town we had never seen—those may well have been just our first steps.

Careful observers have noted that the steeplechase of American life seems to involve some regular or periodic jumps, with a number of them concentrated in adolescence or early maturity. Statistically, the very young and the late teen-agers and young adults are the most mobile. When babies are small they are "captive movers," still transportable and often transported. The arrival of school age may then suggest to the parents resettlement near a better school. From that moment, however, and thereafter for perhaps the next ten years, both parents and children are restrained by educational considerations. After which, for the young boy or girl the normal process of growing up means going away to college—professional training or the first job—induction perhaps into the armed services for a spell—then marriage and striking out on one's own. At about age twenty-six, we again seem to show signs of settling down.[13] But then promotion, or new school-aged children, or a better business opportunity, or death or sickness in the family, or divorce and a new marriage, may trigger a fresh series of moves, a series which normally spaces out and diminishes over the years until old age, and retirement with its problems, may impel one final jump to some milder clime. Such changes of residence measure progress on life's journey: for the tribe called Americans they come close to *rites de passage*.

Not all of us complete this uphill and downhill series, or swing through its gates with the same zest or speed. Yet few of us get by without at least three removes. The first will have been in infancy, and involuntary; the second, for education. For a young man then to move away from his parents and seek his fame and fortune in a new city is an immemorial and almost irresistible prescription—and population studies show that between the ages of seventeen and twenty-seven the young woman is more mobile still. After that, however, marriage will put restraints on her movement, and for him the particular job or the general character of his vocation will either encourage or discourage further migration. This differentiation by vocation can be quite marked. Thus lawyers and doctors and politicians tend to stay with their clients; whereas musicians, actors, impresarios, and theater producers practice a spasmodic displacement almost as a matter of course; and some university professors are now turned almost nomad.

For people generally, education is also "a major determinant," it has been reported, with both the rate and the distance of migration rising with each increase in education. Not only do migrants tend to be better educated than nonmigrants, but "the highest migration rates are for those at the top of the educational ladder." * Vice versa, persons at (or near?) the bottom of the economic ladder seem to be the least mobile or, in moving, move only short distances, often just around and around.

Not surprisingly, it appears that "next to education, perhaps the best asset a worker can have is willingness to move . . . to improve his employment status." Lateral mobility and vertical mobility are often intimately connected and will operate independently (sometimes in dis-

---

* It is worth noting that most academic retirement benefits now have to be transferable, i.e., the professor has been learning to take his security with him (though some state systems, like some corporations, try by nonvesting to tie their staffs to their jobs). In unconscious tribute to the restlessness of our intellectuals, in 1968 The New York Review of Books told its subscribers that over 40% of them were changing their address each year. See the summary in "America: A Nation of Migrants," Vital Issues (March 1967); also William C. Greenough on "Have Brains, Will Travel" attitude, TIAA-CREF 1962 Annual Report.

regard) of the periodic transfer stations on life's journey.

Long-distance moves (over 100 miles) may be motivated by marriage or retirement, but almost 90 per cent of such household moves, according to the American Movers Conference, are being paid for by the government or large corporations, with the corporations alone accounting for two-thirds of the transfers.[14] So a good deal of our transcontinental experience is economically stimulated and controlled. In business and industry we move and have moved so much that we even take it for granted, shift employees about without scruple, build new factories in the back country, relocate the head office, order our junior executives to change departments and territories, and hardly hesitate to integrate business concerns many hundreds, even thousands of miles apart. Sometimes the man goes on the road: from Yankee peddler to Fuller Brush man, the traveling salesman has achieved a legendary reputation. But more often than many of us realize, the whole family becomes involved. Some while ago, in a two-page advertisement in *The New Yorker*, the Bank of New York showed a man and his family about to set out, with station wagon loaded and an open truck waiting for their dishwasher and furniture. The caption read (emphasis in the original):

AMBITION
. . . to move ahead
The typical American is eager to take on new responsibilities . . . ready to travel . . . to move his home or business to a new city when it is required.

Eighteen per cent of us—34 million Americans—change our address every year. And behind this mobility is one of the driving forces of our dynamic economy—*the ability to change . . . the desire to move ahead.*

Change is so much a part of our social and economic environment, our organic pattern of growth, that we accept it without thinking of its significance to our way of life. This year American business will spend in the range of $38 billion on new plant and equipment. . . .

Make no mistake—America is *on the move*. . . .*

Small wonder that the banks send out change-of-address blanks with every dividend check, or else ask you to correct the address in the space provided right on the check: "Have you moved recently? If so, please complete and mail this notice." And if we are now required to supply our Social Security number as well, may this not be at least in part because it seems a more stable identification than a transient address? Crazy as it sounds, people move so often and so carelessly that even close relatives may not know what's become of them. Hence bequests will go unclaimed, and tracing firms have to be created to run down cousins and grandnephews and other descendants, to protect them from losing their share of an estate under the escheat laws. Meanwhile, the Bell Telephone people claim that they have done their part "to make fluidity more fluid" by an "Easy Move Plan": to disconnect your old phone and get one in another territory served by the Bell system, you need only make a single call.

The effects of all this regular or irregular residential displacement? Just as with travel, the business of moving

* As long ago as 1921, in writing about "the neighborhood" for the *American Journal of Sociology* (27:161), R. D. McKenzie said the wage earner was "fast becoming a sort of tourist who spends but a short period in each community during his trip around the country." And commentators, both here and abroad, have often remarked the intimate link between mobility and economic change: fluidity of men and of skills has been indispensable to industrialization. "Lucky the country," observed *The Economist* (Jan. 18, 1964), "in which workers move smoothly from declining to expanding industries, from stagnating communities to growing ones, from obsolete crafts to the skills currently in demand. The American economy has always been thought to possess this key. . . ."

74

has some consequences for our political economy so substantial that we can hardly ignore them.* For example, with the elements of our population in such flux and with so many families moving and moving again, great demographic and political drifts have become possible: witness

REASON CHECKED
Unclaimed......Refused....
Unknown.................
Insufficient address.........
Moved, Left no address. ▶....
No such office in state.......
Do not remail in this envelope

the cumulative rush to the West Coast, the boom growth of Florida, the siphoning away of the preponderance of the Middle West.[15] Meanwhile, a thousand petty rural streams feed population into the reservoirs we call cities. The Southern Negroes stream off the land in such numbers that they swamp and bankrupt our metropolitan centers.

* Because it is professionally and intellectually selective, mobility causes qualitative as well as quantitative shifts, draws talents of many kinds to our great centers, and stimulates a "brain drain" from the Old World to the New, from rural to urban environment, and from middle America to the East and West coasts.

Of course not all our removals are geographically purposeful or in the same directions; they may be and often are reciprocal, back and forth, around and around. People also guess wrong in moving, and come back, or go off in some new direction. So the net balance of the population or the talents may be altered only fractionally. The point remains, however, that people are not sitting still: no matter which way the ball bounces, the populations of our towns are changing from day to day. Their age, their I.Q.'s, their ambitions, and their jobs make it impossible not to move. It makes one shiver a little to be told that perhaps one out of four of one's immediate neighbors, and on the average one-quarter or more of the residents on the nearby streets, won't even be living in the same state ten years from now.

And three-quarters of our counties register a net loss of population by migration. So by and by a congressional reapportionment makes it plain that in rather dramatic and uncomfortable ways the national centers of gravity have shifted.

A second major socioeconomic by-product of all this shifting about is that astonishing and sometimes sordid trade in second- and third-hand houses which we call the real estate business.*

A third is the strengthening of the trucking industry and the Teamsters Union by all that the moving vans and long-distance hauling can add (our *Mayflowers* of today have ten to fourteen wheels; and it is said to take some 12,000 companies and 19,000 warehouses to keep our migrating millions on the road).[16] Still a fourth consequence is a construction industry far more active (and powerful) than might otherwise be expected. In 1955, an industrial economist predicted that in the next decade more than 12 million new houses would be built and $450 billion would be spent for new construction, with another $150 billion for maintenance and repair[17]—all this in part because of population growth, but also because we are "traditionally restless and . . . eight or nine million families have moved their homes annually." The year before, it had been predicted that 31 million persons would pull up stakes and move, with at least 3 per cent of them going to some other state. And though Vietnam may have qualified some of these expectations, it has hardly arrested mobility. In 1963, our annual migration appears to have been estimated at at least 40 million. We may never know the exact

* The realtor is a European bird, of quasi-predatory disposition, who has multiplied prodigiously in the American wilderness. His ancestors exploited the first settlements, then in three hundred years helped sell and resell the continent. Could lots be sold only once, he would now be as extinct as the carrier pigeon.

number: our census schedules yield only sample-based tabulations. "Accurate statistics on the intra-national migrations in the United States are not available," stated the *Encyclopedia of the Social Sciences* back in 1933; "it is known, however, that American workers are far more mobile than the European."

So, even more strikingly, are our farmers. In traditional societies the men on the land, the peasant classes, have seemed the guarantors of stability. Hardly so, today, over here. Even disregarding the seasonal ebb and flow of migratory labor following the specialized crops, the instability of twentieth-century farm residence and occupation has been phenomenal. According to the 1935 Census of Agriculture, only 28 per cent of all the farm operators and sharecroppers had been on their farms for as much as ten years, and 26 per cent had been there less than two.[18] And the Department of Agriculture estimated that the average farm family remained on the same farm only five or six years.

A little later, André Siegfried, in *America at Mid-Century* (1955), reported that mass migrations within the country had

> made instability a dominant trait. People were moving from town to town, from job to job, and very often did not know who their grandfathers had been. . . . In 1947 only 44 per cent of American households lived in the same house as they had in 1940. . . . It is not surprising that, as families lose their territorial stability, psychological instability should become one of the predominant characteristics of the American, and that the dream that one might be born, live, and die in the same house should now be considered old-fashioned.[19]

Bypassing any psychological effects for the moment, we may well ask: Did anyone any longer really dream of dying in the house where he was born? Certainly not the recent immigrants. For with them, as Siegfried also noted, lateral movement was a means of vertical movement as well. With the older immigrants moving up the industrial ladder, as fresh arrivals took the lowest jobs, the same lodging might shelter in turn Irishmen, Italians, Russians, Negroes. And even after immigration restriction this movement appeared to continue, "for it is recorded that in the space of five years, in a certain district of New York 78 per cent of the inhabitants changed their address."

Not to be outdone by farmer or immigrant worker, our blue-collar and white-collar workers in the service professions have taken to living in the suburbs, commuting each day to work, and making a major move from house to house or suburb to suburb sometimes as often as once a year. The suburbs, after all, have been created by mobility, and for suburbanites the oscillations of which we have been speaking are built in.

Half traveler, half permanent transient is the commuter, with some special problems of his own thrown in.* His is the Rush Hour. His is much of the traffic we encounter on the expressways; and his are the accidents, too. Each morning and evening the metropolitan helicopters keep watch over his antlike writhings; and each day the

---

* Perhaps we should even treat the commuting suburbanite as a distinct species of *homo ambulans?* For commuting represents a kind of compromise with migration. And out of this bifocal existence seems to have sprung a special subculture: that of the country club—a younger generation preternaturally unruly and irresponsible—a daytime women's society of jitneying mothers and lonely wives, uncomfortable enough in their frustrations to galvanize the welfare organizations (or inspire a considerable erotic subliterature).

Still another subspecies is the mini-commuter, who lives in the city and takes the subway to work. And then there are the types who have inspired the weather forecasters to announce the temperatures and cloud conditions in our "shuttle cities"!

battered and abandoned remains of what were once two hundred shiny new cars have to be hauled from New York's streets and parkways and expressways by the Department of Sanitation.[20]

The suburbs themselves are unstable. As dormitory towns, as socially segregated or segregating enclaves in the retreating countryside, theirs would seem a quite durable function. Yet their character is rather as perches for people on the way up or the way down. Even as favored a "stopping-off" place as Greenwich, Connecticut, sees the same houses on the market every three or four years.*

"By now, haven't we got enough status to move *out* of Westport?"
—By John A. Ruge, in *The Saturday Review*, February 9, 1963

* Clarence Dean, in *The New York Times* (Nov. 24, 1964) quoted the New Canaan branch of the Deerfield County Trust Company as estimating the average turnover in mortgages at 7½ years. At a cocktail party, it was found that most of the twenty guests had moved their homes four or five times since marriage. The couple of longest residence had been in New Canaan for only five years. " 'They come and they go,'

But let us rather turn to the great centers of our population, to our cities. The dependence of our cities upon communication and transportation is beyond previous experience, and far greater than that of ancient Rome on its fleets and the Roman roads. Without the American style of movement,[21] New York, Chicago, and their sisters could hardly have been imagined, or created, let alone maintained. Nor is this simply to call attention to the millions siphoned in and out each day, as commuters or as visitors, as young conquerors or as dispirited refugees. We might perhaps notice the relative magnitude of these transfusions, and the suffocation that sets in the moment our asphalt arteries become clotted and the life-giving traffic crawls to a halt. But let us rather think for a moment about a special burden laid on our cities by mobility. I refer to the poignant problem of our American slums.

How is it that in this land of opportunity, among this people of plenty, and especially in our "affluent" generation, we have such shameful slums? The maldistribution of wealth? No doubt in part. The influx of poverty-stricken populations? Without question—that has been our history: "Give me your poor . . .", as Emma Lazarus voiced it. Then overcrowding, discrimination, and exploitation? Certainly. Yet do not these answers miss one of the fundamental peculiarities of our American slums?

Why, after all, are they so hard to deal with? And why do they seem to threaten not just one part but every part of our modern city? Is it not perhaps because, when a district starts to become unattractive, many of the "better" people begin to move away, while the "minority groups"

---

said the manager of a fancy foods store pensively. 'You miss them one day and then you learn they've moved to Dallas.' 'Different faces all the time,' said the conductor of a New Haven commuter train."

irresistibly seep in? In our society it is relatively so easy to find new or better housing elsewhere that the substantial citizens choose to escape while there is time, instead of staying to fight the grim battle against decay. Hence the heart and civic pride can go out of a ward with a disconcerting and irresistible suddenness. Within one generation, New York can lose the population and stability of its Upper West Side, and have gangs now roaming the streets near its Riverside vistas, while within the imposing shells of its blocked buildings Puerto Ricans and Southern blacks swarm. In Europe such things move, or used to move, more slowly. In an Old World port one knew where the slums would be. In Paris the arrondissements seem to be tenacious of character and resistant to change. Whereas over here the slum is a disease that cannot be quarantined, a cancer that spreads, almost a galloping blight.

In this process one is struck by a second peculiarity of our slums: the conscienceless neglect of the dwellings. The housing need not be poor to start with; all too often a fine residential district becomes involved. Nor is it entirely the fault of landlords, rapacious as many prove themselves in exploiting the underprivileged. Nor is it because these new tenants are too poor (or have no pride). No. Rather the answer is that they don't seem to care where they live, or how they live, or what their place looks like—so long as they can have a television set, *and a car* to park at the curb. In that car they can escape to greener pastures now and again? Yes. But also to a higher level of aspiration. The hot-rod, the maroon Pontiac, the (third-hand) lavender Cadillac: these have been status symbols. It is even sometimes more important to have a car that is shiny than to be sure it will run. So we see how deeply the image of mobility has been absorbed into the American dream. For the underprivileged it is not the real estate but the transportation, not good cooking and home comforts but bucket seats and the car radio, not the family domicile but the power to move, that really matter.

It may be granted that at least a few slum dwellers obviously take pride in a neat personal appearance, and for them a shiny car also represents a personal protest against an almost intolerable environment. Again, better housing may not be too easy to come by, given the added factor of simple ignorance on the part of the recent arrivals. On top of this last, I have been told,

> a slum infects the people in it with a gradual loss of interest in trying to keep their places clean. There is a progressive hopelessness about the condition of the buildings, the litter and refuse in backyards, sidewalks and gutters. Why bother fighting dirt? You can't beat the system.[22]

But why doesn't a city make landlords and tenants clean up the refuse by simply enforcing the sanitary regulations? "Because this would be politically unpopular—or so it is believed." Yet car registrations and drivers' licenses are required of everyone, regardless of status or party vote, or residence in an "area of degeneration." Which brings us back to the naked fact that people just don't care enough about the look and smell of the slums to clean them up.

The resulting neglect of the slum dwelling makes understandable, though not necessarily successful, our great efforts at slum clearance and urban renewal by low-cost public housing. But will the tenants of the old dilapidated rookeries pay even what such tax-supported apartments will cost? And will they then stay, and help the social agencies to create in the district a new sense of community pride? Some better elements may, but the rest will probably drift off, to honeycomb the neighboring sections of the city. Ironically, when a slum is torn down, no small portion of the human population just "slopes" off and disappears. So resettlement can be made to work perhaps only because a substantial part of the problem is not heard of again, or is only later discovered, in some "gray" area of the city, sharing unpainted flats with some new race of transients just arrived.* The most discouraging thing about social work, in the premises, must be that it deals with an endless procession, and its human salvage operations must forever be started over.

By contrast one might note the effort at urban renewal in New Haven, Connecticut. I take it as a symbol of our spatial instability that, when Mayor Richard C. Lee faced the flight of industry, population, and trade from his city, and moved to cut out the rot that was eating at its vitals, he first tore down the worst slum section, then built in its place an eight-lane concrete "Connector" to the new Connecticut turnpike, then on the edge of the Connector and in the very heart of New Haven commissioned the creation of a spectacular multi-level, open-air parking garage. Next to which was then erected a gleaming hotel. The salvation of a city by circulation? No less.

On and On: The Plaint of the Open Road

Movement means life. To the American it is not "I think, therefore I am," but "I move, so I'm alive." [23] The generations and the occupations demand it. Our urban concentrations would suffocate without it. Our social ambitions are only possible in these terms.

---

* It seems to me that the reformers and the economists, sociologists, public health people, and politicians have been too slow to recognize and too timid to face the unstable reality of the American slum. Obviously they haven't paid nearly enough attention to mobility: to population flows which can overwhelm the best planned city, to group instabilities which will make mockery of welfare budgets or public housing plans.

So, look where we will, society is in motion. To Americans old or new, from farm or city, in business or the professions, to move has become almost as natural as to breathe. And if by some freak accident you or I live where our ancestors did, or have become attached to our residences and not anxious to leave, a new superhighway, or condemnation by public authority, may simply force us to go—with only such compensation as the loss of house and lot may suggest. No damage can be done to the psyche, or none that will be recognized by the courts or public opinion. Moving, after all, is no hardship.

On the contrary, the American psyche would really suffer if it were made to sit still. As Lyman Bryson remarked, "We are restless because of incessant change, but we would be frightened if change were stopped." [24] Just so. Motion has become to many of us an emotional necessity. There is in us an unconquerable restlessness: a "third force" in our lives.

We may "travel," or we may "move," but why do we KEEP ON MOVING? Presumably each kind of motion has its reasons. Each year we may take a trip and return, and be moved to these journeys by curiosity or sense of adventure, by the hope of recreation and fun, by renewal of family ties(!), by the romance of far places and visions of unknown splendor—and all this we may simply call travel. Alternatively—being put in motion by professional opportunity or hope of gain, social ambition, administrative necessity, or public compulsion—we may go so far as to change our residence: a second and more substantial rationale of movement. Yet some Americans keep moving also when there is no reason, no fun or gain in prospect, no necessity. In season or out, they keep on and on and seem helpless to stop.

Are we to call this habit? Have we moved so much,

for good reasons, that we keep on in a sort of mindless, good-natured way? Or is it not more often a strange restlessness, a sort of gnawing uneasiness, an inner instability or psychological compulsion? Whatever the name, or the emotions involved, this urge can be pervasive and surprisingly powerful. Few of us have escaped it entirely. And some have been so infected by this fever, this recurrent spatial itch, that they have become homeless wanderers all their lives. John Steinbeck described the breed. Possibly he was one himself. He began his *Travels with Charley: In Search of America:*

> When I was very young and *the urge to be someplace else* was on me, I was assured by mature people that maturity would cure this itch. When years described me as mature, the remedy prescribed was middle age. In middle age I was assured that greater age would calm my fever and now that I am fifty-eight perhaps senility will do the job. Nothing has worked. Four hoarse blasts of a ship's whistle still raise the hair on my neck and set my feet to tapping. The sound of a jet, an engine warming up, even the clopping of shod hooves on pavement brings on the ancient shudder, the dry mouth and vacant eye, the hot palms and the churn of stomach high up under the rib cage. In other words, I don't improve; in further words, once a bum always a bum. I fear the disease is incurable. . . .

Again:

> When the virus of restlessness begins to take possession of a wayward man, and the road from Here seems broad and straight and sweet, the victim must first find in himself a good and sufficient reason for going. This to the practical bum is not difficult. He has a built-in garden of reasons to choose from. . . .

And again:

> We find after years of struggle that we do not take a trip; a trip takes us. . . . I was to see over and over in every

part of the nation—a burning desire to go, to move, to get under way, anyplace away from Here. They spoke quietly of how they wanted to go someday, to move about, free and unanchored, not toward something but away from something. I saw this look and heard this yearning everywhere in every state I visited. Nearly every American hungers to move. . . .

"Lord! I wish I could go."
"Don't you like it here?"
"Sure. It's all right, but I wish I could go."
"You don't even know where I'm going."
"I don't care. I'd like to go anywhere." . . .[25]

Historically, this breed is not unfamiliar. By all accounts the old frontier knew many unstable characters. In our westward expansion through America's rich farmlands, it wasn't just the hired hands who kept moving. Indeed, the Yankee instinct to move on was said to be so irresistible that "if hell lay in the west, they would cross heaven to reach it" [26] —and hell, or another purgatory of restlessness, was often exactly what they found. On the Kansas plains and elsewhere, the frontier was so unstable that even the minimal five-year residence requirement of the Homestead Act proved malsuited (the "farmers" just wouldn't wait that long). Then in California, as the overland trail ended, the vagrants accumulated.* And yester-

* "Pick up the United States by the state of Maine, and everything loose will roll down to Los Angeles"?

Correspondent Michael Frayn reported for *The Observer* (London) that: "Humbert Humbert, driving Lolita endlessly from motel to motel, lived out one of the most fundamental of all American myths, the idea that *you can always move on* . . . people pack up and move on an impulse; one of the first people I spoke to here [L.A.] had left Buffalo because there was a snowstorm on, driven 1,000 miles with his family to Memphis, Tennessee, got stuck in a traffic jam there, and decided somewhere in the jam to turn right and continue the odd 1,800 miles out to the coast." A lot of people then seemed to feel that California was the

day in our cities, which are the end and the beginning of so many journeyings, the beatnik temperaments were following Kerouac, or dreaming of the open road. For the "hippie" generation, we are told, music and marijuana are the preferred opiates. But is there not also a good deal of moving about, of sudden arrivals and departures, of psychic restlessness seeking release? [27] Pain can be stilled by keeping going, their actions would seem to say. To the sullen and unfulfilled there comes always the word of some other place. In the words that Alan Jay Lerner put in the mouth of an old gold seeker in *Paint Your Wagon* (1952), "some folks ain't never meant to have a home . . ." [28]

> I was born under a wand'rin star.
> I was born under a wand'rin star.
> Stayin' put can kill ya,
> Standin' still's a curse,
> To settle down can drive ya mad
> But movin' on is worse.
> I was born under a wand'rin star.
>
> When I learned to talk the word they taught me was
>   "good-by"
> That and "Where's my hat?" are all I'll need until I die
> Achin' for to stop and always achin' for to go;

---

end of the line and, if they didn't like it, "turned to religion or drugs or shot themselves. But there seem to be plenty who keep circulating—from one part of California to another, from California to Arizona, from Arizona back to California, and perhaps out to Florida for their holidays. . . ." "Frayn in America: On the Road," *The Observer* (London), Nov. 20, 1966. The remark about the Homestead Act I take from James Malin, "Mobility and History," *Agricultural History* (October 1943), XVII:181. From a century ago comes: "There are three wants which can never be satisfied: that of the rich who want something more; that of the sick who want something different; and that of the traveller who says 'Anywhere but here.' " Emerson, *Conduct of Life*.

Searchin' but for what I never will know.
I was born under a wand'rin star . . .*

Who are our wanderers today? They are of many kinds. Excluding the Gypsies (who are alleged to flourish in American social conditions and to swarm in our open campsites[29]), one can still identify a handful of old hobos or "wobblies": men who rode the rods and followed the rails from town to town—men like "Bigtown" Gorman, who was elected king of the hobos and who supported himself with odd jobs for sixty years—men like Scissors Sam, who is no longer running from anything but traveling just to be traveling: "It's a disease," says Sam. There are also the types they scorned: the tramps or bums or drifters who do no work but become mission stiffs and winos, or "Sally Tramps" (going from one Salvation Army post to another).[30]

In succession to the freight train hobos, our automobile culture has given rise to the hitchhiker, who may be just a youngster trying to save money, or a soldier on leave, or a man looking for a job, but who may instead turn out to be a bemused dreamer, or a perpetual "loser," or even someone quite unpleasant and dangerous.

Perhaps hundreds of thousands of our modern wanderers have been on the road for years, in their own cars, begging from gas station attendants and obsessed with moving on. These "jalopy nomads," on their endless trips

* Those who love such music (old and new) tell us that folk songs are full of the sad plaints of wandering: "Look down, look down that lonesome road, / Hang down your head and cry." "Man's gotta go somewhere, can't stay where he is."
> Nail your shoes to the kitchen floor,
> Lace them up and bar the door . . .
> For I can't help but wonder where I'm bound,
>   where I'm bound.

"Aye, 'tis said when New York's sales tax jumped to seven per cent he slipped across the line into Connecticut. And when Connecticut passed its tax package he fled to New Hampshire. And now, the legend goes, he flees from state to state forever."

—*The New Yorker,* September 25, 1971
Drawing by Ed Fisher; Copyright ©
1971 The New Yorker Magazine, Inc.

to nowhere, seem to be increasing in numbers and often they may travel in families or groups. As Barbara Carter has described them,

> . . . they are Southern tenant farmers who have been pushed off the land by mechanization; skilled and semi-skilled workers displaced by automation; families from distressed areas such as parts of Pennsylvania, West Virginia, and the mountains of Kentucky; teen-age school dropouts hitchhiking across the country; abandoned young mothers with children looking for relatives to help them; occasional schizophrenics who have been released from hospitals under the new drug therapy—in short, any

of the various combinations of the unemployed, the unskilled, and the unwanted. Many of them are Negro, and many of them are illiterate.[31]

Many, perhaps all too many, are sick: eroded or erratic personalities, visionaries without anchorage in reality, lost souls. Does constant movement attract the unbalanced —and perhaps increase the unbalance? Our demographers and sociologists have not yet decided these issues, but I am convinced it does both. The pathological restlessness, the refusal to face problems, the inability to plan, the rejection of friends and neighbors, the self-separation from mankind, the resort to loneliness as to a drug: these are signs of less than good health. Rates of admission to mental hospitals seem to be higher for migrants. Homeless men turn out to have deviant histories. Migratory children not only develop behavioral difficulties, but then contribute out of proportion to crimes of violence, and perhaps later to a second generation of disturbed vagrants.[32]

In common experience, the misfits and failures, the petty gangsters and confidence men, all follow a wandering star. Yet so, too, do many crusaders and missionaries in search of new sinners, new sufferings, and new visions of perfection. The star does beckon to some with hope, for it can mean freedom, and another chance at goodness or power. But for many it is a lodestone whose influence is baleful and ultimately destructive. It draws men away from society and civilization; it sets experience and authority at defiance; it evades the law and disintegrates convention. Many travelers under this sign travel light, for they have abjured the past; they have abandoned the arts, the ethical codes, and the power systems, along with many of the creature comforts and emotional reassurances which civilized communities have painfully put together. Wander-

ing is for the "marginal man." [33] It selects the anonymous
and the defeated: "beat up in one place where nobody
loves me—moved to another place where nobody knows
me."

Repeated displacement also has a simplifying and exag-
gerative effect. Like our westward movement, or some
great oilcracking process, it seems to distill out special
types. Often the detached individual is driven to brooding
fixations, or is encouraged to go to extremes. At the end of
such lonely trails have emerged the Daniel Boones and the
wilderness prophets, the Johnny Appleseeds and Billy
Sundays, the Joseph Smiths and John Browns and Lee
Harvey Oswalds, the men who find salvation in some ob-
sessive idea.

In fairness we should also note some accidental benefits. As has been suggested (by Sorokin in *Social Mobility*), the individual encounters, the unexpected atomic
collisions, the stepped-up reciprocal bombardment of
ideas conduce to comparisons, imitations, even inventions
by analogy or the creation of new ideas. May not at least
one good reason for the proverbial inventive ingenuity of
the Yankees have been a release from provincial assumptions and unthinking repetitions by an intense circulation
of miscellaneous ideas, and by all sorts of encounters with
odd customs and strange devices—experiences which
came from or were stimulated by their own restless travels?

If restlessness leads to experimentation, to an acceptance of change, and a special fondness for the new, no
doubt it may also be said to widen our opportunities, encourage our optimism, give us a rebirth of freedom and a
reassuring sense of elbow room. Unquestionably, mobility
encourages activity. We are an activist, not a sedentary
people.

Yet when our actions are successful, then are we often still not content—but must improve upon what works, abandon what is old. For such spirits, one suspects, Heaven would be a suffocation—unless indeed it had many mansions,* each a little further on and promising to be different from the last. Meanwhile, on earth, "our national motion sickness" seems to have a deleterious effect on our earthly abodes. "Moving On . . . encourages the impermanent, makeshift atmosphere which renders some places in America so ripe to be Moved On from." [34] Wandering feeds on itself?

However such mysteries may be decided, long ago movement became for some an end in itself, an incurable longing, a narcotic loneliness, whose victims were always achin' for to stop and always achin' for to go: searchin' for what they never did know. As Edna St. Vincent Millay put it in her poem, "Departure":

> It's little I know what's in my heart,
> What's in my mind is little I know,
> But there's that in me must up and start,
> And it's little I care where my feet go.

So mobility today is hardly a simple or an innocent way of living. Rather, reflection suggests that movement with us derives from no one source. It can be of markedly different kinds. It serves a diversity of ends. Turn by turn its mood

* The same goes for Greek islands, as witness the Special Travel Issue of *Vogue*, April 15, 1971. "We find nowadays that staying in one place for more than—shall we say—three months is intolerable" (Richard Burton on "Travelling with Elizabeth"). "I dream of going to a Greek Island to stay months on end, but after a week I can't wait to move on. . . . My tempo has been established. . . . The treacherous thing about travelling so much is that it becomes a way of life" (Valerian Rybar).

may be playful, purposeful, or psychotic. We may take to the road for recreation, occupation, or evasion, or simply because it has become an obsession, alternative to something even more impossible, that is, standing still. "Refugees," Lenin has been credited with saying, "refugees are people who vote with their feet." And in America nearly everyone votes, but with wheels, and for the most extraordinary conglomeration of programs, social, economic, political, or strictly neurotic.

In this headlong world of ours, our emotional and cultural drives have become so blended and confused and so intimately involved with spatial activity that moving and moving again have become almost second nature. The displacement of men is an indispensable component in our technology. Without spatial movement, no social improvement, either. Our work and our play, our cities and our countrysides, our taxes and our eating habits, our pleasures and our pains, our hopes and our fears are inextricably tied up with mobility.

Perhaps we must also face the fact that continuity in place has never been what most of us New World characters have been looking for, but rather freedom, opportunity, novelty, change. So, on our perpetual quest, stability has come to seem somehow reprehensible, and "permanent" a dirty word.[35] As has been noted by foreigners, but not always with understanding, the American seems to have no foundation, and few ties with the past. Here today, he will be gone tomorrow—and he couldn't care less for yesterday. To put this a little differently, either by accident or by design, engagement with motion has produced disengagement from memory. Indeed, with many of us, what is past has been passed and deliberately left behind. "He is an American," observed Crèvecoeur almost two hundred years ago, "who leaves behind his ancient prejudices and manners." "Let the dead past bury its dead," was Longfellow's very American advice. "The past is a bucket of ashes," insisted Carl Sandburg in his century. And only recently Margaret Mead found herself explaining our ability to block out the past with a kind of innocence staggering to the European: "Nostalgia for the past is out of place among a people who must always be moving, to a better job, a better house, a new way of life. To the immigrant from Poland . . . nostalgia for the past way of life is an acute threat to good adjustment." [36] And so it is to wanderers of every kind: to the hippie or the traveling salesman, to the young man on the make or the blue-collar couple who have just moved to the suburbs, to the rising young executive and his wife, or to our ambitious scientists and professionals.

The American must look forward, not back. His memory must be as short as his trail is long. For he was born under the sign for the uprooted and the homeless, the sign of the wandering star.

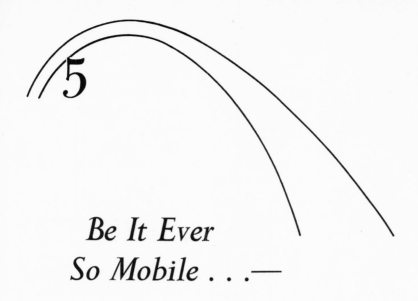

5

Be It Ever So Mobile . . .—

Reflections on the home that moves

Writing home from England, a century ago, Edward Everett Hale explained to his young son about the Hale family ancestry:

> . . . I believe it was from . . . Canterbury that Robert Hale came who was a good blacksmith who lived at Charlestown. . . . Then his son [John] went to Beverly, and his son Samuel went to Newburyport, and his son Richard went to Coventry [Conn.], and his son Enoch went to Westhampton, and his son Nathan went to Boston, and his son Edward went to Roxbury; where his son Philip will go I do not know,—but they all seem to have a disposition to live in a different place from their father's.[1]

In seven generations the English Hales had got as far as Roxbury. Possibly that was because they were still revolving about Boston, the hub of the Brahmin universe. In the same generation but out of a quite different State (and state of restlessness and feeling about ancestors), an Illinois railsplitter with the equally English name of Lincoln opined: "I don't know who my grandfather was; I'm much more concerned to know what his grandson will be." *

Over and over again the older families, the intellectuals and the Eastern élites, had been converted to or swamped by this human restlessness and social instability. In 1917, President Hadley of Yale, congratulating a Superintendent of Schools for half a century of public service, wrote mournfully: "In these days of change, fifty years of continuous service anywhere indicates the sort of thing that our country needs and of which it gets far too little. I remember President Eliot saying that the most ominous thing to him about the future of the republic was the fact that so few lived in the same houses where their grandfathers did." [2] The presidents of Harvard and Yale evidently agreed as to the drift—and regretted it. But of course not everyone thought about it the same way. Thus,

---

* The tribal wanderings of the forgotten Lincolns had begun in 1636 with a landing at Salem and settlement at Hingham by Samuel Lincoln, weaver; removal to Cohasset by his son Mordecai, ironmaster and miller; removal of his son, Mordecai II, also a blacksmith, first to Covell's Hill in New Jersey, then to the vicinity of Reading, Pennsylvania. His son John, a weaver, had acquired "the roving spirit" and lit out for Linville Creek in the Shenandoah; John's son Abraham bought land from his friend, Daniel Boone, along the Wilderness Road near Louisville in Kentucky, and while clearing it was killed by an Indian arrow. What next happened to his young son Thomas, and to Thomas's son Abraham, is recorded in our histories.

Lincoln's remark about ancestors is quoted in Edmund Fuller, *Thesaurus of Epigrams* (as is the characteristic American sentiment: "A man who boasts only of his ancestors confesses that he belongs to a family that is better dead than alive"). The migrations of the early Lincolns are retraced in W. H. Van Hoesen, "The Lincoln Family Trek," *My Country* (Litchfield, Conn., Spring 1971), vol. V, no. 2, pp. 9–14.

the future Yale graduate and musical iconoclast Charles Ives, *aet.* ten, when told by his father that it was customary to start and finish pieces in the same key, said "that was as silly as having to die in the same house you were born in." [3]

THE BRADSTREET FARM
Rowley, Mass.
ESTABLISHED IN 1635
BY HUMPHREY BRADSTREET
AND OWNED BY
THE SAME FAMILY
CONTINUOUSLY
FOR 316 YEARS!*

—Ripley, *Believe-It-or-Not,* 1952

"We can put our children on wheels to see the world," reflected H. S. Canby in 1934, "but we cannot give them the kind of home that any town provided in the nineties, not at any price." ** [4]

---

* The exclamation mark is authentic American.—G.W.P.

** By 1963 Hamilton Fish Armstrong was confessing (*Those Days* [New York, 1963], p. 7): "I once thought that an easy way to become president of something would be to form a society of New Yorkers still inhabiting the houses where they were born, but I could discover no

Home? "Home" is a lovely old English word. It speaks to the heart of inexpressible things. The lawyers and justices of old England had made it a bastion of individual liberty: a man's home was his castle—*Domus sua cuique tutissimum refugium*[5]—and not to be searched without warrant. Our own forefathers had shaped it into the basic industrial unit of our free society and an almost sacred institution: the hearth of affection, the nursery of idealism, the fountainhead of morality, *and* the focus of personal freedom. Here the young had been taught their first letters and their responsibilities. Wishing to expand our republic and to multiply our independent families, our fathers had then voted themselves free homesteads. Feeling so strongly, they made songs for the world to sing, about "Home, Sweet Home":

> 'Mid pleasures and palaces though we may roam,
> Be it ever so humble, there's no place like home.

One thinks of Stephen C. Foster's "My Old Kentucky Home," and perhaps also of that World War I song: "Keep the Home Fires Burning."

Yet over those same centuries some odd things had apparently been happening to that symbol or family dream. Back in the Old World, "home" had acquired a second major meaning:* to empire builders and to trav-

---

members." Which stimulated a country editor to add: "You don't hear about 'family homesteads' because they aren't."—Brighton-Pittsford *Post*, March 5, 1964.

* *The Shorter Oxford English Dictionary* gives nine distinct definitions: "1. A village or town (OE & ME); 2. A dwelling place, house, abode—the fixed residence of a family or household—one's own abode . . . 3. The place of one's dwelling or nurturing, with its associations; 4. The grave, or future state (as in 'his long home'); 5. A place, region or state, in which one properly belongs, in which one's affections centre, or where one finds rest, refuge, or satisfaction; 6. One's own country, one's native land, the place where one's ancestors dwelt; 7. The seat,

elers it meant their native land—to Englishmen particularly as they began to venture out from their tight little isle. One stumbles on this usage in their songs, and in their books. Shakespeare had the foreknowledge:

> Ay, now I am in Arden: the more fool I.
> When I was at home I was in a better place; but
> travellers must be content.
>
> *As You Like It*

In Oliver Goldsmith's *The Traveller* one finds:

> Such is the patriot's boast, where'er he roam,
> His first best country ever is at home.

In Scott's *Lay of the Last Minstrel* echoes the homesick cry of those who die abroad: "unwept, unhonored, and unsung":

> Breathes there a man with soul so dead,
>   Who never to himself hath said,
>   This is my own my native land!
>
> Whose heart has ne'er within him burn'd
>   As home his footsteps he hath turn'd
>   From wandering in a foreign strand? . . .

Alexander Pope insisted that homebodies were more content:

> Happy the man, whose wish and care
> A few paternal acres bound,
> Content to breathe his native air
> In his own ground.
>
> *Ode on Solitude*

And Pope also spotted something else. In leaving home,

---

centre, or native habitat; 8. An institution providing refuge or rest; and 9. In games: the place in which one is free from attack, the goal."

Englishmen risked losing it: a house was not a home, unless dwelt in:

> I find by all you have been telling
> That 'tis a house, but not a dwelling.
>
> *Upon the Duke of Marlborough's*
> *House at Woodstock*

So in going abroad Englishmen were substituting country for home—and perhaps losing both?

> Horses, oxen, have a home
> When from daily toil they come;
>
> . . . .
>
> All things have a home but one—
> Thou, O Englishman, hast none!
>
> SHELLEY,
> *The Mask of Anarchy*

Unless of course his religion offered him an ultimate and truer "home." For Jesus had gone ahead "to prepare a place" for all believers, in God's house of many mansions. After the life temporal, the life eternal. And after sin and suffering in this vale of tears, the hope of immortality and a heavenly home. In a sense both symbolic and real, ever since the fall of Adam and Eve and their expulsion from the Garden of Eden, the people of the Hebraic tradition had always felt themselves in physical and spiritual exile —while over and over again the believing Christian had been reassured that he was on a pilgrimage toward a more perfect resting place or "home."

> Here in the body pent,
> Absent from Him I roam,
> Yet nightly pitch my moving tent
> A day's march nearer home.
>
> JAMES MONTGOMERY,
> *At Home in Heaven*

One thinks also of Cardinal Newman's "The night is dark and I am far from home; Lead Thou me on!"

From such memories, devotionals, and fragments of song, does one not get the suggestion that the colonizing Englishmen were already somewhat detached from their abodes? At the very least, in crossing the Atlantic, they would have to try to resettle and *make new homes* in a savage New World. And if they were at the same time Dissenters, outcasts both political and religious, expatriated by the Reformation, in exile like the Children of Israel but on a Pilgrim's Progress, then these new homes might from the start seem rather temporal dwellings on that journey toward a better life hereafter. For Heaven was their destination. Inevitably to both Pilgrims and Adventurers there was something makeshift and transitory about their first New World dwellings.

Then as the original colonists died, and the generations passed and the fervor of the Reformation cooled, and fur trade and farming drew people inland, there came the experience of the second and third transplanting and before long an acceptance of detachment from the ancestral hearth. The young would rather make their homes farther on. They would subdue the forest wilderness, plow the prairies, "settle" the whole West. For increasing numbers, the continent rather than Heaven became the manifest destination. By the 1850's, our homely poet John Greenleaf Whittier was celebrating the new mission:

> We crossed the prairies as of old
> The pilgrims crossed the sea,
> To make the West, as they the East,
> The homestead of the free!
>
> *The Kansas Emigrants*

For many footloose children and their children's children their home became the whole landscape or the great out-of-doors. This American tendency to make one's country rather than one's house one's home had already been justified by that lofty transcendentalist, Ralph Waldo Emerson:

> Go where he will, the wise man is at home,
> His hearth the earth,—his hall the azure dome;*
>
> *Wood Notes,* I, 1, 3.

Oliver Wendell Holmes also felt called upon to defend our earth-cruising habits:

> Where we love is home,
> Home that our feet may leave but not our hearts.
>
> *Homesick in Heaven*

A prophet of a different order was Nathaniel Hawthorne, who could see in stability a kind of enemy, and in a home the implication of a prison. In his *The House of*

---

* As Earl H. Rovit has so suggestively put it in his "The American Concept of Home": "And the individual traveler—the American—is seen in this current of American literature and painting as man against the sky, man in the open air, exposed directly to the vast elemental forces of nature without the cover of houses or social institutions or established traditions over his head. If he is to have a home, it can be nothing less than the entire universe; and if he is to be at home, he must be at one with all time and space."

Rovit goes on: "A historic American problem which has become universal for Western man in our century, has centered around the difficulties of establishing a settlement in the wilderness, or wresting out of the chaos and flux of life a secure dwelling place for the spirit—a home, a community, a civilization . . .

"From 1607 to about 1917, and probably past that date[!], the dominant habit of American life has been movement—migration first from the Old World to the New, and migration unceasingly since within the shifting social context of the New World. This movement, characterized by a mobility not only through geographical space, but also through the intangible barriers of class and caste, has made permanence, solidity and rootedness anomalies in the American scene, artificially achieved on a temporary basis under certain conditions . . . but achieved only to be destroyed by time and resurrected by nostalgia. . . ." *The American Scholar* (Autumn 1960), XXIX:521, 523, 526–7.

the Seven Gables, one of the inmates, a moving American named Holgrave, had this to say:

"But we shall live to see the day, I trust, when no man shall build his house for posterity. Why should he? He might just as reasonably order a durable suit of clothes, —leather, gutta percha, or whatever else lasts longest,— so that his great-grandchildren should have the benefit of them, and cut precisely the same figure in the world that he himself does. If each generation were allowed and ex- pected to build its own houses, that single change, com- paratively unimportant in itself, would imply almost every reform which society is now suffering for. I doubt whether even our public edifices—our capitols, state-houses, city- halls, and churches—ought to be built of such permanent materials as stone or brick. It were better that they should crumble to ruin, once in twenty years, or thereabouts, as a hint to the people to examine into and reform the institu- tions which they symbolize."

Again, Hawthorne had Clifford explain as he escapes on the train from Colonel Pyncheon's gabled monument:

". . . this admirable invention of the railroad—with the vast and inevitable improvements to be looked for, both as to speed and convenience—is destined to do away with those stale ideas of home and fireside, and substitute something better."

"In the name of common sense," asked [the ticket collector], "what can be better for a man than his own parlor and chimney-corner?"

"These things have not the merit which many good people attribute to them" replied Clifford. "They may be said, in few and pithy words, to have ill-served a poor purpose. My impression is, that our wonderfully increased and still increasing facilities of locomotion are destined to bring us round again to the nomadic state.

". . . These railroads . . . are positively the greatest blessing that the ages have wrought out for us. They give

103

us wings; they annihilate the toil and dust of pilgrimage; they spiritualize travel! Transition being so facile, what can be any man's inducement to tarry in one spot? Why, therefore, should he build a more cumbrous habitation than can readily be carried off with him? Why should he make himself a prisoner for life in brick, and stone, and old worm-eaten timber, when he may just as easily dwell, in one sense, nowhere,—in a better sense wherever the fit and beautiful shall offer him a home?" [6]

So memories, habits, and institutions might become a handicap? And homes were the enemies of change? As the prophet of living everywhere and nowhere, Hawthorne was anticipating the twentieth century. Americans were to be pilgrims of a different sort, he seemed to suggest, on the road to a better life here on earth. Our true progress would be toward happiness and prosperity; from generation to generation everything would improve; after the conquest of nature would come many other changes; and man-made structures would grow obsolete fast. It would follow that the homes of the future would be temporary domiciles, shelters for the raising of children, not much else. At best, home would be where you were born, brought up, loved and cared for—and a place you then abruptly left behind.

A hundred years after Hawthorne, Thornton Wilder would have this to say:

> Americans are disconnected. . . . Taking tea with a friend in London, I am told that I must return to dine and go to the opera.
>
> "All right," I say, "I'll hurry home and change my clothes."
>
> "What?"
>
> "I say: I'll go back to the hotel and change my clothes."

"Home! *Home!* How can you Americans keep calling a hotel home?"

Because a home is not an edifice, but an interior and transportable adjustment. In Chicago—in the good old days—my friends used to change their apartment on the first of May. They were not discontented with the old one; they simply liked to impress their home-making faculty on some new rooms.[7]

Inevitably, one is reminded of the standard vulgarism: "The Missus and I make our home in ———"; and somehow one can almost visualize that article.

"It takes a heap o' livin' in a house t' make it home," argued Edgar A. Guest.[8] But also two parents and self-discipline. [*] With the ease of escape and the prevalence of desertion and divorce, too many of our dwelling sites are now littered with broken homes. "Home is where there's one to love us"? Perhaps. But some of the young seem pretty disillusioned. They get out early. "Home," one heard Robert Frost saying, "Home is the place where, when you have to go there, they have to take you in" (*The Death of the Hired Man*). Yet will "they" be there to take you in? If some prodigal son's heart grows weary, far from the old folks at home, won't he discover the old folks at that moment perhaps wintering in Florida? A shrewd and thoughtful friend of mine, now retired, called my attention to the way the elderly people of some means are behaving. Reaching retirement, they give up their house or apartment in town and move out to their summer place, which was prudently winterized some years before. Family reunions with married children and grandchildren— once automatically held at Christmas—will now more

---

[*] "Hit takes two birds fer to make a nes'." Joel Chandler Harris, *Uncle Remus, Plantation Proverbs* (1880).

likely take place in vacation time, "at the spot where Grandpa makes his domicile and pays his taxes"; in other words, in summer, especially as the old folks have now joined some Georgia colony or Florida club for the long winters. "Happy New Year," my friend concluded his homily, "we're off to Sea Island tomorrow." [9]

"For Americans," wrote the English-educated observer T. S. Matthews,[10] "home is where you come from, home is the place you leave. If you want to go back, quite often it has changed out of all knowledge or even ceased to exist. . . ." And John Steinbeck agreed: "Tom Wolfe was right. You can't go home again because home has ceased to exist except in the mothballs of memory." *

Some go so far as to accuse us of home denial—and triumphantly or regretfully celebrate the independent American on his lonely journey through our technological wonderland. Others seem cynical or indifferent: "There's

---

* *Travels with Charley*, p. 183. See also Steinbeck's disillusionment as expressed in his article on "America and the Americans" (*Saturday Evening Post*, July 2, 1966): "Consider the dream and the hunger for home. The very word can reduce nearly all of my compatriots to tears. Builders and developers never build houses—they build homes. The dream home is either in a small town or in a suburban area where grass and trees simulate the country. This dream home is a permanent seat, not rented but owned. It is a center where a man and his wife grow graciously old, warmed by the radiance of well-washed children and grandchildren. Many thousands of these homes are built every year; built, planted, advertised, and sold—and yet the American family rarely stays in one place for more than five years."

Also sooner or later—usually sooner—the family scatters. In the same year of Steinbeck's lament, my "home town" newspaper carried a story of how Clarence E. Dibble of Long Beach, *aet.* ninety, had picked up the phone to hear his ten younger brothers and sisters, on a hook-up that linked eight states from California to Florida to Connecticut to Rhode Island, wish him a happy birthday. They concluded their reunion by singing a traditional family hymn: "Blest Be the Ties That Bind." Apparently the last Dibble reunion had been before the turn of the century. (New Haven *Register*, Oct. 24, 1966). And the ties were now telephone wires.

no place like home, and many a man is glad of it." "Any
old place I can hang my hat is home sweet home to
me." Home, after all, is "the place one goes from the
garage . . ."

Long ago aging relicts learned to dread the Old People's Home; and now the "homebody," and being "at
home," and "homework," and "God Bless Our Home!" and
even "homesickness" seem to have followed the homestead
into oblivion. Inquiring about some distant and errant
family connection, we may be told: "Oh, he found a home
in the Army." [11]

What such impermanence and indifference may have
done or be doing to the American family[12]—to the nurture
and discipline of the young, to the moral assurance of
their elders, to the concept of neighborliness and the character of old neighborhoods—I must leave for the observation and experience of the reader. But we might notice
that the federal tax authorities have been forced to reshape
their own definition of "home" * and architects their con-

* "2. Redefinition of 'Home'

"One of the problems under existing law is the definition of a taxpayer's 'home.' The Internal Revenue Service has defined 'home' as a
taxpayer's principal place of business. Although this definition is proper
as a matter of statutory interpretation, it is at variance with the com-
monly accepted meaning of the term 'home.'

"The word 'home' would be replaced by the term 'duty area.' The
taxpayer's duty area would be defined as a circular area of 20-mile
radius with the taxpayer's principal business post as its center. A taxpayer's principal business post would be the place at which he reasonably
anticipates that, during the future course of his present employment, he
will principally work or report for work (i.e., the place where he reasonably believes he will work or report for work more than any other place
and at least one-third of his working days). If a taxpayer did not have
a principal business post within this definition, then his duty area would
be centered around his principal residence. Any taxpayer who did not
have a principal business post or a principal residence would be classified
as an itinerant.—*From the Ways and Means Committee printing of the
President's 1963 Tax Message.*

"Or bum." [said *The New Yorker*[13]]

cepts of housing. "With this constant change," Peter Blake once complained, "a man no longer builds a 'house for the ages' but moves around as fast as a pea in a shell game." Hence "modern American architecture is still suffering from an adolescent attitude of structural exhibitionism" [14] (a trait, shall we say, not invisible in Frank Lloyd Wright?).

Has our moving about, young and old, brought us finally to this, that we, who had the warmest word for home and perhaps one of its finest realizations, are now almost without the genuine article? Have we lost the gift of home?

Have we lost the gift of home? Not yet, or at least not quite. For if we can move, can't our homes move too? Most of us, as Thornton Wilder said, make several homes by taking our home-making faculty along and impressing it on some new rooms. But a number—an increasing number—put their houses on wheels and drag or drive them along to wherever they want to go. As André Maurois explained to his erudite fellow *Académiciens*, many Americans were now carrying their shelters with them like turtles:

> Dix pour cent des Américains trainent avec eux leur maison, comme les tortues. Au début la "caravane" était simplement un remorque utilisée par l'automobiliste pendant ses vacances. Maintenant, la caravane devient à la fois stable et mobile. Elle se transforme en maison. Des parois mobiles permettent d'en doubler la superficie. Si le nomade aime le climat, les voisins, il reste et cultive son jardin. Sinon, il replie sa maison, fait sortir ses roues et va plus loin. [15]

"Nothing like a well-built home to give you a feeling of
permanence and stability, folks! . . . In addition,
it's ready to roll!"
—© 1963 by Publishers Newspaper Syndicate
Courtesy George Lichty and Publishers
Newspaper Syndicate.

Maurois thought that this was a survival from pioneer cov-
ered-wagon days. John Steinbeck speculated that it might

be a joyful resurgence of the prehistoric nomadism in which human kind had lived for hundreds of thousands of years.

Whatever the nostalgic components, in 1940 some 16,000 trailers were manufactured in the United States. Twenty years later, we are told,[16] the number was 160,000. Already by 1958, some thirteen out of every one hundred people buying homes bought mobile ones. And it was estimated that soon one in every five new housing units would be on wheels. By 1965, the ratio had reached one in seven for all primary dwelling units, and for those costing less than $12,500 the proportion was three out of four. California, said Steinbeck, was spawning them like herrings. "In a 1969 Department of Commerce study, mobile homes represented 48 per cent of all new homes built that year, 94 per cent of those under $15,000, 79 per cent of those under $20,000 and 67 per cent of those under $25,000." [17]

Clearly the low cost was a powerful attraction, though the range could be considerable. Virginia Held was able to cite a special job with a swimming pool on the roof and a price tag of $50,000. And we all began to see prefabs so large they had to be sawed in two to be towed anywhere. But generally the typical new mobile home in 1960 was about 10 feet wide (the maximum allowed in some states) and 50 feet long, and cost perhaps $7,400 (all conveniences included). By 1967, most customers were reported to be paying between $6,000 and $7,000 for a 12 by 60 foot home (with brand name appliances). By 1971, the trend was toward 14 by 70 foot rolling palaces at only $8.50 a square foot. Financing was also clearly easier on a mobile home, as on automobiles. And people were beginning to trade them in for new models, garish gimmicks and all.

"Sleeping cars used to run on railroad tracks," began a

1971 report; but now the "recreational vehicle industry is doing better than a billion dollar yearly business." [18] The yearly production was over 400,000 home units (the manufacturers were also going into modular, sectional, prefabricated housing). And there now seem to be models and prices to fit every need. One can begin with a travel trailer ("the little house on wheels that you pull behind the family car"), or with the truck-mount camper (sleeping quarters that fit into a pick-up truck and can be unloaded when vacation is over). These are acceptable in trailer camps. Next above in cost and prestige are the mobile homes, in a wide range of sizes and brand names; they require a professional mover in a hauling cab, and are welcome in trailer courts or "mobile home resorts." And then come the self-powered "motor homes," the Cadillacs of the industry. "Does *your* home have power-steering?" asks one producer. "We make a self-propelled, self-contained, fifty-two week funhouse on wheels," proclaims another, "in 10 different models, 5 different lengths, 7 different floor plans, and from standard to luxurious." *

---

* "We make them so you can go places, do things, meet people, and have a downright good time while you're at it. Like touring wherever and whenever you wish. Vacationing with your family. Taking the gang to the ball game, or your cronies out duck hunting. It's your lounge, your kitchen, your dining room. Your shower and bedroom. Plus—your transportation. Your ——— motor home is anything you want it to be. Anytime you want it to be"—*Holiday* (April 1970). Trying to blend the best of both worlds, and inviting their customers to fairly wallow in wish-fulfillment, one enterprising company advertised: "Live carefree and comfortable on your own one-quarter acre homesite in a fully furnished Mobile Home in sunny Florida. . . . Your home is nestled amid unspoiled scenic countryside and waterways. . . . Step from your patio into adventure every day . . . ringed by water, warmed by the year 'round golden sun, a multi-sports natural arena . . . secluded from, yet close-by big city conveniences. . . ." As Steinbeck put it, "if they can double the dream—have a symbol home and mobility at the same time—they have it made."—*Saturday Evening Post*, July 2, 1966.

Who buys and uses these inventions? A number of distinct groups in our population. According to Virginia Held,

> there are the skilled migratory workers, like carpenters, electricians, and engineers, who set up factories or missile bases and then move on—this is the largest group; there are career servicemen with families who may have to move to new bases where housing is inadequate; there are retired people who may want to spend part of the year in a warm climate; and there are people vacationing with small travel trailers.

But there are also the newly-weds, with precarious income, in search of good jobs. And let us not forget the adventurers or the spasmodically restless or the inveterate wanderers.

Even to these last, something may then happen that is

"Look at it this way. You'll have a place to live while you're looking for a place to park."
—By William P. Hoest, in *Saturday Review,* January 15, 1972
Copyright © 1972 by Saturday Review, Inc.

rather curious. Having a trailer for a home, these gypsy Americans begin looking for trailer parks or places where they can feel that they "sort of belong." Of course, they also appreciate the conveniences which the trailer court operator or mobile park owner quickly learns to provide. They come to like the friendliness and hospitality and the sense of shared adventure. There are games and movies and parties; and many of the worries and concerns of land ownership and housekeeping are lifted off their shoulders. Best of all, they can move on. They are not tied down—or they think they aren't.*

Actually, a good many are in intermittent motion, South and North or across the country, especially those with travel trailers who stop for a night or two and then pull out again. But the mobility of mobile homes is in part illusory. Often they are too big—or it costs too much to hire a tractor—or one has planted a small garden, and built an addition. In 1960, it was estimated, the average mobile home owner was moving hardly more than apartment dwellers, or every twenty-seven months. Some compromised by buying a small trailer as well, so that they could go and come back (and have a home away from home). But by 1967 it could be remarked with only modest exaggeration that a "mobile home only moves twice— from the factory to a dealer's lot, then from the lot to the prepared 'pad' in a mobile park." [19]

By 1971, "Expandables" were in vogue, but "Double-

---

* "The first impression forced on me," wrote John Steinbeck, "was that permanence is neither achieved nor desired by mobile people, they do not buy for the generations. . . ."

. . .

" 'Don't you miss some kind of permanence?'

" 'Who's got permanence? Factory closes down, you move on. Good times and things opening up, you move on where it's better. You got roots you sit and starve. . . .' "—*Travels with Charley*, pp. 89, 91.

Wides" were more popular still—and obviously harder to put back on the road. A market study[20] now indicated that mobile home owners were moving on the average 1.14 times in five years, and so were able to become registered voters (88% of the mobile homes claiming one or two voters): "A mobile home is considered a permanent residence by most owners." About half of these owners were locating on individually owned property, but there were also at least 12,800 registered and inspected parks with more than a million sites, for which from $30 to $90 a month was being charged. New cities were beginning to build such parks into their planning. Credit corporations were beginning to cultivate these "wheel estate" developments. And almost 6 million people, it was estimated, were currently enjoying this NOW WAY OF LIFE.[21]

Typically it will be a retired couple, living on a fixed income, who will buy the home with the pleasant idea that they can sell it and then go roving again whenever they want. They won't be tied down. Meanwhile they will have company, recreation, a nice climate, police protection, and no taxes.[22] Then further adventures are postponed, once or twice, and before they know it they become too friendly with their neighbors to want to leave. So the wheels come off. The couple settles down. And the American odyssey ends where it began—in a "home." [23]

Perhaps we should add a sober epilogue. Evidently most Americans share a need of belonging, and all but the most restless still crave some sort of place to belong in. But in the last two centuries the once extended family has shrunk; the grandparents and maiden aunts are no longer built in, the parents know only a nuclear family, soon broken up, with the children turned loose on the world. And the house itself, now crammed with gadgets and even self-moving power, has been stripped of its ancestral memories, detached from its local setting, quite largely deprived of its family character.

More citizens of the United States may own their own dwellings than in any other civilized society. But what they own has been drained of much of its human feeling and associations. Be it ever so mobile, it's an emptier article.

6

The Fifth Freedom—

And its impact on
our institutions

In 1954, in two international conferences under the aegis of UNESCO, a group of European intellectuals devoted themselves to the discussion of *Le Nouveau Monde et l'Europe*. Characteristically, several of the participants dropped quickly into attacks on United States civilization in its more deplorable manifestations. American materialism (our mechanization and technocracy, the gadgetry and "emptiness" of our lives), American infantilism and conformism, and the sad state of American arts were arraigned with such mordant fervor that the three Americans present, and the sympathetic André Maurois, must have been troubled to keep their calm.

Now and again, but without systematic connection, allusions were made to our mobility: to the *manie itinérante* which was perhaps becoming a national characteristic; to the decline of genuine regionalism under the assaults of invading students, old people, and tourists; to the mournful interchangeable towns; to the nomadism even within our cities; and to the piercing need to conform so as to obliterate an immigrant background. Only this conformity, warned Maurois, was not *immobilisme* but rather conformity to change and improvement, hence an instinct for adaptability carried to extremes. Maurois also observed that Americans use the city just for work, their living they do on the open road:

> La ville, comme la maison, est un instrument de travail. Dès que la journée active est terminée, on s'évade. Aucun peuple n'éprouve plus que celui-ci le besoin de voyager, de prendre des vacances, de se replonger dans la nature. L'état normal de l'Américain c'est le mouvement. C'est lorsqu'il part dans sa voiture avec sa femme et ses enfants, comme jadis ses ancêtres dans leur wagon de pionnier, pour quelque ranch dans le désert ou pour un campement de montagne, pour une cabane au bord d'un lac où il pourra pêcher et chasser, que l'Américain se sent vivre.[1]

Regrettably, these fragmentary perceptions were not linked together, or pursued toward a deeper understanding, as Thornton Wilder had just tried to do with brilliant intuition in his Norton Lectures at Harvard.[2] By way of preface to his study of the peculiar language of American writers, Wilder had insisted on a certain "disequilibrium of the psyche which follows on the American condition." Specifically, "From the point of view of the European an American is nomad in relation to place, disattached in relation to time, lonely in relation to society, and insubmissive to circumstance, destiny or God." The American's relations were not with the past but with the future: his life was one of becoming (like the characters in his Bible, he hung "suspended upon the promises of the imagination").

Again, said Wilder, the American was "differently surrounded"; for he had no fixed abode, but carried his "home" with him; his relations were not to place but "to everywhere, to everyone, and to always." The American was the independent, the lonely man. And he was still engaged in inventing what it is to be an American.

If Wilder was right that a process of invention has been going on—or if Americans have practiced any such extreme adaptiveness as Maurois referred to—then some challenging possibilities confront us. For it would appear that, consciously or unconsciously, we Americans have perhaps been engaged in reconstructing *the entire gamut of relations* for western (or mobile) man. This would mean (1) new institutions patterned in part on free movement; (2) new relations with the physical environment based on a view of nature differing from the European; (3) a new concept of human fellowship or a decalogue of social conduct in some ways deviant from the Greco-Christian tradition; and (4) even possibly a new attitude toward the self.

This is a large order, indeed a new order too vast to be comprehended and described, the more so as these inventions or ventures in adjustment must be still in process, and far from concluded. The new society, if such it is, has not quite crystallized out. Robert Moses and our city planners to the contrary notwithstanding, it is too early for some latterday prophet to codify the commandments of mobility, or make straight the highway for our culture.

Yet are there not signs?

By way of experiment, we might first consider some of our basic institutions and ask ourselves a sober question. The family and the home, the town and the city, our churches, our business and industrial corporations, our governments whether local, state, or federal: are not all of these institutions being shaken, changed, even visibly restructured by the American habits of movement?

It can no longer be any secret, surely, that under the strains of modern living the American family has been showing signs of coming apart. The progressive weakening of the household as an institution, the loosening of the ties of marriage, the seemingly casual ease of desertion and divorce, the all too obvious decline of parental authority, the quick escape of the children: clearly, these derive from no one sickness, no single social cause. Yet clearly they have all been facilitated *and increased* by our ready mobility.

Home? We have already paid our respects to the home that moves. Thornton Wilder may like to think that we Americans have learned to take our homes with us, and enjoy "making" new homes, or impressing a new apartment with our "home-making" ability. But do we really carry with us the substance as well as the word? Can "home" be altogether divorced from place, from neighbors, from memories and ancestral associations? In this grasshopper existence to which we seem addicted, have we not converted "home" into boardinghouse or temporary pad? And who is to measure the moral deprivations to children, the adolescent insecurities?

As for the town, let us recall the strange history of the New England community. Typically, it began as an English village: a congregation and a cluster of homes about a green. Then the settlers moved out upon the land and built homesteads on scattered farms, leaving only the church and the school, the blacksmith and cooper, an inn and general store perhaps, with a few old retired folk in the houses around the green. So by dispersion the residential village had been converted into a trading town, a crossroads of services and communications. Then came the nineteenth-century Industrial Revolution. Half the farm sons took off for the West. A railroad crept up the valley. A depot was built down the hill, a mill at the waterfall, a bank or two, and much housing across the tracks, as the Yankee mill owners began affecting stone mansions on Prospect Street. A generation or two more and the railroad seemed to be drawing town talents and capital away to the greater centers, sucking the vitality out of the local communities along its line. Once again the young men were leaving; the future belonged to our cities. But then came the automobile, new turnpikes and thruways, and a renewed but different dispersion. Within the last thirty years, especially, the congestion and deterioration of the inner city, the ease of escape, the invasion of poverty-stricken minority groups, the breakdown of rapid transit and police protection and other public services have gutted the residential heart of many a city, converted nearby towns into skyscraper suburbs, and plastered the once smiling countryside between with endless "villages" of ranch-type or split-level houses, in dreary monotony mile after mile.

Viewed from the air, or from abroad, the tents of our people now cut a strange pattern. No doubt a changing technology, better incomes, social ambition, higher standards of privacy, and the tyranny of fashion—as well as that characteristic independence of the younger generation—have helped trigger this rush outward from our urban centers. Yet such large-scale "developments" would never have been possible but for expressways and commutation tickets, *and the habits* that make their use possible. As a rather obvious corollary, it proves hard now to give to these Levittowns any pride of place or community life of their own. As with the family and the home, no little vitality and moral force have been siphoned out of the American town. And even in our bankrupt cities the desperate plea for fiscal "home rule" sounds a little artificial and hollow.

By contrast, at the other end of the political structure, let us note the growing centralization of the whole nation. Of course, the failures of the Jeffersonian vision—the decline of localism, the paring away of states' rights, and the steady enlargement of the sovereignty and activity of the national government—have been stimulated by many strong forces, not least the victory of the North in the Civil War, the triumph of industrial capitalism, the development of telecommunications, then press services and radio and TV, to say nothing of the emotional demands of two world wars, and now the daily dangers of the international situation. Yet has our growing nationalism of feeling and action and administration not had a more than casual connection with the ever-mounting movement of people from state to state? With the long inflow of immigrants whose aim was to be Americans, not Pennsylvanians or New Yorkers? With our astonishing interstate commerce and its regulation? With the siphoning of tax monies, industries, and employment from one section to another? And most recently with the channeling of defense orders into places whither the plants can be moved or where the labor and voting forces have already arrived? People have been moving too much to allow of an effective regionalism.

Looked at in the large, our empty continent was supposed to foster individualism of action and belief. And, in retrospect, space-plus-mobility may have begun with dispersion and freedom to differ, that is, with decentralization. But in the longer run mobility overruns space, and the circulation and recirculation of people induces conformity. As once the nineteenth-century utopian colonists and the Mormons learned to their sorrow, wherever they could flee others could follow, and in a surprisingly short time there were no hiding places left. Nor ought there to be, in the eyes of our vigilant moralists. As once the abolitionists and Radical Reconstructionists demonstrated, and then the prohibitionists and child labor crusaders learned, and recently the freedom riders rediscovered, space-plus-mobility may begin by offering escape and freedom for peculiar institutions, but ultimately it brings on the need for federal intervention and big government. You cannot quarantine personal liberties, they say; you cannot prevent the desire for equality from crossing state lines; and you cannot forever segregate schools and public places. Why not? Because ideals speak to the heart; because free speech will carry their message across regional barriers; and finally because people are moving so much back and forth. The Bill of Rights and interstate commerce will prevent.*

Thus, from anarchy to conformity, from home rule to centralization, has been the story. And where once the idealist might have founded a utopian colony, now he asks for a constitutional amendment.

The same progress, or radical zigzag of development, has been known by our churches. Our first settlers brought in the Church of England, in either orthodox or dissenting

---

* In President Kennedy's message to Congress on civil rights (as printed in *The New York Times,* June 20, 1963) one read: "In a society which is increasingly mobile and in an economy which is increasingly interdependent, business establishments which serve the public—such as hotels, restaurants, theaters, stores and others—serve not only the members of their immediate communities but travelers from other states and visitors from abroad. Their goods come from all over the nation. This participation in the flow of interstate commerce has given these business establishments both increased prosperity and an increased responsibility to provide equal access and service to all citizens."

form, and tried to perpetuate what they had brought. But soon the dispersion of the Tidewater tobacco plantations so weakened the episcopal hierarchy in Virginia that it was almost destroyed; while the spread of self-governing towns through New England greatly encouraged Congregational home rule. Meanwhile, the ease of access made it almost impossible to prevent the entry of other sects like the Quakers and the Baptists, especially as such heretics could always escape to Rhode Island or go directly to the middle colonies. So the competition for settlers and for prosperity gradually forced on each colony an unanticipated toleration. In the Revolution the resistance to established authority disestablished the churches, too. The first amendment to the Constitution forbade Congress to make any laws "respecting an establishment of religion, or prohibiting the free exercise thereof. . . ." And so was initiated a free-for-all competition among all religious come-outers, with the home-mission movement, and a race westward to keep up with the migrating pioneers.

Today our churches still seem geared to the expectation of movement, but in its concentrating phase. Witness chapels on wheels and drive-in churches, or the astonishing circulation of ministerial talent and the growing homogenization of the Protestant believers. To speak merely of the dissenting churches, in the eighteenth and nineteenth centuries the unprecedented American freedom of movement undoubtedly encouraged sectarianism and accelerated the splintering of congregations; but lately interdenominational communication, based on an intensified interchange both personal and intellectual, seems to be promoting consolidation. How powerfully the cooperative movement among the Protestant sects may derive from weakness and a fear of Roman Catholicism, or the ecumenical movement among all Christians from the menace of Marxism, should not be underestimated. Yet when one hears on Sunday in a suburban congregation a "letter" (of transfer) read, or when twelve people stand up before the minister to be received into membership, and not one enters by confession but all twelve turn out to be communicants from other churches, at that moment the traditional substance seems to leak out of the word "congregation."* And the individual church becomes merely one cell in a church universal, a standardized unit for us pilgrims, not unlike a service station for the convenience of the passers-by.** The effective congregation seems to be following the town meeting into oblivion.

If we turn next to the vast area of the American economy, the emphasis on transportation and the extraordinary flow of our interstate commerce surely challenge reflection. To the casual motorist the Pennsylvania turnpikes and the Los Angeles freeways, the Holland Tunnels and Golden Gate Bridges, the Greyhounds and vista domes, the drive-it-yourself services and the U-Hauls, the mastodon trucks and the Teamsters Union: these may seem too familiar, practical, and economic to have any larger implications for our culture. Yet, in the impressions of a visiting Frenchman, symbolically entitled *La Grande Parade Américaine,* one might recall what was said not so very

---

* A few Sundays after these lines were penned, the minister in our local Congregational Church stated that fifteen members had left the choir within the year as a result of moving away.

** In their analysis of "Institutions in Motion," McKitrick and Elkins propose that survival requires portability, while the habit of moving generates improvisation along habitual lines, hence the indefinite multiplication of institutions, with duplicate organizations or interchangeable parts (e.g., the American Army, or units of Bell Telephone).—Eric L. McKitrick and Stanley Elkins, "Institutions in Motion," *American Quarterly* (Summer 1960), XII, no. 2. pt. 1: 187–97. Wright Morris rather emphasized the American vitality of improvisation: "Made in U.S.A.", *The American Scholar* (Autumn 1960), XXIX, no. 4, 493.

long ago about our railroads—they had entered into the national emotions as well as the lives of Americans:

> pour l'Européen, ce n'est qu'un moyen de transport; mais l'Américain éprouve un sentiment voisin de l'amour patri-otique pour le train qui est à la fois un ami, un témoin unique, un champion aimé et un lien national. . . . Sans le chemin de fer, il n'y a pas d'Etats-Unis.
>
> . . . les villes sont nées sur ses bords, comme en Europe le long des rives des fleuves. Cette rivière de metal amenait avec elle la vie et déposait sur ses verges des alluvions: campements, puis cités.[3]

To H.-J. Duteil, not only had the railroads created the nation, they expressed the grandeur of American concep-tions; and he went on to quote from Freeman Hubbard's *Railroad Avenue . . .* , the C & O prose poem:

> Listen . . . From across the sleeping countryside
> Comes the steady, rhythmic rumble of the trains,
> The great, husky trains of America.
> They've talked to you since childhood,
> They've told you, in the lonely silence of the night,
> Of far-off places, of romance and adventure!

Sadly, our own generation has had to watch the de-mise of the steam engine, the ossification of railroad man-agement, and the threatened ruin by featherbedding. Those old arteries celebrated by Duteil have hardened and deteriorated. And so today it is the automobiles and planes that breathe of romance and adventure, that speak to us of distant lands, that carry the mystic numbers and the names from interstellar space: Nova and Vega, Comet and Galaxie, Impala and Mustang, Riviera and Bonneville, JetStar and 747. Yet even now the threat of a national rail-road strike can shake President and Congress.

Back in 1936 Philip Guedalla, in reviewing American development, ventured his celebrated judgment: "The true history of the United States is the history of transportation . . . in which the names of railroad presidents are more significant than those of Presidents of the United States." [4]

Then came Henry Ford. And what his system of production and his Tin Lizzie did to the transport, the roads, the tax structure, the work habits, and the lives of Americans has become part of the American legend. From sport to transport to unifier of the nation: what the railroads had initiated, the automobile completed. It made us one people out of many: "We became more alike than we were different." It generated the richest and most productive economy of all time; without the mobility given us by our cars, first on tracks and then on rubber, these technological miracles and this affluent society would not have been possible. The motor industry also fed our aspirations and fueled our dynamism: mobility meant experiment and opportunity to grow. With the disappearance of free land in the West it even gave us new elbow room.

Unfortunately not without costs. With the automobile, said George Kennan, "we have done untold damage to our society." Charged Lewis Mumford: "The assumed right of the private motor car to go any place in the city and park anywhere is nothing less than a license to destroy the city." A third critic has written of this country as *God's Own Junkyard*. And from a fourth we hear that "the automobile's promise of pleasure and liberation turned into dismemberment of the city, the defiling of nature, and the compounding of chaos with congestion." [5] Obviously, the junking of cars and the abandonment of derelict jalopies on the parkways and streets have become serious problems. On top of that it has dawned on us that the automobile industry has been filling our air with leaded exhaust vapors, and now is threatening to choke the circulation of both men and goods by just too many cars. Will most of us soon be "sitting in a perpetual traffic jam"?* And must we soon bar private automobiles from most of our cities? I do not think so. The price would be much too high. As one defender has written,

> Eliminate the car and you must eliminate privacy and the single home with a bedroom for each child, a lawn and a tree; scratch the shopping center and the clean, one-story suburban factory and office; forget the dancing lessons for junior three miles away, the suburban college campus and the weekend trip to the country or the wilderness. Kill the supermarket, too, and tell each woman to shop each day for the night's meal instead of loading up on groceries once a week.
>
> Even the protesters drive to their rallies. . . .[6]

In sober fact, the car has rearranged and in some degree damaged the quality of American life, but also has become a part of it, an indispensable part. For it is now the vehicle for our passions as well as for transportation. People will do almost anything rather than give up this outlet for feeling. As Harry Golden stated it,[7] "They simply pack their tensions, their frustrations and unfulfilled yearnings into the automobile and they're off." ** Many

---

* Already in 1964, one could read that ". . . there are some 180 million people in the United States, each occupying about 2 square feet of our land surface; there are also close to 70 million private automobiles in the United States, each occupying about 120 square feet of land. (In addition, there are 15 million trucks and buses.)

"In short, only 360 million square feet of America are being used (at any given moment) by people; but 8.4 *billion* square feet of this country, or 23 times as many square feet, are covered with private automobiles."—Peter Blake, *God's Own Junkyard* (1964), p. 119.

** A colleague and friend has often told me how his father, head of an automobile appliance company on the West Coast, used to harangue his salesmen at the annual banquet: "Well, boys, go out and sell 'em [the things to put in their cars]. Times may be tough but people

people drive (it is obvious) to satisfy their longings for power; others make it their whole recreation; still others use it as an almost perfect way of escape. Yet of all the car's gifts perhaps the greatest gift is freedom. It satisfies an ancient and fundamental American urge. By simply turning a key we can now go almost anywhere we please.

> Q. Why are passenger services on the railroads virtually doomed?
> A. Because they are so much slower than the planes and less convenient than automobiles. (The trains are straitjacketed by their tracks.)
> Q. And why will the complete substitution of municipal transportation be fiercely resisted?
> A. Because we'll refuse to allow a monopoly of movement by the public authority. The right to go where we want and when we want is too precious.

As Simeon Strunsky so paradoxically asserted a generation ago: "The more things American change under the impact of the automobile, the more they remain American. . . . The automobile embodies a vigorous restatement of basic national principles. The automobile cannot undermine the old American way of life because it is the product of that way of life and of the spirit that shaped it. It incorporates the aims and impulses that guided our older history. The throb of its engine is the beat of the historic American tempo." [8]

But let us now get out of our cars to examine, for just a moment, one of the outstanding by-products. I refer to that extraordinary flat-topped do-it-yourself store which car-minded Californians sold to the nation and which recently has had our Continental scholar-critics goggling

---

will give up their food, they'll give up their likker, but they'll NEVER give up their cars."

and almost speechless: the *supermarket*. Even with its satellite shopping center, the supermarket may not be so very unprecedented in its concentration of possibilities: one senses a modernized version of Old World market squares; one is reminded of the crowded bazaars which go back to prehistory. Inside this American sales factory there is self-service, which to a European does have some revolutionary implications. But what is it we drop into our wheeled baskets? Why, nothing special: just canned goods, bottled beverages, packaged cereals, and frozen foods—almost all with common names or standard brands. Some of the articles come from a long way off, hardly any from the immeidiate neighborhood, but that is an old story in the American market. We could buy these articles as well five hundred miles away. In fact, we have brought them across the continent, and with time many of the newest brands will seep into the remotest settlements. Why? Because they are cheaper and better? It may be. Because the American production line, with automatic machinery, interchangeable parts, mass production, and high-pressure salesmanship in the mass media inevitably undersells and replaces the local or regional product? Quite probably. With press and radio and television to back up *Good Housekeeping* and a Sears-Roebuck catalogue, what might one not sell?

Yet I wonder a little about local pride or prejudice, and the proverbial sectional antagonisms, not to mention ingrained habits or man's immemorial dislike of accepting things from outsiders. Did our Californians cheerfully take their steel from Pittsburgh? Did traditions of taste and individual workmanship set no limits to the spread of "Grand Rapids"? Do we really like the Western Golden Delicious as well as the New England apples of our boyhood? What standard brand, I want to know, can possibly match the bite and aroma of a Broadleaf Connecticut cigar? And how did those insipid "fifteen-centers" get to New Haven in the first place? Because they were advertised and brought in by salesmen? No doubt, in due course. But first one suspects they came in men's pockets. And then they were asked for, and slowly offered, in the corner drugstores. In my book, it was often the obvious superiority of the mass product that persuaded. But at other times it was the man who helped bring the article.[9] Or, coming in from outside, and not finding what he was used to, he asked to have it brought in. *

So if the standard brands find their way into the remotest settlements, and soon come to dominate the lonely crossroads, may it not be in part because they are what the travelers asked for? When frozen chickens first invade the village grocery, does one not know that an old customer has already been in, or will drop in tomorrow?

Advertising and word of mouth are immeasurably powerful. Ideas can carry packages no less well than men. But things are surer if the man has been by, too. So our cans chase our consumers about the country—and vice versa. In a sense we are in a circular argument. Standard brands make moving from region to region less painful to the traveler, while at the same time the traveler makes it easier for standard brands to cover the whole nation. Take

---

* A few days after first writing these words, I came on the story of how in 1844 the first wholesale pie factory in New England got its start. It appears that a homesick son in New York, with other New Haven lads who longed for "old-fashioned pies," gave Amos Munson back in New Haven the idea of setting up a pie factory and shipping his "Connecticut pies" via steamboat to New York. Within five years Munson's firm was producing one thousand pies a day, and the freight bills by steamboat became so large that Munson opened a plant in New York City. Eventually three of his workers "started their own pie-making factories after learning the trade. They were H. H. Olds who stayed in New Haven; Elisha Case who went to Chicago; and J. E. Perry who settled in Providence."—New Haven *Register*, Feb. 3, 1963. See also the article, "New Haven Pie Industry," in the same newspaper, Oct. 22, 1967.

away the moving consumer, and the standard brand will not "move" so well either. *C'est fou? Eh bien, monsieur.* Which are your favorite chain stores in France?

No doubt this seems a long way around to a simple fact, but that fact is worth pondering. Whether as cause or coincidence or consequence, mobility is built into our social economy. And if we have achieved not only a certain uniformity of speech, but a generalization of consumer taste and an agreed-on vocabulary of comfort across the nation, it is because *both* men and ideas have been in almost constant motion everywhere.[10]

To put this another way, our regional economies and peculiarities have followed our local loyalties—just as our cities have followed our towns, and our homes our splintered families—into increasing disrepair, giving way to an ever more generalized, homogenized, and effervescent American style of life. Because of motion.

One would, of course, like to know much more about the impact of mobility on our institutions—most especially on politics and the law. How has mobility entered into our common or statute law? What changes has it produced in the laws governing real estate? Of movable possessions? Of domiciliary rights or estate taxes? It would be astonishing if even that tough and resistant mountain complex of accumulated decisions which we call the Law did not show the parallel grooves and occasional water gaps scoured by the slow drifts and sudden freshets of our population within the past two centuries. But, in all candor, I have been able to find few examples.* In our legisla-

---

* When Hetty Green died in 1916, several states struggled ravenously for the privilege of calling her a legal resident, for in the law she could belong to but one. Will not this some day have to be changed?

In the world of farm animals (which also moved) it is instructive

tures and city boards of aldermen we even still cling to the local residence requirements and the district delegate idea rather than shift to the more fluid "virtual representation" long practiced in England and now made feasible by our automobile-airplane age. Possibly the movements of Bobby Kennedy to New York and of Richard Nixon between New York and California may presage a change; but our political parties and patronage habits will obstruct.

What happens when free mobility threatens injury to the public welfare? Obviously any government must try to impose restraints. Thus for presumed reasons of social, physical, moral, or financial health, we have at times restricted immigration, excluded the criminals and the diseased, imposed national origins quotas, and made movement into this country not a little unpleasant as well as far from free. The import of plants and animals into the country or across some state boundaries (e.g., California) is controlled and to a degree restricted by agricultural quarantines. For like reasons there are laws against the carriage of firearms across state lines.

Taking advantage of the interstate commerce clause, the federal government has prohibited the carriage from one state to another of kidnapped persons, strikebreakers,

---

to observe how the English laws of fencing did have to be changed. For where the common law had required each stock raiser to enclose his animals with a legal fence, in the New World, with so much wilderness and free land available for both domesticated cattle and domesticated plants—man's animal and vegetable slaves—it soon came to seem more sensible, in fact necessary, to require farmers to put the fences around their crops. That is, the costs of fencing (and the more mobile four-footed slaves!) got the upper hand. And it was only with the disappearance of the open range in any given area that the agriculturists began to have a chance to restore the balance in their own favor. See Earl W. Hayter, "Livestock-Fencing Conflicts in Rural America," *Agricultural History* (Jan. 1963), 37:11–20.

or women for immoral purposes. The United States has also forbidden the shanghaiing of sailors, or any interstate moving or traveling to avoid prosecution, confinement after conviction, or giving testimony in a criminal case. On a lower plane, tax reasons have acted to inhibit the personal transport of alcohols into one state from another, and when the New York commuter carries city earnings into the suburbs of Connecticut or New Jersey, two states may try to tax him.[11] Yet all this adds up to very little.*

Altogether there seem to be remarkably few "cattle-guards" sunk into the boundaries of our states to keep their human herds from straying. Instead, these sovereign entities find themselves helpless to prevent the passage of strangers across their territories, powerless to block the invasion of Okies or freedom riders or destitute blacks in flight from the Southern uplands, unable even to impede the exodus of their own citizens with their votes, their capital, and their business organizations.

Such has not been the universal human experience. In classical times, we are told, the flight from taxes and perhaps other concerns caused the Romans to tie their colonists to their occupations and residences: hence a start for serfdom. For almost a thousand years men were bound to the soil and taught their obligations of place by the feudal system. Then the Elizabethan Poor Law of 1601 and later Settlement Acts, when feudal estates were breaking up and vagrancy loomed as an interparish problem, set a more limited but harsh precedent, which some of our states have tried to imitate, to protect their own job oppor-

---

* C. Vann Woodward, to whom I owe many useful suggestions, has recalled that before the Civil War some states in the Midwest had laws prohibiting the immigration of free Negroes; until 1886 South and North used different railroad gauges; and the Southern freight rate structure still perpetuates the design to restrict competition. In a degree, the same could be said of the basing point system in industry.

tunities and their welfare funds from destitute itinerants.*

Yet our earliest colonizing charters had encouraged a freedom of movement which the settlement process then converted into a habit. In 1774, the mother country's attempt to exclude our colonists from the West (by the Quebec Act) helped ignite the Revolution. In the Declaration of Independence, George III was accused of interfering with free immigration and naturalization. And in both the Articles of Confederation and the U.S. Constitution (later also in the Constitution of the Confederate States of America!), the citizens of each state were declared "entitled to all the privileges and immunities of the citizens of the several states."** The basic law of our republic should make it safe for a citizen to go. *E Pluribus Unum.* Disunity through the inhibition of movement was to be discouraged. And thereafter the equal application of the Constitution to all sections and states, whether Northern or Southern, whether humid or dry, whether English, French, Spanish, Indian, or African in origin or prevailing culture, would constitute an implicit assumption and endorsement of free movement.

What cognizance has the Supreme Court given to motion? It has struck down taxes and other impediments to interstate circulation. While upholding vagrancy laws as generally valid exercises of a state's police power, it has

---

* "Usually it is formally stipulated that local aid to non-residents can be given only to return them where they came from. Rarely is any provision made to help them settle down."—Barbara Carter ("The Jalopy Nomads," *The Reporter,* May 7, 1964, p. 33). The 1971 renewal of efforts by New York State to require a year's residence for relief is in point.

** In Article IV of the Articles of Confederation was next added this phrase: "and the people of each state shall have free ingress and regress to and from any other state." For some reason (perhaps the slave question, possibly forgetfulness) this was omitted from the otherwise similar article in the Constitution.

limited the residence requirements. And it has repeatedly upheld the citizen's right to travel as an adjunct to such basic rights as voting, association, commerce, contracts, or livelihood. Along a jurisprudential pathway that has had a number of twists and turns, from the Passenger Cases of 1849 to *Shapiro* v. *Thompson* in 1969, the Supreme Court has generally, though for differing reasons, supported freedom of movement. The grounds given (in rough chronological order) have been the "privileges and immunities" clause of Article IV, Section 2, of the Constitution; the commerce clause (Art. I, Sec. 8); the concept of Union; the 14th or Due Process Amendment; the 5th Amendment; and on occasion the 1st Amendment.

Curiously—and this point has been made in a recent study which is worth quoting—the right to travel may be "fundamental to many concepts of the United States citizenship . . . and explicit in our public beliefs, but it is only implicit in our laws. Freedom of movement is not to be taken in the same light as the freedom of speech which is explicitly guaranteed by the words of the First Amendment: 'Congress shall make no law respecting . . . freedom of speech or of the press. . . .' The right to travel has no such protective clause. The very plenitude of ambiguous constitutional interpretations which uphold it weaken its own legal strength." [12] So it *could* be upset tomorrow. But the sentiment against restriction will surely be very strong.

It remains to ask about the United States itself. If the interior and interstate passage of persons has known few impediments, what about the right to enter or to leave the country? Here memories of the Alien and Sedition Acts, the nativist movements of the 1830's and 1850's, and some ninety years of immigration restriction since 1882 would seem to cloud any professed freedom of entry; while some recent efforts of Congress and the State Department to prevent travel to Communist countries, or to withhold passports from some of our own citizens, would clearly seem to threaten free egress. Yet each issue deserves closer inspection.

From the beginning, our nation championed the right of expatriation and offered easy naturalization. In due course, the Supreme Court declared that children born to aliens in this country were citizens of the United States. And finally it has been established that a citizen, whether native or naturalized, can be held to have lost his citizenship neither for residing abroad nor for voting in a foreign election, but only by a voluntary act of renunciation. As another unpublished study[13] remarks, "A nation built on immigration could hardly afford any other rule; only in this way can the country be assured of not creating a class permanently disfavored by the very mobility which characterizes the country as a whole."

As for legal restrictions on entry, these seem to have come surprisingly late, in a piecemeal and hesitant fashion, and with powerful effect only when thrust on our society by massive emotional campaigns. From the start some of the states, inspired by colonial memories, prohibited the immigration of convicts and tried also to exclude foreign paupers. But the immigration regulations of any single state could easily be evaded, and the head taxes to help take care of immigrant paupers were declared unconstitutional. Quite understandably, the increases in numbers and the unequal burdens of cost led the states to seek federal aid, which generated the first federal immigration regulation of 1882, and the exclusion of such undesirables as were "threats to public morals, like prostitutes and thieves, to public finance, like paupers and insane persons, or to public health, like carriers of various contagious diseases." Meanwhile, the job-conscious labor movement had secured the exclusion of Europeans who, prior to departure, had signed contracts to work in the United States. After the assassination of McKinley by an anarchist, immigrants who advocated or believed in the violent overthrow of the government were excluded. And finally, but not until well into the twentieth century and experience with million-a-year inflows largely from southern and eastern Europe, one saw organized labor's drive to reduce numbers (or protect certain job monopolies) fuse with the cultural and ethnic fears of the educated to produce a literacy test, yearly quotas, and a national origins system—that is, an annual legal entry of 150,000 with preference to the older immigration stocks. In the 1920's, Orientals from a large sector of the earth were even totally and permanently excluded. Yet it may be noted that these restrictions seemed somehow unnatural, were adopted during or after catastrophic wars (or socioeconomic crises in California), and tended to be modified as the emergencies receded. Now skilled workers are given priority, temporary sojourns by students and by scholars are almost encouraged, and Orientals are no longer totally excluded; yet the quota system, and within it a preference structure, persists. If the disparities in numbers, economic standards, and cultural attitudes were not so very great, one might look with some confidence for a further liberalization.

As for going abroad, the regulation of exit has been very much slighter but has followed a comparable curve.[14] At first Americans were free to go, and no papers were required. Passports were merely letters of introduction, and until 1856 were issued only on occasion and by a wide range of officials, from a Secretary of State to a local no-tary public. On the Continent of Europe, since Louis XIV, passports had been used to prevent the flight of military conscripts or the smuggling out of industrial secrets, or to prevent invasion by paupers, plague carriers, or wandering Jews. In England itself, in the last quarter of the eighteenth century, Parliament had repeatedly prohibited the export of skilled workmen or industrial machinery. Then, under the pressures of nineteenth-century nationalism, the border inquisitions and the bureaucratic paperwork had multiplied until the paralyzing numbers carried by the new railroads—and laissez-faire, laissez-passer attitudes—had forced relaxation. Yet in the United States, with the brief exception of the Civil War, no passports were required for exit or entry until World War I—after which came relaxation, then re-enforcement in World War II and the Cold War that followed.

Restrictions on travel to particular areas, which began in 1915 as a protection to our travelers, were revived in 1952 with national policy, anti-Communist implications. American Communists themselves could not get a passport between 1917 and 1931; and in 1950 it was made a criminal offense for a member of a Communist action organization to apply for or to use a passport. But soon litigation set in in earnest. First, the withholding of particular passports was held as without congressional authorization and contrary to the due process clause. Then, in the case of Staughton Lynd, who had gone to Hanoi but said he would not take his passport to forbidden areas, the District of Columbia Court of Appeals ruled that a new passport had to be issued and that passports served only to make American diplomatic facilities available; if a citizen wished to do without, that was his affair.[15] So the American passport has been restored to its original function of identification and presumably is required, if at all, only by other governments. No longer, one hopes, will either Congress or the State Department be able arbitrarily to prevent Americans from traveling abroad.

For a short time it seemed almost as if these authorities had revived *Ne Exeat Regno,* that old prerogative and personal writ of the kings of England which, from Magna Carta onward, John and his successors had gradually been forced to surrender.* Yet there was and is something so tyrannical in such a prohibition—and so contrary to the

---

* In 1215 King John was forced to give up the writ of *Ne Exeat Regno* when it was stipulated that except for criminals, outlaws, alien nationals, and briefly in times of war, *liceat unicuique de cetero exire de regno nostro, et redire, salvo et secure, per terram et per aquam.* . . . Because this permission gave the clergy opportunities to appeal in person to Rome, thereby undermining the king's authority, it was promptly omitted from the second issue of Magna Carta in 1216, and Henry III required all persons going abroad to secure a royal license or be fined. But gradually his successors found they could control or arrest only special classes, the rest presumably being free to come and go. In 1606, to accommodate the Scots, *Ne Exeat Regno* was abolished (if indeed the royal prerogative could be limited). More securely, one could say that the writ was diverted from an instrument of the Crown to subserve the interests of private individuals, for *Ne Exeat* was taken over by the Court of Chancery to prevent parties to a suit in equity from withdrawing to a foreign land.

"In many of the American Commonwealths, the writ of *Ne Exeat,* seeming repugnant to American institutions, has been abolished by statute, either expressly or by implication, although in a few jurisdictions it is still in force and recognized by statutory enactment (Fla., Wisc., Va., Ga., U.S.). . . . Probably in a majority of the states wherein the writ has been abolished it has been supplanted by statutory remedies for detaining debtors . . . similar in effect to *Ne Exeat.*" (*American Jurisprudence,* 38:618 ff.)

Whether the writ *Ne Exeat Republica* can now be used by the federal government to prevent exit from the United States for other than causes in equity would seem to be moot. For *Ne Exeat,* see W. S. McKechnie, *Magna Carta* (2nd. ed., 2 vols., New York, 1958) pp. 473–8. For guidance and suggestions on this and other matters of legal history, I am indebted to Professor Alexander M. Bickel of the Yale Law School; also to the former law dean, Eugene V. Rostow, and to my colleagues in history, Professor William H. Dunham and the late Professor Archibald S. Foord.

historic ethos of our society—that only the intense fears of Communist Russia and China could warrant its temporary exercise.

In summary it would be fair to conclude that, though almost 40 million managed to get in, foreigners have enjoyed only a somewhat qualified right of entry to the United States. But our own citizens, save only for emergency situations or military installations or private property protected by laws against trespass, have been free to go anywhere in this country, and almost as free to travel abroad. Indeed, the average American feels he has a natural right to come and go as he pleases. Oddly enough, our Declaration of Independence and our Constitution fail to state this right. So it is to the French Revolutionary Constitution of September 3, 1791, that one must turn to find formally proclaimed among the inalienable human rights "la liberté à tout homme d'aller, de rester, de partir, sans pouvoir être arrêté, ni détenu, que selon les formes déterminées par la Constitution." Yet the French, having declared the principle, proved hesitant in application, and promptly abandoned their own constitutional position. Whereas the Americans, without explicit constitutional declaration, have assumed the existence of the right and in practice have carried it to its logical extremes.

In World War II, as a goal for our century, Franklin Delano Roosevelt proclaimed the Four Freedoms: of speech and religion, from want and fear. He failed to say (possibly because it seemed self-evident?) that basic to these Four Freedoms, and indispensable to each one, had been still another freedom. For the best escape from want and fear, since time out of mind, has been flight; while the freedom to dissent and the separation of Church and State have come, at least in the American experience, largely by means of migration. Whether the institutions of other societies will be reshaped as ours have been, and whether the right of mobility will be found indispensable to human rights everywhere, remains to be seen.[16] But for Americans, and for the societal structures they have created, one of the greatest and most consequential freedoms is, has been, and perhaps ever will be, the Fifth Freedom: our Freedom to Move.

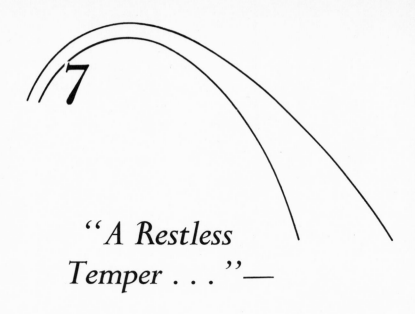

"A Restless Temper ..."—

And its long-range consequences for society, land, and people

Let us now shift the spotlight from the impact of restlessness on our institutions to three other major categories: our relations with things, with each other, and with ourselves.

The élite of Europe accuse us of materialism in many forms, from a childlike delight in shiny gadgets to a willing slavery to labor-saving machinery, from engrossment with creature comforts to a worship of the almighty dollar, from an obsession with material possessions to the debasement or total neglect of the finer arts.

One vivid image of the American home is that of a procession of new dishwashers, freezers, mixers, and other mechanical devices going in the front door, while out the back door comes another procession of the barely used and still serviceable machines of yesterday, on their way to the discard heap.[1] This picture says that we are rich, but also wasteful, not to say careless with our things.

Are all rich peoples so enamored of new things or so careless of the old? The question has only to be asked in the context of the European aristocracy, or of privileged classes anywhere, to suggest that something else must be involved here besides "plenty." And I would propose that this something may lie in one of the peculiarities of the American experience. As a part of that experience, traveling hither and yon, even moving his family from year to year, the American has been subjected to a bombardment of new situations, stimulated by the unexpected, taught to accept and to value new things. Also in moving so often he has had to leave a good deal behind. On the one hand, believing in progress and looking toward the future, he has come to expect change and to assume that change will be good. On the other, he has discovered that yesterday's valuables may safely be discarded. The new model automobile will be more powerful than the old. Technology has already made some of his labor-saving equipment obsolete. Indeed, since the days of the clipper ships, our industrial system has been building obsolescence into its products—just as we consumers have learned to build obsolescence into our household planning. Not all of us, it is true. Yet next year an impressive percentage of our neighbors and acquaintances will either trade in the family car, install a disposal in the kitchen sink, buy a new lawnmower, or perhaps move to an all-electric house.

So by long practice and habituation, we may say, the American has become a neophiliac, a lover of the new. Yet if he keeps chasing new possessions, it should be noticed that his relations with the things themselves do not go very deep. In part for the very reason that he has seen so much that is new and handy and has grown used to changes and improvements, he will be quick to pick up new gadgets and games and the latest fashions, yet as quick to discard them for something different or better.

Reflecting on all this, I find it hard to believe that a sedentary population would show any such gay abandon.

As for our basic pragmatism—our insistence on practicality—our emphasis on engineering—our preference for applied science over basic science—our anti-intellectualism and aversion to theory—have not all these been strengthened by our restlessness? I do not for a moment question the influence of our lower-middle-class inheritance. But is not pragmatism also the natural faith of movers? For they can't afford to wait. If something is to be worthwhile it must work. As Everett S. Lee shrewdly observed a full decade ago: "Migrants are likely to meet their numerous new situations with temporary expedients at the expense of long-run solutions. The most characteristic of American philosophies, pragmatism, which stresses continuous short-term adjustments in the conviction that whatever works is best, is a typically migrant philosophy." [2] To which may be added the thought that successful adjustment breeds confidence. So our pragmatism, our doctrine of works, reinforces our optimism, removes the threat from novelty and change, and makes further movement inviting. [*]

If we now bring into view that rather different category of things we call nature, or the physical environment, have not Americans once again proved themselves avid yet careless of their resources? [3] On landing, our forefathers found the wild continent more terrible than beautiful: a savage wilderness to be feared, brutally fought,

---

[*] For a discussion of our money-mindedness, and its relation to movement, see ch. 10.

and mastered as the price of survival. For almost two centuries it resisted attack. Then the mountain barriers were breached, the great interior opened. And once conquered, or on the way to subjection, the continent began to fascinate our curiosity, our cupidity, and our ambition. Where some dreamed of a better, simpler, bucolic New World society, a new Garden of Eden—and where others saw the wilderness as a challenge to adventure or as a refuge or hiding place—the great majority, North and South, rushed to exploit it. The endless emptiness of its great open spaces lured us forward; the sheer novelty and awesome size of its natural wonders excited national pride; its wealth drew us on. Our forefathers had never seen so much timber or so much virgin land: in a surprisingly short time they overran both. And hard on their heels came the travelers and the sightseers in search of the sublime, the picturesque, the romantic "beauties of nature." Scenically, the Hudson River Palisades were but the curtain raiser to the grand landscapes of the interior. With patriotic fervor we sent foreigners to view Niagara Falls and the Great Lakes, to steamboat down the Ohio and Mississippi, to ride out over the Great Plains to the Rockies, to admire the Badlands and Monument Valley, perhaps, but certainly the Grand Canyon and the giant redwoods of California. We streamed there ourselves, stopping off en route to see the great Salt Lake or the fumaroles of the Yellowstone.

Yet on the way West, unfortunately, the face of nature soon began to show signs of dissipation and human erosion. Just as the Tidewater tobacco plantations had been worn out by rapacious cropping, so the hardwood forests of the Ohio Valley and the magnificent white pine stands of Michigan were soon decimated. In swift progression, the prairie sods were plowed, overplanted, and robbed of much of their fertility; while either side the

Great Divide the ghosts of abandoned mining towns began to haunt the dry gulches and arroyos.

Happily, it will be observed, some of the most spectacular resources have now been wrested in some part from commercial exploitation and "saved for the nation" (along with the modest sand dunes of Cape Cod). Yet this in itself is a curious grand concourse kind of salvation. At best our natural wonders we first admire, then exploit, then reluctantly turn into national parks, not to be lived with but to be visited with, not to become the basis for a distinct and colorful regional society but to be experienced superficially by just about everyone.* The democ-

---

* It is revealing to reread the advertisement for *The American Heritage Book of Natural Wonders* (1963):

"As Robert Frost remarked recently, 'What makes a nation in the beginning is a good piece of geography.'

"That, for certain, we've had in these United States. A land so whopping big and wild and varied that even now—when we can span it in four hours, or scar its remotest corner with a beer can—it can awe and dazzle us.

"You've probably seen a lot of America, because the lovely and barrier-free country has conditioned us all to be easy travelers. And surely you have had the thrill, more than once, of imagining what it was like to be the explorer who saw some great vista for the first time —a Henry Hudson, a Captain John Smith, a Meriwether Lewis.

"View the land as they saw it (and you can still, here and there) stretching westward without end, and it is easy to comprehend why America forged a new kind of man. The primitive continent called for a new way of life, and a new point of view, that marks us all to this day.

"No doubt of it, the American land has been the anvil that has shaped a lot of your belief and character. And no doubt at all, much of the American land is a spectacular sight to see. . . ." American Heritage Publishing Co., Inc. (1963).

One wonders if *American Heritage* really meant to emphasize that this vast continent, without barriers, has shrunk to a mere four hours, with its beauties considerably spoiled, its natural wonders scarred by beer cans, and its grand vistas only here and there still visible. At all events, the uneasy conscience and the commercial instinct both come through. In sober retrospect, if the land did give a little shape and much scope to the American character, it was in its turn almost reshaped by the moving American. And today in many places the face of the land is a dead giveaway: it shows what too many of us have really been like.

racy of movement makes it impossible to deny access. What fragments of unspoiled wilderness remain are now in danger of being "loved out of existence." And if, in our new-found anxiety for conservation, we succeed in stopping ourselves from littering the face of our earth with the wastes of our motorcar culture, how will we protect nature from overabundance of visitors or from pollution by people?

Given our habits, there can obviously be no privilege of locality, no priority for the natives. For so vast and variegated a terrain, this country has known and knows now astonishingly little of that intimacy with the soil, or that interdependence of man with living nature, which we call love of the land. Hence our regionalisms have always proved surprisingly superficial. William Faulkner and Robert Frost* to the contrary notwithstanding, one encounters too rarely that feel for locality which generations of occupancy should nourish. In this sense, after 350 years in geographic North America, we are sojourners still.

Nor has the story been so different with our seasons and our climates. By dint of winter vacations and travel holidays, Americans have pretty thoroughly scrambled their seasons. Even the New England Yankee and the Minnesota farmer have broken out of their winter prisons. Having, on some such journeys, encountered the stimulus of desert or mountain air, the thought then occurs of packaging it, resort-fashion, for rent to later comers. At the same time, Americans have learned to simulate their climates by air conditioning at home. And the denizens of a great metropolis can live for weeks together without once exposing themselves to the weather.

* Robert Lee Frost, New England's poet laureate, was himself born in San Francisco, the son of an Indiana "copperhead," who named him after "Marse" Robert.

All this, of course, is nothing more extraordinary than the conquest of nature. And Americans take that conquest for granted. Yet, as has so often been hinted by puzzled Europeans, the American's relations with nature are neither human nor natural. For where the classical or pagan traditions had given nature a soul, and even endowed each element with a guardian spirit—a god of the sea or of the winds, a goddess of the earth or some wood nymph for the trees—to Americans, somehow, nature's elements were merely things, and things were to be mastered, exploited, manipulated. And where the Christianized hunters and tillers of old Europe had painfully worked out a kind of symbiosis, a man-land and crop-game balance of living, we upset the balance. From the first settlements, the record of our conquest of the continent became one of destruction and exploitation. Somehow the settlers and their successors, the pioneers, did not really want to live with the land and cultivate its soils or make the most of its natural beauties, but rather slaughtered the wildlife, burned the forests, mined the soils, desecrated the landscape—and moved on.

The story is an old one, and sad. Why take time to repeat it? Because it suggests a haunting might-have-been. Might not our pioneers have been more careful if they had had to stay put?

Today we still manipulate the physical environment in ways that would have staggered the Romans. Soils are changed by chemistry, clouds seeded, distances annihilated, or the balance of nature upset by massive applications of sprayed poison. The needed snowfall for skiers a Vermonter accepts from Heaven, or else manufactures with a blower. If the home golf course seems too flat and uninteresting, now that the club members have played the Mid-Ocean and Pebble Beach, the greens committee has the old terrain bulldozed into seaside shape. In a strange juxtaposition, each "ranch house" for a rising young executive must now have a swimming pool. In our real estate "developments," we first skim off the topsoil and cut down the trees; then we plant little bushes and saplings in artificial symmetry. So here again one finds us first admiring, then abusing nature's varieties. We will not be beholden to nature. Neither time nor place must have us in their power. All of which brings even the friendly interpreter face to face with this paradox: that the people who in many regards had the most natural environment to adapt to have yielded to it the least. Perhaps they have moved too much to let it really capture them, or they ate up space too fast to enjoy it?

In a less friendly review, it may be argued that we have become toughened by exposure, hardened to physical environment, superficial in our relations with nature as well as with things. No doubt some pretty careless or indifferent parties came here in the first place, and kept coming, and kept coming, and that must have been a substantial part of the explanation. Yet the American experience of moving and moving again has increased rather than qualified the "detachment."

Without question there is much else to be said about our relations with nature and with "things," but let us move on to another aspect of the "disequilibrium which follows on the American condition": our social relations. "From the point of view of the European," we heard Thornton Wilder say, "an American is nomad in relation to place, disattached in relation to time, lonely in relation to society, and insubmissive to circumstance, destiny or God." [4] In the literary perspective, the American has been called the independent and lonely man: the "American Adam." Has this really been his destiny? Or let me phrase the question in a different way: Have Americans really been working out a new decalogue of social conduct and human fellowship?

In his Harvard lectures, Wilder proposed that Americans (living separately and independently, and finding in the environment "no confirmation of their identity") may engage in a hollow gregariousness, but they only really come alive through action: "There is really only one way in which an American can feel himself to be in relation to other Americans—when he is united with them in a project, caught up in an idea and propelled with them toward the future. . . ."

Another way to describe the same uncertainties and arrive at cooperative activism is to see American social relations as essentially those of friendly strangers. Without ancestry or family tradition, without estates or credentials of place, without privileges of authority or gentility of person, each citizen necessarily has had to stand on his own feet and reciprocally accept his fellow Americans as equal integers, at face value. Knowing little or nothing about his fellows because he has not grown up with them, it seemed wise not to discount them in advance, the more so as, having just arrived in town oneself, one hoped to be accepted on equal terms. Living in an unstable community, with new faces appearing continuously and old faces disappearing before one had really come to know them, a smile had come to seem the required greeting, a handshake and perhaps a clap on the back the best welcome, and the use of first names a brotherly and quite sufficient identification.

Our intimacy with strangers can be an engaging experience, yet ultimately disillusioning, even dangerous for the foreigner. The Englishman, it has been remarked, is notoriously shy, and builds around his personal privacy all sorts of barriers and reserves of manner. The American smiles and invites you in. Yet once you have penetrated the Englishman's defenses, all his aloofness disintegrates, his reserve melts, and he takes you into his heart. Whereas with the American you find yourself only in an ante-chamber, and the deeper you go the harder the going, the stiffer the barriers to real intimacy.

Others have pointed out how surprised, even over-whelmed, Asian students can be by the friendly welcome of the dean or admissions officer of an American univer-sity, but how bitterly disillusioned they become when it turns out that this welcome is standard, not a personal and exclusive concern for the particular soul and body of the visiting student. Never trust a stranger!

Such misunderstandings call attention to a rather pe-culiar characteristic of the "person" in this country, or at least of the work relations of one person with another, or of one individual with the many. It is a commonplace that we pride ourselves on our individualism, but limit it. Indi-vidualism, American style, insists on personal liberty to act, but aims at progress by competition *and* cooperation. No peonage for us: our hero is the free individual. At the same time no man acts alone. Sooner or later even the lone wolf finds that sheer ruthlessness defeats its own ends; there are too many against him. Over here the rugged in-dividualist learns to compromise, and to be cooperative, too—at which point he may discover how much he can get done with the help of others if he trusts them, and even how satisfying it is to be able to make his own personal "contribution."

By contrast, individualism, French style, demands recognition of a unique personality—is ever jealous and full of *"moi"*—instinctively suspects fellow employees and depreciates the outsider. Cooperation with the other fellow is limited. Advancement is sought by inside channels. The great slogan of the French Revolution may have been *Liberté, Égalité, Fraternité,* but when, by American standards, did the French ever learn the first thing about *Fraternité?*

Returning to the paradoxical American brand of individualism: If we believe in free speech and also guarantee free assembly yet seem astonishingly herd-minded and conformist in expression, may this not be at least in part because we find ourselves so often outsiders in a chance gathering of fellow outsiders, rather than insiders fighting for room in a more stable hierarchical society? *

Once again, the relative equality of opportunity—the very absence of inherited privileges and established handicaps, or the ability to walk away from such containments into new and neutral communities—enlarges the field of ambition to John Doe, who soon learns that with luck he may even come to call himself Horatio Alger. In the words of a distinguished historian, "where social relations were

---

* As Everett S. Lee has put it: "In some persons individualism may manifest itself as in Turner's frontiersman, in truculence and uncouthness, but most migrants find that a premium is placed upon the ability to adjust to new situations and new people. They learn the value of outward conformity and may come to place great value upon it, they make acquaintances easily—in short they exhibit many of the characteristics of today's 'organization man' " (Lee, *op. cit.,* p. 81). It's no secret that Americans are afraid to be choosey. For example, in "Nomadic Instincts Still Rule the Americans" (a review of Lord Kinross, *The Innocents at Home, Sunday Times* [London], Nov. 29, 1959), Raymond Mortimer quoted Kinross: " 'There's hospitality because there's warmth and a desire for company, but it isn't selective. Everybody's a grand guy.' " Mortimer added: "Americans . . . seldom complain, or seem even to notice, that anyone is a bore. From the first they are taught the supreme importance of popularity (the most popular boy, or girl, in the school is chosen by regular elections); and one must display a liking for others in orders to be liked onself."

so fluid, the individual was raised to a new power." [5] Or, sociologically speaking, spatial fluidity encourages upward (or downward) flow too. Just how "open" our society is, by comparison with what it used to be, or just what the ratios will be between geographic and social mobility, may be questions for heated argument: the necessary research has not yet been done.[6] What seems unarguable, however, is the absolute necessity of much lateral movement if there is to be any appreciable vertical movement as well. Without other places to go—and those places occupied by strangers—there would be much less opportunity and no second chance.

One of the drawbacks of this rootlessness and vertical mobility, Richard Hofstadter pointed out, has been the personal loss of identity: "this has become a country in which so many people do not know who they are or what they are or what they belong to or what belongs to them. It is a country of people whose status expectations are random and uncertain, and yet whose status aspirations have been whipped up to a high point by our Democratic ethos and our rags-to-riches mythology." [7]

So migration has been a problem-creating phenomenon as well as a problem-solving process. What it offers with one hand it may even partially withdraw with another. After encouraging the self-reliant individualists, it helps turn many of them into organization men. Promising opportunity, it puts insecurity into the bargain. Paradoxically, it seems responsible for much of our proverbial friendliness but also for much personal indifference; for the American accent on sociability but also for our "hollow gregariousness."

Whether for good or ill, I conclude, no inconsiderable fraction of today's social life, and materialistic attitudes, and personal uncertainties, can be understood better if they are seen as geared to the stubborn fact that the average American must live and work among a quasi-anonymous and constantly shifting population. Ask how a stranger might introduce himself and protect himself among fellow strangers, and how he might then employ himself, enrich himself, amuse himself, or organize his social occasions, and one will not only fashion a new decalogue of social conduct, one will come surprisingly close to many accepted American norms.*

All this will perhaps seem commonplace, yet immensely confusing. Is movement cause or consequence or merely coincidence? It may be one or the other or even all three. Is movement coherent in its institutional action and uniform in its social results? Anything but. It is full of paradoxes and contradictions, confusions and uncertainties. As we have noticed earlier, there are many motives for moving and many kinds of movers and movement, and at best they overlap rather than coincide. Nor are the psychic consequences necessarily harmonious. Nor are all our movements, put together, sufficient to explain American divergencies and peculiarities. Far from it. Freedom of movement is but one freedom; it takes many others to make a free society. Yet let us not make the contrary mistake of regarding free movement as merely neutral. It may either heal or hurt, atomize or restructure our civilization. Rarely is it just coincidental. Every day of our lives it affects you and me.

---

* In such communities, for example, will charity be interpersonal, spasmodic, and secretive, or cooperative, regularized, and publicly conducted as through some community drive? Will business be conducted by tacit, traditional rules or by legal contract? Will hospitality be guarded or pretty undiscriminating?

Perhaps most important of all, let us remind ourselves, mobility is *not new,* not an accident nor a temporary state of affairs. As demonstrated by much of the evidence already cited, this moving business, in most of its forms, has been going on here for a long time. Movement has always been a major ligament in our culture, knit into the bone and sinew of that body of experiences which we call our history.

Thus in the field of transportation, we may be now perhaps just past the peak of the automobile age. But before that was the age of steam, of the railroad and the paddlewheeler, and before that the day of canalboat and prairie schooner, and before that the generations of stage-coach and wilderness trail.

As for personal movement, looking backward we can see that in the nineteenth century the westward movement provided a spectacular (though not unique) series of experiments in displacement. For a little more than a hundred years the rough-and-ready frontiersmen, the leapfrogging pioneers, the land speculators, and backwoods evangelists kept surging relentlessly toward the westward horizons.* The expedition of Lewis and Clark,

---

* In "The Turner Thesis Re-examined," Lee makes the point that the true safety valve was not the frontier but migration, while Turner's frontier theory was but "a special case of an as yet undeveloped migration theory."—Lee, *op. cit.,* pp. 80, 83. I find myself in substantial agreement with this suggestion.

The most interesting historical work on the statistics of urban mobility is perhaps that of Stephan Thernstrom. See his article (with Peter R. Knights) "Men in Motion: Some Data and Speculations about Urban Population Mobility in Nineteenth Century America," *Journal of Inter-Disciplinary History* (Autumn 1970), vol. I, no. 1. Thernstrom has also kindly let me see in advance the concluding chapter in his forthcoming book on Boston, in which he argues that the nineteenth-century patterns of fluidity or persistence in American cities generally were astonishingly similar, and like those of Boston.

the great Mormon migration, the sudden rushes of the forty-niners or the Sooners into Indian territory, the sifting of voters across state lines in the battle for Kansas, the Conestoga wagons and the barges drifting downriver, the ox trains and pony express—all these played a part not only in the conquest of the continent but in the forging of an "American" character.

To speak in a riddle, the restlessness of the American character has been and remains one of its most stable characteristics. Foreigners have noticed and called attention to it over and over again; like an endless refrain or ululation the theme has kept sounding through their books. To give one recent example: in the mid-1960's, a Japanese scholar applied for a grant to study the "escape from reality" expressed in the plays of Tennessee Williams and the novels of John Updike, along with the great theme of "on the move" in Steinbeck and Kerouac.* Twelve years earlier, *Réalités* of Paris had recognized that we aren't just frontiersmen but perpetual immigrants:

> On a dit souvent qu' à la base, l'Américain est un pionnier. C'est commode pour l'interpréter mais bien simpliste. Il est surtout un émigrant perpétuel, un homme qui n'est définitivement chez lui ni ici ni ailleurs et encore moins dans les terres épuisées et dans les idées reçues. C'est un être disponible, toujours prêt à prendre la route.[8]

A short generation ago the Englishman James Pope-Hennessy referred to "that profound law of personal development by which one must belong to one place but work in another: if you came from Tampa you must go to San Francisco, if from Alabama, to Illinois. Transplanta-

---

* Almost simultaneously, another Nipponese scholar confessed that he envied the openness of our society, and the way professors could move from university to university; even at a cocktail party, Americans walked around more and talked to strangers.—Application for ACLS fellowship, 1966; and a letter to one of my former students, December 1945.

tion is vital to the making and embellishment of individual character." [9]

From Paris, in the same year (1947), came the voice of Denis de Rougemont, proclaiming us a people of the road:

> L'Européen parle parfois de sa conception de la vie; l'Américain (l'Anglais aussi) de son *way of life*, littéralement: de sa route de vie. Ce qui est pour le Latin concept, forme arrêtée, devient chez eux chemin, voie et mouvement.
> . . . je prendrai les routes d'Amérique comme un symbole du rêve et de la volonté du Nouveau Monde.[10]

Going back to the 1890's one may find another Frenchman, Alphonse de Calonne, identifying us as activists—compelled by tradition, inheritance, and money-mindedness to be always on the move:

> L'Américain du nord est l'homme actif par excellence. La tradition, l'hérédité, son culte pour l'argent, le portent à aller, venir, à remuer sans cesse. Il s'arrête, il ne demeure pas. Où on l'a vu la veille, on ne le retrouvera plus lendemain. S'il s'y trouve c'est qu'il est revenu. . . . S'il se donne un logis stable c'est qu'il ne peut faire autrement.[11]

And going back still another half century, one comes on Domingo Sarmiento, the South American reformer and statesman, taking particular notice of our Yankee propensity for travel:

> The large number of passengers reduces the cost of the fares and low fares in turn tempt people to travel, even though they have no precise object in view. The Yankee leaves home to enjoy a change of air, or just to take a trip, and he travels a hundred and fifty miles by steamboat or train before returning to his work.

In 1847 Sarmiento went so far as to proclaim a connection between travel and other peculiarities of American civilization, in particular our "monstrous hotels," our appalling eating habits, and the explosion of the American population. A little mischievously, he noted that it was the custom for young honeymooners "to take the next train to parade their happiness through woods, towns, cities, and hotels. In the coaches these enchanting couples of twenty summers are to be seen in close embrace, reclining very affectionately against one another to the edification of all the travelers." Hence two effects. All the crusty old bachelors decided to get married: the birth rate became phenomenal. And ". . . I attribute to these ambulant amours in which American flirting ends, the mania for travel which is so characteristic of the Yankee that he is called a born traveler. The rage for traveling is increasing year by year." [12]

Visiting us in the years 1833–5, Michael Chevalier encountered populations not native to their towns, and destined to die elsewhere: "the full-blooded American has this in common with the Tartar, that he is *encamped,* not established, on the soil. . . ." Our emblem should be a locomotive or a steamboat, he suggested. Moreover, these were essentially democratic instruments, for their effect was to promote practical liberty and "to reduce the distance not only between different places, but between different classes." Chevalier was deeply impressed by our restless activism: "An irresistible current sweeps everything away, grinds everything to powder and deposits it again under new forms. Men change their houses, their climate, their trade, their condition, their party, their sect; the States change their laws, their officers, their constitutions." And he went on to describe the American character, the "pure Yankee," as

. . . not only a worker, he is a migratory worker. He has no root in the soil; he is a stranger to the worship of one's birthplace and family home; he is always in the mood to move on, always ready to start in the first steamer that comes along from the place where he had just now landed. He is devoured with a passion for movement, he cannot stay in one place; he must go and come, he must stretch his limbs and keep his muscles in play. When his feet are not in motion, his fingers must be in action; he must be whittling a piece of wood, cutting the back of his chair, or notching the edge of the table, or his jaws must be at work grinding tobacco. Whether it be that continual competition has given him the habit, or that he has an exaggerated estimate of the value of time, or that the unsettled state of everything around him keeps his nervous system in a state of perpetual agitation, or that he has come so from the hands of nature—he always has something to do, he is always in a terrible hurry. . . .[13]

Such was the Jacksonian American. Yet before locomotives and steamboats, and even before the Erie Canal had been dug or the Mississippi reached, Europeans were commenting on a psychology that owed much to movement: on our friendliness and hospitality, our casual informality and lack of deference, our inquisitiveness and our helpfulness with strangers. Already our feverish restlessness and activity, our boastfulness and psychological insecurity, our mental and emotional instability were a familiar story, noticed by our visitors, commented on by many.[14] Yet if a twentieth-century American should wish to assure himself that mobility had always been a large and meaningful factor in the American way of life and in the making of the American character, he could do no better than to consult our most discerning judge and commentator, Alexis de Tocqueville.

In 1831 Tocqueville was astonished by our propensity for movement, by the stagecoaches that went everywhere at breakneck speed over bone-breaking roads, by the phlegmatic way in which Americans took the hardships of travel, and by the extraordinary sight of Americans building roads into the wilderness even ahead of their settlers. While traveling through backwoods Tennessee, Tocqueville got to speculating about some of the effects of such movement for the economy and arrived at the by no means inconsiderable discovery that volume of communications and speed of interchange (that is, turnover) had perhaps as much to do with prosperity as anything else.[15]

Again, on his nine months' journey through the country Tocqueville noted how the English Puritans had planted their institutions and their faith in New England, and how the Connecticut Yankees had then sent their lawmakers, their teachers, and their clocks across the continent. Yet not without alterations. In the migration process the laws changed, the institutions became simpler, more democratic, and freer from ancestral prejudices. The destruction was piecemeal and not complete: it took at least three migrations to destroy or renovate an old English law. But necessarily, he suggested, there was much loss of ancestral baggage on the march. It was almost as if he had said that Europeans could become Americans only by repeatedly moving.

Once again Tocqueville noted the beneficial effects of the continent and of movement in assuring political stability and in preventing revolution. Why were there not more political plots and conspiracies? And how could the state survive, being so weak? Because there was so much land, because careers were all open, because there were so many other avenues to power than the channel of politics, because younger sons could go West, because the frontier was a safety valve for the adventurous and the irresponsible as well as for the ambitious.

Notwithstanding all these advantages and opportunities, the Americans seemed to Tocqueville at once feverish and sad. And in a striking chapter in his *Democracy in America* he finally tried to explain to himself "Why the Americans are so restless in the midst of their prosperity."

> In the United States a man builds a house in which to spend his old age, and he sells it before the roof is on; he plants a garden and lets it just as the trees are coming into bearing; he brings a field into tillage and leaves other men to gather the crops; he embraces a profession and gives it up; he settles in a place, which he soon afterwards leaves to carry his changeable longings elsewhere. . . . Death at length overtakes him, but it is before he is weary of his bootless chase of that complete felicity which forever escapes him.[16]

How account for this strange unrest of so many "happy" men? The taste for physical gratifications, and the hurry to enjoy them because of the shortness of life, seemed to Tocqueville one obvious source. A social condition in which neither laws nor custom retained any person in his place was a great additional stimulus to this restlessness. Still a third was the "equality of conditions" and opportunity, which engendered a feverish competition and ambitions never quite satisfied.

Such passages are informative and suggestive, not least of our physical and emotional instability. Yet if one were to seek even sharper insights into what Tocqueville called the "national character" of the Americans, one should read again the intuitions that he confided to his diary, after only a month in America (June 7, 1831), and before he had seen the frontier, or talked to John Quincy Adams about the West, or come to attribute too much to an all-pervasive egalitarian *démocratie*.

A restless temper [*l'inquiétude du caractère*] seems to me one of the distinctive traits of this people. . . . We have been told that the same man has often tried ten estates. He has appeared successively as merchant, lawyer, doctor, minister of the gospel. He has lived in twenty different places and nowhere found ties to detain him. And how should it be otherwise? In a word, here man has no settled habits, and the scene before his eyes prevents his adopting any. (1) Many have come from Europe, leaving their customs and traditions behind. (2) Even those long established in the country have preserved this difference. There are no American *moeurs* as yet. Each accepts what he likes from the group, but remains a law unto himself. Here the laws vary continuously, magistrates succeed each other, nature itself changes more rapidly than man. Through a singular inversion of the usual order of things, it's nature that appears to change, while man stays immovable. The same man has given his name to a wilderness that none before him had traversed, has seen the first forest tree fall and the first planter's house rise in the solitude, where a community came to group itself, a village grew, and to-day a vast city stretches. In the short space between death and birth he has been present at all these changes, and a thousand others have been able to do the same. In his youth he has lived among nations which no longer exist except in history. In his life-time rivers have changed their courses or diminished their flow, the very climate is other than he knew it, and all that is to him but the first step in a limitless career. . . .

. . . Born often under another sky, placed in the middle of an always moving scene, himself driven by the irresistible torrent which draws all about him, the American has no time to tie himself to anything, he grows accustomed only to change, and ends by regarding it as the natural state of man.[17]

May we not deduce that what we feel today our grandfathers and their grandfathers felt before us? We have been pilgrims and pioneers from the beginning; we were and still are restless almost beyond measure. Has this been a superficial trait? Hardly. Has it done something considerable to shape the American character and society? No matter how uncertain we may feel about the precise nature of the results, I do not see how one can question this. Perhaps the strongest effect has been our very unsettlement: our culture of endless change. In 1831 Tocqueville said there were "no American *moeurs* as yet"—while Wilder in 1952 thought we were still engaged in inventing what it is to be an American!

In any reading, what remains inescapable is this: mobility has been one of the oldest and most continuous themes of the American experience, and its meaning is still to be fully appreciated.

Of course movement, restlessness, and change are not unique to Americans. And the conquests of time and of space: these are not American inventions but the conquests of modern man. Perhaps all we ought to say, therefore, is that in this movement, and in their relations with time and space, Americans have been ahead of Europeans: the first modern auto-mobiles? Americanism, after all, can be in part just a matter of timing: for example, a society behind in the arts but ahead in its gadgets.

Yet does one not feel just a little uneasy about the adequacy of such an explanation? The mobility that America has today, Europe will have tomorrow? Not quite. For it is hard to escape the conviction that somehow, for some strange reason, Americans have had a special affinity for mobility, have known it, used it, enjoyed it, and suffered its agonies, with a devotion and an intimacy no other people has experienced. We are, and will remain, a more fluid society. In times past, we have been so swept along in the vast currents of movement that we have taken movement itself for granted. Now it is in our institutions and our economy, in our social actions and attitudes, in our expectations, in our bones. As Tocqueville so shrewdly observed some 140 years ago, "a restless temper seems . . . one of the distinctive traits of this people."

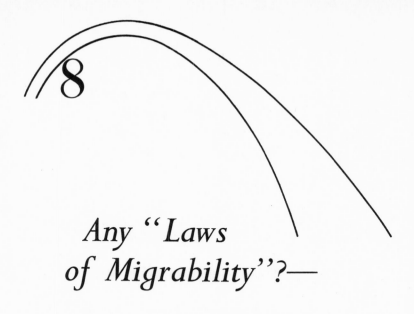

Any "Laws
of Migrability"?—

Who moves? Why? The influence of
push, pull, and roadbed

Are there any laws of human motion? Thus far we have looked on American society and seen that it is moving, and moving in distinct and sometimes peculiar ways. And these restless habits have been reflected (intensified but rarely impeded) in the language and in the laws, in the economy and in the landscape, in the homes, the life style, and the social attitudes of Americans for the past two hundred years. But are there any statistical probabilities, any social tendencies, any cultural predictabilities or psychological syndromes of a sufficient regularity and reliability so that we can formulate a structure of rules or code for spatial migration—and then perhaps apply that code to the case history of the Americans?

We have had and still have no such code. Back in 1885 an Englishman, E. G. Ravenstein, after studying the statistics of the drift of Irish laborers toward London, presented to the Royal Statistical Society seven (largely quantitative) probabilities which he called "The Laws of Migration." [1] He was greeted with skepticism and attracted no followers. Again in the 1920's, Ellsworth Huntington became interested in the biological and cultural selectivity of migration,[2] Pitirim Sorokin explored briefly the psychological consequences of detachment,[3] and Rudolf Heberle, a young German scholar, after a study grant in the United States wrote an interesting book on the American habit of movement and on some of its social, political, and personal effects.[4] Once again, in the Depression, Warren S. Thompson and Rupert B. Vance tried to summarize the knowledge of population flows and redistributions in the United States; and Dorothy Swaine Thomas asked about the migration differentials of age, sex, health, intelligence, and occupation—with quite tentative and inconclusive results.[5] Since 1930 our historians of immigration, our students of acculturation, and our demographers—from Commons and Wittke to Blegen, Thistlethwaite, and Scott; from Davie and Hansen to Handlin, Glazer, Moynihan, and Thernstrom; from Walter F. Willcox to Everett S. Lee—have illuminated the larger story of the peopling of this country.[6] And in the past generation, sociologists and social psychologists have been compiling a wide range of case histories on the displacement of the blacks and on many mini-movements from place to place within the United States.[7] Yet, except for a thoughtful beginning recently made by Everett S. Lee,[8] no great framework has emerged, no substantial schema.

Taking my courage in my hands, leaning on the work of many scholars, and borrowing wherever I can from a vast and often difficult literature, I therefore venture to propose some *Laws*. These will be probabilities, not certainties—sometimes even speculative possibilities rather than probabilities—and they will hardly be original or new. Indeed, perhaps the only novelty will lie in the comprehensiveness of the attempt. They are for trying: for reflection, application, rejection, or improvement.

I. My first Law or basic proposition is obvious, and I am quite confident of it: *Movement means change.* To transfer is in some part to transform. *Wanderung meint Wandlung,* as the Germans put it. And all forms of movement, from expulsion to flight, or from mass exodus to simple milling around, have shared in this subtle process of alteration.

II. Why should motion cause change? Because *Institutions do not move easily. A few can't be moved at all, or perhaps have to be left behind. Many more are damaged in transit. Nearly all are shaken, and have to be pruned, simplified, or otherwise adjusted to survive the transplanting. To a degree, displacement will mean replacement of institutions.* The organizations that survive may then either gradually wither or else expand by taking over the functions of other defunct organizations. If displacements continue, then the institutions will have to be made portable, or at least imitatable and duplicatable, that is, interchangeable. And the homogenization of culture will be institutionally reinforced.*

III. Why again should migration cause modification? Because *Migrants are not average people. As a group they do not represent a fair cross section of the society they are leaving. As individuals they tend toward exaggerations of one sort or another. As settlers they won't wish to reproduce the entire society they have left, or succeed in re-*

---

* Quite a few ranges of institutional change or adjustment or homogenization have already been cited, but we will return to this theme in chs. 9 and 11.

producing it even should they so desire. A process of personal selection has been at work. So changes, both planned and unplanned, there will have to be. (The only possibility of holding such changes to a minimum, as far as I can see, will be at the two extremes of mobility: either the single, quick, short move by an intensely self-centered clan or sect; or the repetition of movement into such a habit of nomadism that the tribal company comes to stabilize its customs on the basis of motion.) After some hesitation I think I am prepared to go along with Huntington, who was persuaded that migration has a selective appeal: selective of the physical stock and of the intellectual equipment and of the psychological temperament, as well as of the institutions or culture. I mean to say a good deal more about this in a moment. But first we must recognize a fourth major probability, or Law.

IV. *The process of moving alters the stock, temperament, and culture of the movers, not only by an original selection but on the road as well and also at journey's end.* Inevitably, migrants are affected by their new circumstances and prospects: that is, by the hardships and accidents of the flight or crossing, by the strange people and ideas encountered on the voyage, by the unaccustomed climate and geography, and last but not least by some of the odd practices and beliefs stumbled into in the new environment or receiving society.*

So why can we say dogmatically that migration means change? Because not everyone or everything moves, and moving does things to both the mover and his goods—and so does the process of resettlement. Such is the crude message of our major quartet.

Let us now first look more deeply into that fundamental and most important operation: the process of detach-

* For more on this Law, see the end of this chapter, and also ch. 10.

ment at the point of origin, or the original selection of the movers (Law III). If not everyone moves, who moves? That will depend in part on (A) the Home Index, or "Push Factors"—in part on (B) the Colony Index, or "Pull Factors"—and in part on (C) the Journey Index, or "Roadbed Factor." [9] And let us not forget (D) Selection by Accident. Each of these is a complex or composite of variables.

What are the migration possibilities or "migrabilities" under differing conditions at home?

III. A. *Who Moves? The Home Index, or Push Factors*

III. A.1. *In the case of expulsion by a physical event —by war, by flood or famine or other natural disaster— who moves?*

(1) One is tempted to believe that *after a natural disaster* everyone will have moved, but historic experience suggests otherwise: the most one can say is that almost everyone may try to move, *perhaps all but the very obstinate or the weaklings.* Even in a predictable catastrophe, some don't or won't get away. Illustration: a great flood in China—a "dust bowl" in Oklahoma—the potato blight in Ireland which pushed half (but only half) of the Irish abroad.

(2) *During or after a great war, or a civil war, who moves?* One can predict it will be *many innocent bystanders* (e.g., the Palatinate Germans in the Thirty Years' War, or the Laotians and Cambodians today); also *the persecuted and displaced minorities* (e.g., the Jews of Middle Europe since 1880, or the Arabs in Palestine since 1945); and of course *the losers* (e.g., the American aborigines, or the Tories in the American Revolution). But also it will be *the fighters themselves,* and especially at the end of a war the unemployed soldiers (one thinks of the Hessians in our Revolution, of the many Confederate soldiers

who went abroad after Appomattox, and of the G.I. rush to California after World War II). With soldiers perhaps this will be because the army forcibly detached them from their homes; they were kept on the move and got used to being uprooted; or had they glimpsed greener pastures?

III. A.2. *In the case of an economic event* (*hard times, good times*), *who moves?*

(1) *In hard times,* it will not automatically be the poor or the unemployed. It is not so simple. Rather, the probability is that *fewer will move than usual:* it is not panics or depressions or hard times that create great migrations. Perhaps a few of the richer will take off, and perhaps also a scattering of the desperate: the sudden bankrupts, the hopeless debtors. Yet *the main group of movers will be middle-class people with savings, who are threatened by a relative loss of status or increase of wants, and see it.*[10] Let me emphasize those last words: the fear of hardship seems to be more important than the hardship itself (Thornton Wilder has said the same thing about the shadow of a coming persecution). The foreknowledge of trouble, or the apprehension of hard times ahead, is what matters—witness the flight of the Scots after the union with England, or the run-off of Yankee farmers from the hilltops of New England into the Ohio Valley.

(2) *In good times more people move,* but generally not from the top classes (not lords and gentlemen, not princes and bishops, not bankers or great lawyers) and not from the bottom classes either (unless aided or driven). Rather, it will be *the rising middle classes* generally, and especially the more energetic and ambitious and hopeful.

So we reach two further generalizations about prosperity and depression:

(3) They change the amounts but not the kinds of

migration. A *depression may slow up* or partially dam the flow to town and rejuvenate a little the return flow to the farm, *but it hardly changes the basic pattern.*

(4) *Prosperity is encouraging psychologically: economic migrations are therefore a function of prosperity, and of hope.* So America was the product of a rising Europe in two ways: of the rising economic classes, and of the rising temperaments and expectations.

III. A.3. *In the case of the social event—in times of stagnation or rapid change—who moves?*

(1) *In stable or reactionary times, they tend to move who are out of step,* that is, the political rebels, the economic radicals, the religious reformers, the socially discontent. In a slowly declining feudalism, it may be the traders and the fast-rising middle classes. In Stuart England, the three breeds of Puritan—the Parliamentarians, the economic adventurers, and the devout iconoclasts— each discovered their reasons for going. As Thistlethwaite has observed, the dissenter became an archetypal American personality.[11]

In any sober, serious, slow-moving age it will be the idealists, the visionaries, the utopians who will get restless. And to these will be added the self-reliant individualists, and the extra-curious, the excitement-hungry.

(2) *But in times of change, or rapid and prolonged transition?* Again, the movers will tend to be *those who are out of step.* This will not necessarily be the enterprising and adventurous and excitement-hungry, for they may be finding opportunity and excitement enough at home. Rather, the movers will include many conservatives, anxious to preserve their position, their occupations, their ways, their beliefs. So the sturdy yeomen of old England, in the face of the new factories, began thinking of lands

across the Atlantic. So the frontiersmen and the pioneer farmers made our westward movement occupationally and socially an oddly conservative affair. In times of rapid change, such migrations attract not only the conservative but also the disgruntled and the reactionaries, the primitives of old Europe or the Atlantic seaboard. So there came to the New World, or later to the Mississippi Valley, the German pietists and sectarians, the Scots fundamentalists and hell-fire preachers, the baptists and methodists and revivalists to the peopling of our Southern Bible Belt, and the Mormons to Illinois and Utah. Yet always on the fringe of even a fast-changing society will be found those for whom fast change is still not fast enough: the very impatient radicals, the prophets and absolute visionaries, the shaking Quakers and the New Harmony folk. Surprisingly, often the extremes of radical and conservative impulse seem to combine into some new mixture of authority and freedom, or of free love with community property and paternalism, as with the Oneida perfectionists.

Reflecting on these paradoxes, one is led to entertain certain additional conclusions about change:

(3) *Social change frees elements of the populations for moving,* and especially the extremes;

(4) *These migrants then tend to draw their own kind after them;* the elastic pull of the forerunners, once in action, may not quickly stop (compare the two early streams from Massachusetts: to Connecticut, "the land of steady habits," or to Rhode Island, "the home of the otherwise-minded").

(5) *Immigrants are probably already uprooted.* Those who crossed the Atlantic had already crossed other bridges; those who got on the boat were already adrift. As Thistlethwaite has so clearly demonstrated, migration had already acquired momentum in Europe. Or as Lewis

Mumford once put it: "The Settlement of America was the product of the Unsettlement of Europe." [12] Yet all these considerations also apply to the settlement of our West, or to the feverish milling around we know today. So, in this sense,

(6) *The conquest of our continent was the by-product of the transformation of our early republican society*—just as the current instability represents myriad personal responses to the revolutionary changes of the last fifty years.

III. A.4. *Can we also classify migrants by their social motivation:* by their main interests or occupations? It is clear that group interests differ and that the opportunity which appeals to one class or industrial group or religious faith may not appeal to others. Different personal ambitions also respond differently. And both personal and cultural quality are always hard to measure. This subjects any "lawmaker" to the risk of value judgments, and to the accusation of prejudice. So perhaps the best way to state certain possibilities may be to phrase them as questions. [13]

(1) If the ambition in moving has been *military:* Has the class appeal been to the rulers, the aristocrats, and the strongest young men (the Cortés, Frontenac, Walter Raleigh breeds)—and has the cultural type been power-hungry, managerial, literate, but emotional?

(2) If the ambition was *political:* Was not the appeal to the top and the next-to-top classes; or if the ambition was for liberty and self-government, was it not to the best of the middle classes—and were not the political movers ambitious and managerial like the soldiers, but perhaps more highly educated and idealistic?

(3) If the prime motive in moving was *economic:* Did it not appeal to a few younger sons from the aristoc-

racy or big trader families, but chiefly to the numerous middle class, and to the upper levels of the lower class—and were not the participants pragmatic in temperament, materialistic in values, and distinctly nonintellectual?

(4) If the real reason for moving was *religious:* Did it not draw from all classes, but predominantly the moral consciences and the emotional temperaments?

(5) Again, if the reasons were *mixed:* Were not the respondents also of mixed origins, but prevailingly out of the middle class, and from the more vigorous and enterprising?

With none of these suggestions do I find myself entirely comfortable. Yet two conclusions about social motivation (which I originally drew, I think, from Huntington) seem to me firmer and quite defensible:

(6) *The more abstract the appeal, the higher the type of respondent;*

(7) *The greater the sacrifice, the higher the type.* For if a man is willing to sacrifice, and postpone his rewards, that shows imagination, faith, endurance, and self-discipline.

(8) *Whereas if something is free, a handout, you get trash.*[14]

III. A.5. Using a *psychological classification:* If now we ask what temperaments or kinds of individual—out of any class or occupation or church or community—will move most frequently and easily, we get a kind of *Index of Detachability. Who are most easily moved?*

(1) *Those who are most easily moved:* the emotional, volatile, suggestible, enthusiastic.

(2) The *optimists* of all kinds, all the way to the wishful thinkers: the *future-minded,* those who "never carry an umbrella."

(3) The *curious*, the *natural explorers*, the *adventurous*, and the *gamblers:* those who will try anything once, the happy-go-lucky ("In God we trusted, in Kansas we busted").

(4) The *persons with a burning faith*, the *men with a mission*, the prophets and crusaders, the people touched by an "Awakening," whether their cause be religious or social or economic. From Whitefield and Jonathan Edwards to Billy Graham, from John Brown to Malcolm X and some of the Black Panthers, from Henry George to Staughton Lynd, from Frances Wright to Carrie Nation and perhaps some women's liberators still alive and kicking, one keeps bumping into such characters on our national road.

(5) Next (though the order of counting no longer matters) one might name the *resolute individualists*, the courageous and self-reliant, the "inner-directed" parties or groups, the self-contained congregations: those with their gyroscopes built in.

(6) The *doers*, the activists, the energetic.

(7) The *restless*, the uneasy, the people with itching feet: those who were born under a wandering star.

(8) The *maladjusted*, the marginal men and groups, the perpetually discontented, and the demoralized.

(9) The *criminals* and *outlaws*, the perennially *delinquent*, and the persistent *failures*.

(10) The *insane* and *mentally disturbed*.[15]

Isn't this about everyone? Haven't we covered the full range of temperaments or psychological types? Absolutely not. For, as is demonstrated by this very listing, if movement appeals to, or promises to satisfy, certain emotional types, to others it seems positively unattractive. Thus, in a free migration we are decidedly not likely to get our fair share of the stable and well-balanced temperaments, of the skeptical, of the pessimistic, of the prudent and thoughtful. Again, the lazy and the easily discouraged and the fearful either don't start or soon drop out. The dependent may only go if they can ride on someone else's coattails. So, other things being equal, it is the men with high emotional potential, all the way from the wishful thinkers through the activists and the revolutionaries to the refugees, who most readily take to the road.[16] Leaving behind the thoughtful—and the weak.

III. A.6. *Is there an order of moving?* A timing in mobility's appeal? A differential vulnerability as between ages, sexes, occupations, talents?

Here our sociologists, economists, demographers, and behavioral scientists have long been doing a good deal of work, especially with regard to internal migration, and some of their major conclusions, while not yet given classic expression, may perhaps be broadly summarized as follows:[17]

(1) *Adolescents and young adults and the productive workers* have almost always constituted the large majority in any free migration. For mobility offers opportunity.

(2) *Mobility becomes almost automatic at certain moments, or transfer points, on life's journey.* It seems to be built into our American *rites de passage:* as with going away to school or college, or the first job, or getting married, etc., until there comes the moment of retirement (see above, ch. 4).

(3) *Occupations have a differential mobility,* and certain professions (e.g., academic scholarship and the performing arts, or law and politics) seem to either encourage or discourage moving (again see ch. 4).

(4) *The longer and harder the journey, the more selective it is in favor of the young, the males, the energetic and courageous, the able, and (recently) the highly educated.* "The cowards never started, the weak ones died on the way," is an old proverb. But the weak are also slower to start and stop sooner. So our successive waves of immigration were each in their early phases overwhelmingly youthful and masculine—and the same could be said of our frontiersmen moving West. Yet certain immigrant groups, having got across the Atlantic, lacked the strength to go on into the continent and so got bogged down in our coast cities (and the westward movement must have dropped a good many weaklings along the way?). In internal population flows, at all events, it is becoming evident that the movers seem to show a higher average level of education than those who stay behind.

(5) *Women? Historically, they have moved later* across the Atlantic or across the continent—in part no doubt because it was a man's world, and they constituted a somewhat unfree or semi-captive class. Many women followed their husbands across, or came to find husbands in our more fluid young society, or swelled the after-flows to Ohio and Texas and the Mormon empire. Yet in this country perhaps more women have entered our cities than men; they outnumber the men in short-distance movement; and they seem to begin moving a bit earlier, perhaps because they reach marriage or the job stage sooner.

(6) What about the *second-comers?* The people who make up the bulk of a major immigration? If a general judgment can be hazarded, it would be that *they are*

177

likely to be less able. For it takes less courage and imagination to follow, to copy, to be a filler-in. Perhaps such parties also are less independent, more inclined to go with the crowd, more "other-directed"? At that, the late movers may be showing more initiative than those who stay behind. Yet if they are sent for, or subsidized, or arranged for by others, clearly their journey requires less personal get-up-and-go.

(7) Can we say anything qualitative about *speed and timing?* Here the returns are not all in. But it looks as if Huntington was right. In a slow disaster to an occupation, or a class, or a region, the *more intelligent start sooner and go farther,* for example, in the flight from the farms, or the dispersion of the coal miners from the stricken anthracite region[18] (I sometimes think I can see a parallel in the transfer of ministerial types from the clergy into academic life, social welfare, or certain kinds of journalism).

The further application of some of these probabilities to our own immigration history, or the westward movement, or the rise of our cities, or the cumulative flow of blacks into our Northern centers, should add understanding and significance to our demographic experience—as well as some teasing might-have-beens. For example, in our immigration we drew talent from a very wide spectrum of peoples. But for the recruitment of energy and initiative and ability, would we not have done better to admit still more nationalities—and restrict the later comers or cut off the after-flows much sooner?

III. A.7. *What about unfree migration—or immigrations that have been aided or forced? Who moves then?*

At first, it might seem that unfree migration just reverses the conditions, hence must reverse the type of migrant, too. One remembers the attempts at "Resettlement" in the Great Depression, and their failure; the timid and weak may be willing, but the proud and independent resent dictation and are slow to accept such aid. Again, one recalls the indenture system of colonial times, or the prepaid tickets of the nineteenth century, or the recruitment by steamship and railroad companies of the disposable populations of southern Italy and the Balkans in the first decade of this century. Yet care is needed; there are distinctions to be made.

(1) *State aid,* being mostly impersonal "push," may disregard personal inclinations. So a state-generated migration *may reverse the normal expectations, or instead it may prove almost entirely undiscriminating,* as with war or a natural disaster. In the seventeenth and eighteenth centuries, the mother countries of Europe dumped a good many criminals and undesirables on their American colonies. And both Spain and France (but not England) sent a good many soldiers. Again, the forced migration of the slave trade hardly consulted the wishes of its victims.

(2) *Private aid for profit,* however, is apt to be less drastic. It *may merely lower the level of the appeal.* Thus an aided or "impelled" immigration seems to step down the class, of those likely to be moved, one or two rungs on the social ladder, without otherwise changing the pattern. He who sold himself into indenture for seven years showed at least some initiative and hopefulness and resolution?

III. B. *The Colony Index, or Pull Factors*

Let us turn now to the destination, to the receiving station or "colony." What influence has the colony had on the quantity or quality or social distribution of the take-off population? Presumably, the land freely sought should have had all the influence in the world. Yet this appears not to be so.

III. B.1. *Quantity*. The colony's influence on numbers can only be stated in elementary and rather impressionistic terms:

(1) If the colony is empty (or sparsely settled) and poor in natural resources (for a given level of the arts), the settlement will tend to be sparse and to continue at a slow rate. Witness the immigration into New England, after the first religious generation—or the later settlement of the Dakotas—or Russian Siberia.

(2) If the colony is empty and rich in resources, history suggests that the population will be light at first but may become great (either through migration or birth or both).

(3) If the colony—the receiving station or city—is already crowded with a native population, of a different color and markedly lower level of the arts, then the immigration will be quite limited in numbers, and historically such migrations have developed into ruling oligarchies, sometimes absentee.

(4) If the colony (or region or town) is already crowded with a native population on a comparable level of the arts, then the invasion of newcomers is likely to be large, and to enter the lower levels of each occupation.[19]

(5) If the colony or city is growing rapidly (Ravenstein), or if it offers a variety of conditions, hence a wide spectrum of opportunities and incentives (Lee), then more different types will find it interesting, and the influx will also tend to be larger.

(6) Economic pressures? Some economists and some of the older historians have assigned an overmastering influence to population pressures, or to job opportuni-

ties, or to relative economic development, or to capital flows; but I find the Malthusian doctrine and almost the entire range of materialistic explanations of immigration either partially misleading or false.[20] In our own historic experience, it has only occasionally been the relative population densities which have determined the direction or the size of the movement (witness the farm-to-city flow). Again, it has not been the relative economic advantage that has been determinant, however powerful the economic motivation, but rather (at most) what was *supposed* to be the economic advantage. And often the migrant was mistaken. Or he made a compromise move, with weight given to other strong impulses and considerations. Even Vance's relative occupational density seems inadequate, for so much depends on what the potential migrant *wants*. In the nineteenth century if he wanted virgin land, then he went West. But if he wanted some other things, then perhaps he became a millhand and followed the mills.

(7) In general, between destination and expectation, *it is the expectation that counts*. In mobility, we should remember, what one supposes to be the fact is more important than the fact. True, the imagined fact may in large part be based on, or may later be corrected by, experience at the destination. Yet such corrections only imperfectly get back to the point of departure. Much of what one thinks of the colony or destination—and perhaps a very large part of its emotional image—will continue to be made at home. Our El Dorados and our Fountains of Youth were essentially manufactured in Europe.

So I conclude that the quantitative, the economic, and the occupational appeals of any New World may become distorted and exaggerated; but the real economic compulsions will be more qualified and limited than most of our commentators have assumed. The massive migrations from Europe to the United States were at times almost overwhelmingly economic; yet that in my judgment was due perhaps less to the North American continent than to the fact that the lower-middle-class populations of Europe were being freed for movement without ceasing to be economically minded. They wanted to "better themselves"—and the promises of quick affluence had been somewhat exaggerated.

III. B.2. *Quality factors.* The colony's influence on the qualities of the newcomers? What attractions will be exercised by the rich land or the poor?

(1) Offhand it might seem that a poor natural environment will tend to wind up with a low quality of settlers—and this trend is observable socially in the poorer sections of our cities. Yet difficult Iceland, and stony New England, and desert Utah hardly wound up with low-quality populations. Evidently other motivations can result in almost complete disregard or defiance of the natural and social environments at destination. *Just possibly poor environments attract the extremes?*

(2) *Rich environments evidently attract (and support) all kinds;* they are relatively nonselective. So with time the American wilderness changed from the eliminator to the catch-all receiving station and "melting pot" for European types.

(3) This shift draws attention to the fact that *the same environment will perhaps play host to quite different civilizations at different times.* The isles of Greece, the isles of Greece! Or we can think of Texas, from its early days of mission and presidio, to the invasion of slaveholding planters and ranchers, to the cattle kingdom, and then the

great empire of oil. Once Texas attracted more than its share of outlaws . . .

All of which makes one question or downgrade the importance of the colony factor.[21]

But surely, someone will argue, the colony was always supremely important as a challenge. The very difficulties of the American wilderness called out the qualities of courage, optimism, and enterprise which have so distinguished our people. Does not discomfort generate improvement? Perhaps—but chiefly if the discomfort is mental.

(4) *Psychological discomfort seems by all odds more powerful than physical discomfort in stimulating reaction.* The wilderness "calls out" certain qualities, yes, but only if they are strong to start with and waiting to be called, that is, only if it clashes with the settlers' expectations and hopes.

Imperceptibly, this train of thought has led me to speak of the colony not only as a lure but as a receiving station. Yet the passage will be justified if it reminds us of another fundamental influence or complex of impulses.

(5) *The first influence in any quality drift is the state of the mover's mind.* Even more than in the attraction of numbers, the decisive original factor in determining the quality of the immigrant is his bundle of expectations. And these expectations will be the product of his personal character and disposition; his education; his situation in family, community, occupation, class, and nation; the many societal "pushes" or impulses building up behind him; and his vision of the colony, his information about America, his "feel" of what it will be like, *for him*. Only the last—the feel or the anticipations—derives from the colony; and this has to be fitted to what he, himself, is like: to what he wants.

III. B.3. *The Moving Fever?* What about the migrants' dreams? Their visions of the promised land? Their emotional convictions about tomorrow in a different place? Now and again these aspirations have been unmistakably strong. According to all testimonies, the yearning for America—the famous "America Fever"—*could be almost irresistible.* A simple advertisement or a small item of news might spark the interest. Glowing letters might come back from relatives who had gone before. Some earlier emigrant would return with silver in his pocket and a gleam of independence in his eye—and suddenly a whole neighborhood would become infected. From family to family the infection would spread, and from village to village. Soon the epidemic would be sweeping through a whole province or countryside and a landslide of migration would be under way. In the mid-nineteenth century, the moving epidemic raged through Ireland and the Germanies; at the turn of the century, through southeastern Europe. Observers have called this "America Fever" the most powerful of all the impulses to emigration. And I do not see how one can question the verdict. Yet it points less to the land of destination than to a quite different terrain: not so much to the New World as to the interior world of the emotions. And it suggests that:

(1) *Moving can be* (and very often is, to a greater or a lesser degree) *an irrational performance.* Man is an emotional animal, and suggestible, too. Moreover, his emotions can become his most powerful spurs to action. So, since good sense is not necessarily in command, and moving requires action or force, we can neglect the emotional incentives or propellants to migration only at our peril. First and last, moving has often been an intensely emotional business. In that phrase "America Fever," the second word has meant more than the first. And even

though "America" did conjure up special visions, these were impressionistic, imperfect, second-hand, distorted, and built up into a moving impulse *at home.* I therefore conclude that:

(2) *In the first stages* (and perhaps even later on), *the magnetic or selective influence of the colony has been less than many of us have been tempted to believe. Except as an emotional image, a mirage or a myth, it has been relatively helpless to attract or to reject.* Our cities are finding this true today.

III. C. *The Journey Index, or Roadbed Factor*

What influence has the journey itself had in selecting the movers—or in culling or conditioning them in transit? As a people, we seem hardly to have considered the first of these possibilities. And—with certain fabulous exceptions —we have also ignored the second.

The influence of the journey? I suppose that the most conscious and the best-remembered and the most influential journey of the American experience was not theirs at all, but the story of the forty years the Children of Israel spent wandering in the Sinai wilderness: a religious memory turned metaphor and admonition. Romantically, in long retrospect, we would go on to enshrine the voyage of Christopher Columbus, the Pilgrim story, the exploits of Captain John Smith perhaps, or the mysterious lost settlement at Roanoke. But what all the early settlers, and especially the colonial redemptioners, must have endured in their tiny storm-buffeted Atlantic cattle boats was soon forgotten. Somehow the horrors of the "middle passage" in the infamous slave trade, like the vanishing redskins' "trail of tears," were effectively blotted out. Later would come the romantic engagement with the wilderness, the venturous explorations of Zebulon Pike or Lewis and Clark—and in our folklore the feckless wanderings of a pioneer like Daniel Boone, or the grubby hardships of the Oregon Trail, are blown up into legends twice lifesize. Meanwhile privately, for at least the first generation, our immigrating ancestors must have remembered the dangers and the sufferings of their particular crossings, the death of kin and loss of friend, the desperate homesickness, and the gnawing doubts. But one faced forward, not back; to survive one rose above such unhappy memories and self-questionings (just as visually the Statue of Liberty would quite obliterate Ellis Island). Moreover, those who died on ship, or failed the transfer and went home, left no mementos. Meanwhile, of course, the Atlantic passage was getting easier. So since the coming of modern transportation the journey has been treated, even by historians and social scientists, as merely one exposure among many in the resettlement process. Especially in our studies of internal migration, the transit phase has now almost been obliterated. Notwithstanding, I propose that:

III. C.1. *The journey or middle passage in migration has influenced and continues to influence the movers before they start, in transit, and afterwards as well.*

(1) To begin with, the journey occupied a much larger place in the hesitating migrant's mind than he would later remember. Its costs and dangers, its promise of excitement and adventure, its threat of change and the unknown, its prospect of loneliness and deprivation, the exhilarating prospect of being on one's own: all these impressions either encouraged or discouraged the idea of emigration. Though diminished, they still do so today—and they will balance out in different ways with different people.

Typically, the journey will appeal more to the optimistic and adventurous, less to the timid; more to the independent and healthy, less to the foreboding and ailing; more to the gambler, less to the careful. Again, the prospect of a journey, almost any journey, has a great appeal to the young. The journey factor is therefore selective, or strongly influential in the decision of who does or does not finally make the move. Out of many potential candidates not a few are repelled, or so torn that they finally decide to stay home. So *the journey has either encouraged or weeded out some putative migrants even before the start.*

(2) Again, *once they are launched, the migrants are at the mercy in some degree of their venture.* How vulnerable they become will depend perhaps on four circumstances: (a) their personal equilibrium; (b) their state of community or of social disorganization; (c) the natural difficulties and accidents of the passage; and (d) the opportunities they are given for new contacts and ideas and social exposures. This phase of migration carries us once again beyond the question of "Who moves?" to the question of "What happens to him next?" (Law IV). And I mean to speak more pointedly to the question of human adaptation or erosion in chapters 10 and 11. So perhaps we may content ourselves here with a simple balance of aphorisms.

(e) The moving will influence the movers more if the journey is hard (1600–1850), less if it is easy (1880–1914); more if it is long and slow, less if it is short and fast; more if it is interrupted or by stages, less if it is continuous; more if it is by land, less if by sea;[22] more if it is made in small numbers or by the young and single, less if it is made en masse or by the elderly, the firmly wedded, or by infants; more if the migrants come in broken groups, less if they come in working organizations under discipline (one can hardly fail to note the difference between the

New England congregations and the settlers in Virginia, or the Yankee towns planted in the Old Northwest as against the frontiersmen and pioneers who infiltrated the Kentucky-Tennessee woods). Finally, it should be added that the impact will be greater if it is the first such migration, less great if it is the second or third.

(f) The distance? "The distance is nothing," Mme du Deffand is credited with saying; "it is only the first step that counts." Admittedly the first step away from home can give a person or a people a traumatic shock. But *the distance counts, too. Especially if the distance is so great* that intercourse and later communications become difficult or next to impossible. And especially, too, if the receiving station is so strange, *and the cultural differences between home and colony are so profound,* that the migrant recognizes, very early or even perhaps before setting out, *that he has reached the point of no return.* Such voyages force on the traveler an unexpected independence, and encourage him thereafter to "fare forward" on his own.[23]

What kinds of people move out of one nation or community into another? If many are called, who are "chosen"? The answers, we have suggested, will be shaped by push, pull, and roadbed—all three—and most of all by push, by the native character, background, ambitions, and social circumstances of the person at home. But also there will be selection by accident.

III. D. *Selection by Accident*

III. D.1. *Especially the accident of individual personality.* Not all who go will be one kind—and at least a few of the going kind will almost always stay behind. They will not have been in the mood; their personal circumstances will have differed; the temptation will have encountered some unexpected obstacles; perhaps the person himself was ill, or not ready, or had already waited too long. Or perhaps he just missed the boat.

III. D.2. *Again, the accident may be one of social pace or timing*—with its paradoxical production of discontents, its repulsion of those "out of step," its export of extremes (see above, III. A.3).

III. D.3. *Alternatively, the accident may take the shape of some great psychological storm*, some tidal wave of feeling, some sudden landslide of the emotions. One thinks of that irrational, irresistible "America Fever" which swirled and danced across the face of Europe, sometimes emptying whole countrysides yet leaving neighboring villages almost untouched.

III. D.4. *And there are the thousand accidents of daily living*. Migration is a human affair, and the web of human history is interlaced with accidents. So there can be no certain predictabilities, no perfect patterns, no "Laws" without their exceptions.

In conclusion, let me also say again that, en masse or in clusters, *migrants are a mixed lot,* even as is the nation or community from which they come. *Yet they are a selection from, not a cross section of, the parental society.* Their assortment of human types and capacities will tend to be more limited; the emphasis will be different, the average intentions not quite the same. So both the personal character and the social potential of the migrants will produce changes in the transplanted culture. And ultimately, even though no single migrant was unique, there will emerge a new and different civilization.

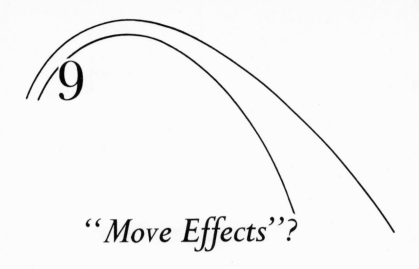

"Move Effects"?

On some probable consequences of migration, at home and abroad

I propose to proceed from the "Laws" governing the selection of the movers to the results of the migrations that follow.[1] Are there any historical experiences or sociological observations which will enable us to identify and even predict the probable aftereffects? Are there any warrantable generalizations about what will happen to the home country or place of origin? To the colony or place of destination?

Effects at Home

Without pretense of finality, let me first tackle the theoretical prospects for the parent society, and state my fifth "Law":

V. *In a large emigration, the parent society suffers certain immediate and substantial losses—with the uncertain possibility of some only partially compensatory returns, later.* To elucidate,

V. A. *The Immediate Losses Are Both Substantial and Enduring.*

V. A.1. *The most certain losses are of youthful brawn and brains.* Because movement appeals so strongly to the adolescents, the young adults, the ambitious workers, the men of adventurous imagination and constructive enterprise, the country or community of origin will inevitably face *a disproportionate outflow of ability, industrial energy, technical skills, and innovative dispositions from its younger generation.*

V. A.2. *Altogether lost also will be a great deal of money and effort* previously invested in child care, that is, in raising that generation to the age when they would begin making some social returns.

V. A.3. *Presumably these losses will be followed— after an interval—by a series of after-shocks,* as the weakened generation in its maturity fails to supply its share of leadership to the society, and then proves to have generated a below-average successor population class.

V. A.4. *Good-riddances?* Unquestionably we should note the other end of the J-curve: the flight of the outlaws and criminals, and the out-seepage of the ne'er-do-wells and the drifters. Also in times of rapid change the departure of some of the reactionaries and the disgruntled—to say nothing of a larger than normal draft on the emotional, the suggestible, the excitement-hungry (about whom the stay-at-homes may entertain mixed feelings). Yet on balance the real losses will outweigh the welcome departures. And even in persecutions or "impelled" migrations, these real losses may be spectacular. One thinks of the desiccation of great Spain, after the driving out of the Jews and Moriscos; of what France lost in the flight of the Huguenots; or of Albert Einstein, and the transfer of so much science and learning out of Germany after the rise of Hitler.

V. B. *Change in proportions? Does emigration, by subtraction, force a change of proportions on the parental society?* [2] For example, did the great seventeenth-century exodus of English Puritans to Virginia, New England, and the West Indies eliminate or reduce the strength of Puritanism in old England? Or again, how serious was the drainage of Yankees out of New England in 1800–50? Experience counsels caution. Apparently one must say:

V. B.1. *It is rare that an entire social type is eliminated by emigration.* Obviously, quite a few Puritans were left in old England. And as for the Yankees, even after the double draft to the Ohio Valley and the seaboard cities, quite a noticeable number of such characters still stiffened the social discourse in Connecticut and Vermont. It is observable also that though the lower-middle and lower classes of the continent kept flowing year after year by hundreds of thousands across the Atlantic—to help make and keep us almost exclusively a middle-class society—still the middle classes captured Europe, too, after a time; and today the industrialists and the bankers, the shopkeepers and the bureaucrats, the labor unions and the splinter parties of the Socialist left seem to share the rule. Incidentally, if it can be argued that European democracy was delayed, it would still have to be conceded that the inheritances from aristocracy, monarchy, and authoritarian

Catholicism were at least as responsible as the departure of many hopeful republicans. So, after a relatively free migration,

V. B.2. *Perhaps we can expect at most a slow change of proportions in the parent society:* Such a loss of vigor as the Romans must have suffered from sending so many fighters and governors into the provinces; such a change as became visible when the brighter American farm boys began turning to the cities; such a diminution of enterprise as overtook the flourishing inventor-society of New Haven after the Civil War; or such a human shrinkage as today seems visible in Appalachia.

V. C. *Emigration as a Safety Valve?* It has often been so regarded, and so advertised and administered, by persuasion or by force. If England is overpopulated (one can hear the voices) . . . "and the dogs do bark" . . . there is reason for colonies. Encourage your evicted tenants and your yeomen displaced by enclosure to go abroad so they may find fresh land. Sentence your criminals and disturbers of the king's peace to Virginia. Or again, in our Revolution and after: Hound out the Tory Loyalists. Let our younger sons find farms in the West. "Ship or shoot" (Attorney General Palmer's solution for the Reds of 1921). Deport the Communists and their sympathizers . . . Unfortunately,

V. C.1. *Emigration is an overrated economic or demographic safety valve.* Some departures do help; and emigration does seem to diminish the visible surplus of vagabonds on the roads or of unemployed in the streets. Yet experience shows that colonies are rarely advanced enough to absorb great numbers; in hard times the sparsely settled countryside will not support a fraction of the city's poor; and even in prosperity the many diverse job openings in the metropolis fill up long before the tenant farmers, who are being tractored off the land, can stop moving in. In sober fact, aided or unaided, *emigration will not remedy unemployment or equalize occupational opportunities or relieve population pressures or guarantee improved home standards of living.* It may do a little of each of these things. It may also remove some of the problem to another place; or it may diffuse the surplus over a wider area; and in so doing it may help the individual movers, especially if they are prompt. But the home society seems to benefit, economically or socially or politically, in a somewhat different way:

V. C.2. *Emigration is a much better psychological safety valve.* It does relieve some of the anxiety and emotional pressure. For the unemployed the thought that finally one can always try somewhere else will keep hope alive, encourage further job-seeking, even strengthen the worker's hand in bargaining. For the socially disadvantaged or the politically discontented, the alternative of departure—the assurance that one is not finally defeated or forever condemned—will prevent desperation, postpone the political explosion, buy time for reforms, and perhaps enable the old society to avoid revolution altogether. So the knowledge that one can go, even if few take advantage of that knowledge, is a remarkable safety valve. And *pragmatically the home community benefits more from the idea of emigration than from emigration itself.*[3]

To this paradoxical probability there are likely to be at least two modifiers or exceptions:

V. D. *There Will Be a Return Flow or Counter-Current, and with time the feedback may bring some unexpected returns.* As already noted (by Ravenstein and

Lee especially) any substantial human stream tends to generate a lesser but similar counter-stream. There will be emigrants who return; there will be visitors from the receiving society who, having heard about "the old country," will want to see it, perhaps even come to live in it themselves. And there will be a new flow of communications, perhaps also of trade.

V. D.1. *The economic and social benefits.* The letters home from successful sons and brothers will bring new ideas, cash remittances, and hope for a better tomorrow. The emigrant who has made his fortune and returned will have suggestions to make and savings to invest. So will the foreigner backtracking the trail, be he missionary or tourist, professor or romantic expatriate. And so will the New World capitalists or businessmen. It is perhaps fair to say that no man could have predicted and no man has since been able to measure the economic and social and emotional dividends—the unexpected and sometimes overwhelming benefits—that Europe would ultimately derive from its original colonial plantations and its later tidal flows of emigration to our strange and hopeful New World.[4]

Of course not all of these returns proved welcome or even tolerable: they tended to upset Europe's more ordered society quite as much as they invigorated it. Can we at least say that,

V. D.2. *The return flow will be a stimulus to reform and to change?* Historically, such a proposition seems debatable, and sometimes rather dubious. As Franklin D. Scott has shown, the Scandinavians learned a lot from their experience with emigration to America, and moderated many of their inherited rigidities and social or religious discriminations in order not to suffer repeatedly the loss of their ablest youth.[5] Did the German Junkers and ruling families learn as much from the century-long out-flow of peasants, skilled artisans, and political idealists? It would hardly seem so. And what about the Irish or the Italians or the Greeks? Across the Pacific, some fifty years after Yung Wing at Yale became the first Chinese boy to earn a B.A. in the western world, the intelligentsia of the Middle Kingdom finally did take advantage of the flow and counter-flow of persons and of goods to study the scientific and technological secrets of western power. But what did the czars get in return for their pogroms? And what were their successors, the organized party Marxists under Lenin and Stalin, ever willing to receive from the West—beyond the atom bomb and other such secrets? One concludes perhaps that the most effective exterior stimulus to change may be technological, but the impulse to reform will depend far more on the cultural psychology of a parent society than on the departure or the criticisms and later suggestions of its wandering sons.[6]

Colony Effects

If generalizations can be based on the history of western colonization, it would seem that we are now warranted in formulating a sixth major Law:

VI. *A major stream of migration will have immediate, strong, limited, but mostly positive and quite tangible effects on the receiving society. Later will come ambiguity. Then, finally, some disguised but surprisingly powerful aftereffects.*

I confess that I base this projection primarily on what has been observable in the largest and longest continuous flow of men in modern times, the peopling of North America. But these observations can be checked against the evolution of colonization and immigration elsewhere and of course also against our knowledge of internal population movements. All will, I believe, confirm the first part of our projection, that migration inevitably makes recognizable additions to the empty land or the receiving society. These we may call,

VI. A. *The Positive Gains.* They are of several kinds.

VI. A.1. *The added population and labor.* Especially the manpower, the young males and the young families, the new hands and new skills, the energy and productive capacity—all acquired without the costs of training. In short, the colony gains what the mother country loses—with one notable difference. The men who land are not quite the same as the men who sailed: some of the weaklings will have been eliminated; the tougher, more persistent, and more adaptable will have survived, though themselves subtly changed by the journey. By and large, we can say that a free immigration (in contrast to starving refugees) brings a marked increment to the available energy. The new arrivals benefit the receiving society also in a distinct but related way:

VI. A.2. *The natives are hastened upstairs.* Migrants are fillers-in. Being strangers to the country, needing food and employment immediately, they cannot wait or refuse, but have to take the available opening, the offered job. This enables the native worker to move up. He can sell his worn acres and buy virgin land farther on. He can expand his production by taking on a hired hand. He can turn over the heavy work in the shop or factory to men fresh off the boats and himself become a foreman or step into a managerial position. The same elevator effect is observable in internal migration. As students have discovered, the later comers tend to move into the lower ranks of a trade or profession, almost automatically promoting some of the locals or earlier arrivals to higher positions. So, historically, the continuing Atlantic migration enabled the first settlers to prosper and to move West. The greatest profits accrued to the early arrivals. Our westward movement became in some part a race to get there first. And in the building of our cities it didn't hurt to be on hand early.

VI. A.3. *Quick cultural contributions.* In colonizing an empty area, the settlers will bring the powerful apparatus of their culture—though less than they left behind. By the time the second stream of migration arrives, presumably the language, the laws, and the customs will already have been established. The later comers will therefore be handicapped. Their "alien" ways will generate suspicion; their young workers will compete for the scarce jobs or housing; and the initial attitudes of some or many of the natives may be guarded or quite hostile. Yet in short order even a secondary or trailing migration seems to make at least a few quite tangible cultural additions to the receiving society: new words and expressions for the language, new foods and recipes, new games or social observances, new congregations of faith or religious practices, new crops or systems of tillage, new skills in mining or in manufacture. Even slaves from Africa or coolies from Canton or refugees from some belated and poverty-stricken Middle Eastern population seem to manage a few "gifts."

Yet as the second wave of immigrants continues coming, the receiving society seems to experience

VI. B. *Feelings of Growing Ambiguity.* Even if, or perhaps especially if, the society is democratic in disposition. The more friendly to strangers, the more "open" and spatially mobile, the more uncertain or divided may become the attitudes of the older stock. The sons of the most recent immigrants (craving recognition and wanting to fit in) will themselves become critical of their parents' "un-American" habits. Then the sheer number of later arrivals —perhaps a noticeable decline in quality—more certainly their clinging together (in Germantowns and Irish wards, in Chinatowns and Little Italies) will generate local misgivings. Success in local politics will spark wider alarm. The organization into ethnic work gangs or occupational families, the "clanning up" for some special crop or harvesting or service function, will seem to drive out the older practitioners; and the next to last immigrant group is sure to object to the wage competition of the most recent arrivals, etc. But we need hardly rehearse the oft-experienced trials and obstacles to full citizenship. And the deceptions of the "melting pot" theory of culture contacts and diffusion are too complex and difficult for discussion here. Suffice it to notice that there will be divided counsels: on the one hand, nativist movements, with demands for immigration restriction and 100 per cent assimilation; on the other, more tolerance of the newcomers, and interest in using them, and satisfaction with a democratic live-and-let-live, or cultural pluralism. (One could cite the experience of the West Indians in England or the Algerians in France today.)

VI. C. *The Aftereffects?* With time and familiarity and spatial intermingling and multiplication and intermarriage of the generations one may expect a considerable diffusion, acceptance, and surface homogenization. But gradually, quietly, two great changes will have been taking place. The first is:

VI. C.1. *Displacement and replacement of the natives.* For reasons that are not altogether clear, the recent migrants tend to multiply, the oldest start to dry up. Whether because the new aliens are willing to work for lower wages and have more children, while the natives spend more time preparing for higher jobs and more money educating fewer children—or whether there is some genuine difference in vigor or knowledge of contraception—or whether a higher percentage of immigrant women are of a child-bearing age—for whatever reason or reasons, the new arrivals tend to expand their share in the population in the second and third generations. A similar drying up of the locals, and infusion of fresh numbers and energy from the outside, is to be seen in the growth of our cities. A second change follows:

VI. C.2. *Contamination and change in the value systems.* As gradually the majority comes to be composed of postcolonial immigrants or later comers and their descendants, the original value system or great basic body of assumptions imperceptibly begins to suffer alteration. And suddenly some event, some cultural happening or spectacular political change, makes it clear that it is no longer the Anglo-Americans or descendants of the founders of the city who are setting the standards. First the Brahmins may find themselves outnumbered and outvoted. Next, an American cardinal is appointed and the Roman Catholic Church emerges as the largest single church in the United States. Then, in the politics of our cities and our national parties, the influence of German social idealism or of Irish ward bosses begins to make itself felt. Perhaps we can say that the first thirty years of this century saw the unmistakable achievement of real power by the older immigration

(1820–80), however hyphenated their loyalties. Then the newer immigration (1881–1917) floated irresistibly toward the top. Remember Hollywood? Hollywood was (and is) hardly an Anglo-Saxon institution. In sports, always a sensitive barometer, the old English-style gentleman amateur had disappeared, and even the football juggernauts of once Congregational Yale—with stars by the name of Heffelfinger or Corbin, Hinkey or Coy—had given way to Notre Dame, whose "Fighting Irish," under Knute Rockne, soon sprouted almost unpronounceable Polish and Czech names. Again in the great urban game of cops and robbers, the police forces and styles of civility might still be overwhelmingly from the "old sod," but the new warlords of the underworld seemed to have names ending in "o" or "i" or "-one." and to be playing the game by rules straight out of Sicily. Meanwhile, in quiet offices uptown, bearded doctors were beginning to prescribe therapies for the Yankee psyche that had been invented by and for Jews in Vienna. And after World War II, our Puritan sex code gives a helpless gasp as people of all ages, origins, and social positions begin indulging in a license that can only be called pagan, and in a premarital freedom reminiscent of the European working class.

In short, if one may judge at all by the American experience, after two or three generations an immigrant tributary, which was supposedly absorbed into the mainstream of national life, may re-emerge with no little of its value system, its habits of mind and conduct still powerful. Like some great submarine current suddenly welling up from the depths to break the surface of the Pacific with a startling visibility, the immigrant rivers of lower-middle-class culture have recently come pouring to the surface of our national life. The inference? Somehow neither the dynamite of dispersion nor the solvents of assimilation will quite decompose the basic attitudes of a substantial and continuing immigrant stream.

So in such a migration the country of destination will be in for some delayed surprises. The drastic shifts in the American value system since 1945 are surely strong testimony. And what has already happened to our Northern cities, under the influx of the blacks from the South, may only be the second act in that American tragedy.

Because of the massive transplanting of peoples that we have known, there will be other delayed dividends of surprise and pain and change of standards to come.

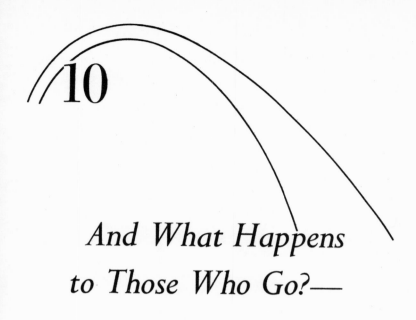

10

And What Happens to Those Who Go?—

On certain social and psychological implications for the movers

We come finally to the effects of movement on the movers. And I will say at once that (after the original pre-selection of the movers) these effects seem to me as important and interesting as all the others put together. In Law IV it was laid down that *The process of moving alters the stock, temperament, and culture of the movers, not only by an original selection but on the road as well and also at journey's end.* I propose now to elaborate that statement. For we should recognize that wanderers are not magically protected. Moving will mark or even scar the mover. The simplest travel has its costs; each traveler, his baggage and his expectations. And for migrants, or those who move and move again, the experience will have consequences— social consequences, institutional consequences, psychological consequences—of a decisive and often enduring character. Let us look first at the social predictabilities.

IV. A. *Migration Means Great Social Losses to the Migrant, especially in the goods of community—but also a number of reciprocal gains, especially in freedom and self-command.* The "losses" may be extremely hurtful, or of mixed portent.

IV. A.1. *The major losses are those of community and social roots.* When a man moves for good he has to tear up his roots, and he has to leave many people, many accustomed activities and participations, many familiar sights and sounds behind. Thus,

IV. A.2. *The mover will lose his friends and associates,* his village or town, perhaps even his family but in any event *his social envelope,* his group frame.

IV. A.3. *He will of course lose his old job and any expectations of promotion;* and in migrating to virgin land, or into a less advanced economy, he will probably lose *the fine edge of his skills* and be unable to carry with him his most sophisticated tools. Historically, the most advanced technologies have not been found on the frontier or in underdeveloped countries.

IV. A.4. *The higher arts of all kinds may have to be left behind,* for there will not be enough fellow travelers with either the skills or the appreciation to sustain them.

IV. A.5. *Almost certain to be lost will be the high art of leisure.* For the majority of the migrants will be workers, and almost all will have to be active to survive. Perpetual movers may then acquire a distaste for inactivity.

IV. A.6. *Inevitably, there will be a loss of background:* ceremonies can no longer be observed; traditions are one by one forgotten; the past is put behind. So for the believing and remembering man, emigration becomes indeed a "form of suicide." For the loyal and devoted, the separation cannot help but yield some "dividends of pain."

IV. A.7. Again, in moving out of a community, the mover will move out of the sight of his peers, the supervision of his elders and his betters. The old social restraints will drop away; and there will be *a loss of moral sanctions.*

To put all these consequences of uprooting a little differently, we may say that migrants typically suffer certain great losses: their sense of identity, their settled expectations and security, the earned regard and human sympathies of their friends, the discipline of the old social order, the variety and depth of the parental culture.

The loss of discipline and social restraints, however, may not all be for the worse; escape from the old order and way of living can have its compensations. So the migrant will soon recognize that,

IV. B. *Some Losses Bring Their Compensating Gains.* To escape from authority may be

IV. B.1. *An escape from tyrants and social tyrannies:* from political oppression, from economic dictation, from social discrimination, from religious persecution.

IV. B.2. Or departure may mean *delivery* from a rigid society, from a decaying old order under *the dead hand of the past.*

IV. B.3. Or by flight one can *escape a poisoned atmosphere* of opinion: the bad blood of family feuds, or a village perhaps torn by jealousies and suspicion.

IV. B.4. The loss of social order and the increase of social disorder in the company of fellow migrants may at the same time open the way toward *a more fluid and flexible society.*

IV. B.5. In any case, it offers *a chance to start over.* The man handicapped by his birth or by accident; the ambitious worker locked into the slow motion of his trade or craft; the failure; and the delinquent: all are given a second chance. By decamping a man may be able to leave behind his family origins, his class, his hostile superiors, his old reputation, even his criminal record—and make a fresh start.

IV. C. *Migration Also Brings Great Gains—gains often almost without their compensatory deficits.* Thus,

IV. C.1. *The mover gains a new physical environment,* with its material resources.

IV. C.2. *The mover enters a new social environment* and gains contact with new people and different cultural resources.

IV. C.3. *The mover gains a new simplicity and directness.* Since he cannot take all his clothes or tools or associations or obligations with him on the journey, he has to strip down and is forced to part with many nonessentials.

IV. C.4. As already implied, *the mover gains a new freedom from authority, and chance to govern himself.* Whatever the suffrage opportunities in the society he joins, he gains a voting power over himself. Perhaps for the first time in his life he begins making his own decisions. Being on his own, among strangers,

IV. C.5. *The mover also has the chance to stand on his own feet economically, and to better himself.* With detachment from some tradition-minded social order come insecurity and disequilibrium but also almost providential opportunities to rise: to break out of the old hierarchy into a society where one wears no label; to escape from old jobs into new and more profitable occupations; to get out of some stiff and limited class system into new and more open competitions. In any age or civilization, *freedom to move must mean for the individual a greater freedom to rise.*

IV. C.6. *All this means an invitation to enterprise and an enormous release of human energies.* The migrant moves toward a world where ideally every man can be his own master, and every church a self-governing congregation. He realizes that what happens will depend, more largely than ever before in his experience, on himself. With hard work and some luck he will prosper, and so will gain in confidence and persistence as well as in self-command.

IV. C.7. Finally, *the migrant is given an opportunity* —far too often neglected in our histories—*the opportunity to choose:* to choose first what he will bring along, next what he will accept from his traveling companions or new neighbors, lastly what he will send back home for, once he gets his feet on the ground, or can afford the latest tools and notions from the East Coast or from Europe. It might be illuminating to pose this question to our immigration record: which ethnic or cultural group, among the many that have come to these shores, chose well in the moving or later on? For surely there were marked differences in the choosing.

IV. C.8. However such a judgment might go, one thing is clear: *The greater the fluidity and opportunities and individual initiatives and personal choices, the greater the chances of new social combinations*—and also, one hopes, of a *"better society."* And whether that "better society" was to be defined in terms of personal freedom, or of material possessions, or of moral goodness—the three visions of greatness which have wrestled in the American conscience and struggled for the command of the American experiment from the beginning—was to be in large measure decided by the migrants' choosing. The mix we now have was not inevitable.

What was inevitable was a changed social order—and changed not just from the accidents of the crossing, the mixtures of nations, the new physical environment, and our historical experiences accumulated across three centuries. No. A new social order arose ineluctably out of the losses, omissions, releases, opportunities, and options of peoples who had moved and who had kept on moving. Since these migrants were overwhelmingly of European origin, so would their New World society be European in character. But it would be different, very different, in balance. From the very start it could have been predicted that *America would be Europe—but in disproportion.*

America would also be different in its institutions: those particular social instruments which men have created to survive the life span of individuals, organize them into working groups, preserve the social inheritance, and project the group purposes into the future. And because the institutions which migrants bring with them or transplant afterwards will give limit or shape to their later existence, it is now time to remind ourselves of our second great Law of motion:

II. *Institutions do not move easily. A few can't be moved at all, or perhaps have to be left behind. Many* *more are damaged in transit. Nearly all are shaken, and have to be pruned, simplified, or otherwise adjusted to survive the transplanting. To a degree, displacement will mean replacement of institutions.*

Remembering the character of our own beginnings, and assuming that migrations are often movements outward, from the centers of civilization to the empty areas or the less advanced societies, we may begin with the colonizing mission: the effort to carry institutions across space and through time. Space may prove difficult at first, for one or both of two reasons: because it is rough and dangerous or because it is vast. Institutions by their very structural complexity or their relations to the society as a whole may not lend themselves to export. Thus we can say that in a free migration,

II. A. *Some Institutions Will Have to Be Left Behind,* for example, the central organs or the most advanced social structures. One does not export the Pope and the Vatican, unless by some Avignon capture. One does not carry the Royal Family abroad, save by exile as with the Stuart Pretenders. Opera companies and orchestras need players, instruments, composers, singers, and patrons. And out of the necessity of using the most advanced learning and technology, the most highly skilled personnel, one keeps the most specialized scientific laboratories, the highest courts, the institutions of the highest learning at home.

II. B. *Many Institutions Are Damaged in the Transplanting.*

II. B.1. *They then either die or have to be cut back to survive.* Thus the great device of the English merchant adventurers, the joint-stock company—so indispensable for the raising of capital, so useful for long-distance trading, and apparently so ideally suited for the work of colonization—proved nonviable in the Virginia and Plymouth colonies because the returns from investment in the wilderness were too slow and they could not hope to monopolize all the land. So the New World meant bankruptcy for the joint-stock companies; and the modern corporation would have to wait almost two hundred years to jump the Atlantic successfully. A like fate almost overtook the monopolistic labor unions, the guilds. For the governors (the master craftsmen) mostly stayed home and the learners (the apprentices) found in America more demand for their physical labor than for their skills, and a freer life everywhere than the guild rules contemplated. So the apprenticeship system made the passage and survived but only as a fragment, an isolated and personal relationship to some smith or cooper or joiner without guild sanctions; or else the apprenticeship was converted and debased into a system of selling one's labor for a few years in return for the passage money. And much the same could be said of many of the forms and legal arrangements for landholding and conveyance. If feudal dues, and entail or primogeniture, in skeletal form lingered on here and there until the Revolution, that was due to special circumstances; generally, the men were too few and the acres too many and the distances too great and the social hierarchies too weak and the ease of escape all too obvious for the successful transfer of these medieval devices—as for a host of other Elizabethan institutions. Again, in a related way, we must observe that,

II. B.2. *The transplanting of Old World institutions into New World space brings disorganization, atomization, simplification, and even primitivization.* In a raw young country elaborate codes cannot be maintained, the niceties will suffer, the citified habits and the ecclesiastical rituals have to be simplified. There isn't the time or the manpower or the consuming public to maintain them. Complex relationships also cannot subsist on infrequent encounters. So, for example, the family, as a unit of parents and children, was successfully transplanted across the Atlantic—but the larger "extended family" of the landed squirearchy or the continental peasantry began to shrink. For many near relatives and remote relations were perforce left behind, and the new cousins and relations by marriage lived too far away for easy reunion, then perhaps moved again and entirely disappeared. The process of simplification and atomization can be seen everywhere in our colonial societies: in the way the transplanted manorial village exploded into freehold farms or the established churches into self-governing congregations; in the way the college-clustered university of Oxford or Cambridge shrank down into a single lonely college here or there; in the way the English army system, with its aristocratic officers and its hired troops, reverted in colonial hands into a citizens' militia (old Anglo-Saxon style); in the way the law and lawyers had to get on without their own schools or Inns of Court; in the way colonial doctoring often had to be carried on by the Puritan ministers, without formal training or benefit of hospitals. So sometimes in a transplanting, what is quite crude enough to start with becomes even cruder. And this on top of the fact that,

II. B.3. *Often the culture of the settlers is decidedly backward and primitive to start with, and seems to come to an abrupt halt.* For the migrants come out of the lower and middle classes in the main, not from the most highly educated or the cultural aristocracy. Again, a free migration will tend to draw from the rural shires rather than from the bustling towns. So much of what is instinctively carried along will be old-fashioned and a little behind the times even at the moment of departure. And when the settlers get over they will be too busy for a while to try to catch up; instead, they will keep living on their inherited culture. So *in the first years of settlement many institutions will tend to stand still.* It is almost as if the culture suffered a shock on transplanting. Such expertness as is brought proves hard to maintain. Improvements have to wait. Yet meanwhile the folk at home go on changing and innovating. And presently the colony seems more than ever old-fashioned and provincial. Such was certainly the fate of the English colonies in America in the first generations. While old England was becoming new, New England became old. The colonists made do with what they had, maintained what they could, improvised when they had to, and abandoned or simplified what was too refined or complex. Facing the savage wilderness, they adapted as best they could. Feeling social needs, they borrowed rather than invented. In the simple extractive economy, they became jacks-of-all-trades and masters of none. We may conclude that *relapses and atavisms are among the hallmarks of the colonial adventure.* One can see this in their language which, as Mencken so entertainingly demonstrated, was not only pre-Shakespearean and full of old Anglo-Saxonisms, but tended to stand still, and so to fall still further behind the advancing English of the mother country. Only in its hasty improvisations, its journeyman's slang, its metaphors out of the new landscape, its vulgar energy and liveliness and irreverence did the American speech give promise of a more powerful future. And might not similar things be said of some of the institutions of local self-government out of the remote Anglo-Saxon inheritance?

II. C. *Dispersion Promotes Decentralization.* With time added to space as a hazard, the transplanted institutions will next show a series of delayed or secondary effects. Many of these stem directly from the movement outward, the dispersion of the migrants into wider territories, and the consequent decentralization. Unless there is some single port of entry, some bottleneck through which men and goods must flow, some natural point of control where autocratic authority may center its power to choose and to reject, to govern and to punish (in which case the migration loses much of its freedom), it is difficult to preserve the graduated hierarchies within an institution or instrument of government. The distances are too great for the necessary supervision or procedures of deference and appeal. One town or court or college will resemble another and claim the same rights, to be exercised locally. Indeed, the given instrument will not be socially viable unless it can be transplanted, necessarily in miniature:

II. C.1. *In a colonial dispersion, institutions have to be miniaturized or made portable to survive.* And, reciprocally, those communities with portable organizations will be stronger, more durable, better able to carry their civilization with them. This point is extremely important, but has been suggested or implied so often in our discussions* that it is perhaps sufficient here simply to remind ourselves of what the Puritans were able to accomplish with

* See chs. 4, 8, and 9, and above, sec. II.B.2. In the post-colonial phase of flow and counter-flow into already settled areas or going societies, the same requirement of portability will obtain if the migrants are to carry their chosen occupational systems or ways of life with them—except that (as Elkins and McKitrick have pointed out) institutions can be re-created as well as carried, i.e., it is enough if they can be so standardized and well understood that they can be simulated or duplicated indefinitely, like some unit of the U.S. Army or Bell Telephone.

their town meeting and congregational discipline, and not only in New England but all across the Old Northwest.

II. C.2. *Dispersion and decentralization lead toward the division of sovereignty.* In theory, sovereignty has been supposed to be singular, indivisible, and from the top down. The divine right of kings rested squarely on this supposition. But in practice, migration has meant a kind of escape from the king's presence. He may send out viceroys and governors, but even those agents cannot be everywhere. The stretch of space, as we say, proves too powerful for the span of control. And some royal powers have to lapse, or have to be transferred to intermediate authorities, or will even be taken over by local groups. In theory, the king still rules supreme, and the mother country is superior to its colonies. But in practice, the colonial legislatures may also be legislating and coming to think of themselves as Parliaments (and in New England a still further decentralization and takeover of sovereignty came to favor the locality or town meeting). In Madras the East India Company acted for—indeed almost instead of—the government at home. Even in jealously supervised New Spain the viceroys became so uncontrollable that visitors and inspectors general had to be sent.

II. C.3. *Out of dispersion and decentralization may also come a federal concept,* as the dependencies begin exercising some sovereign powers. Whether this will always follow seems doubtful; but in the English experience (whether American colonial or later Commonwealth), the exercise of some local authority seems to have led to the idea of participatory authority and an operative federalism. Again, in the English experience,

II. C.4. *Dispersion and competitive settlement seem to lead toward toleration,*[1] and the abandonment of a good many prohibitions, restraints, and political controls. Once the beachheads had been established, being dependent upon their produce and land sales, each group of English settlers became eager for more settlers—hence anxious to attract them by favorable treatment. In such a competition only the most dedicated could cling to strict religious prescriptions; feudal dues became handicaps; and exclusion from landholding and from the suffrage were jeopardized. With both old and new settlers all too willing to move on, into the back woods, or to some other colony, grievances perhaps had to be listened to, and authority could not be too arbitrary. So an original dispersion, reinforced by many later movements, almost forced the abandonment of monopolistic rules, reduced the practical authority of the rulers, made taxes and duties difficult to collect, encouraged religious toleration, and generally operated to favor the individual subject against the governing state. In the English colonies, at least, the freedom to keep moving became, so to speak, a basic colonial freedom. (And one may note that the sovereign but competitive states in the federal Union of the United States would find themselves unable to legislate an effective system of taxation until the twentieth century.)

II. C.5. *Repeated migration also encourages the abstraction of authority.* Or at least this is one of the things that seems to have distinguished the moving English from their more sedentary rivals. The argument here would be that in the moving and intermingling of peoples from all over the British Isles, local habits and peculiar shire customs could no longer be maintained. County families and hereditary authorities of all descriptions were left behind. The protection afforded by the realm became remote. The king himself failed to visit his colonies and became invisible. So both the force of tradition and rule by God-given rulers were diminished. Hence a natural resort to agreements or compacts—and later a necessary resort in each colony (or state) to statute law. But statute law itself is burdensome and requires enforcement and re-enactment in each fresh jurisdiction. Statutes were indeed duplicatable. But was there any truly portable law? Statutes required human force. Were there not unarmed laws? Given the intense moralism of the Protestant Reformation, the dependence of the Puritans on sacred scripture, and the insistence of the Enlightenment on "right reason," it was perhaps not surprising that the restless colonists and their successors came to put considerable emphasis on natural rights and moral law. Such concepts or principles were enduring. But principles were also portable. Principles required no expenditures. Principles could be applied abstractly to all men. At least one notes the strong reliance on principles in the Declaration of Independence and in the personal freedoms enumerated in the Constitution's Bill of Rights. The Constitution itself? Here was an agreement or contract, such as contracting parties might make or had made before. Here again was a supreme law to take the place of a supreme sovereign. Yet the Constitution was also an abstract theory of balanced government, which applied to all alike, and which went with the people into each new territory or state. The Constitution was at once a bargain, a law above ordinary law, and it was portable. Ours became, then, a government of laws, not of men—and of two kinds of law.

In due course we became also a nation of "doctrines"— of moral declarations of principle which could be carried, without fresh re-enactment, through both space and time. I do not for a moment wish to deny the strong inheritance from the Protestant Reformation and from English legalism. Yet can one not see both the habits of mind and the personal interests of an extremely mobile people in those principles or doctrines we came to call Freedom of the Seas, Monroe Doctrine, Manifest Destiny, Open Door, and Good Neighbor?

Thus far we have been focusing on the institutional effects of the colonial dispersion. Let us now note (very briefly, because they have been referred to repeatedly in the preceding chapters) the apparent institutional consequences of the continuance and even intensification of movement by almost all hands since the landing.

II. D. *Repeated Movement Shifts the Social Balance and Encourages Institutional Distortion.* At least to judge by the American experience, some institutions and some elements of civilization seem to have had an extremely hard time surviving and getting established, while others have been emphasized and even exaggerated. As already noted,

II. D.1. *Repeated movement is bad for the arts and sciences.* There will be serious omissions. The great libraries do not move. The highest learning and the most sophisticated science are too fine and delicate for the wilderness, or for the early stages of farming, manufacturing, or city-making. The hospitals and laboratories stay behind at the great centers. The liberal arts and humane learning can be transported, but only with difficulty, for those who believe in them will be in a minority among the movers. Even the applied arts and sciences will be slow to establish their schools and advance their subjects. The fine arts? Artists move easily, indeed there is something especially appealing to them in the anti-authoritarianism and indiscipline of displacement. But their schools and their tools, their systems of patronage and the great collections and museums of art are not so readily moved or reproduced. In new societies, again, with the accent on improvisation, theoretical thinking will be neglected, though the art of building should flourish. A pragmatic insistence on quick and inexpensive returns will also handicap institutions and distort the balance of the culture.

II. D.2. *A people in continual motion will improvise or borrow.* Limited in what it can transport or replicate and support, a moving society will tend to make do with cheap substitutes, imitate foreign inventions, beg-borrow-or-steal what it has not the strength to create. Tocqueville saw we were living on European science, and were likely to continue. So also American books and magazines and newspapers were long imitative and second-rate. And if Americans sometimes heard great music, it was from foreign composers and players.

II. D.3. *Repeated movement emphasizes communications.* Word carries. A common language becomes necessary for survival. The curiosity of movers asks for news. Spellers and literacy, or a common education, become important. And eventually it should not be surprising if the media of communication come to occupy a large segment of the day and of the working population.

The accent will also be on physical transportation, on the roads, and on technical devices for more rapid and effective transit for men and goods. But so much has already been said on this subject that it will be enough merely to cite the American emphasis on transportation, on mass production and mass marketing and mass advertising.

II. D.4. *Repeated movement leads toward uniformity and conformity.* As was suggested in chapter 6, space-plus-mobility produces dispersion; but by and by, mobility overruns space and there are no hiding places left. The circulation and recirculation of men and of ideas leads to a common tongue; to national fashions in goods, styles, slogans, and ideologies; to the more equal application of the Constitution and the Bill of Rights; to the decline of regionalisms or local peculiarities. And also to a tyranny of opinion which Tocqueville saw and called the "tyranny of the majority." With instantaneous national media and almost instant interchange of people, we have become subject to more sudden barrages of suasion and seemingly irresistible waves of emotion. One can still find local idiosyncrasies, and quite a number of recognizable regional peculiarities; but these distinguishable ways of living seem today only minor variants in the overwhelming, inescapable "American Way."

II. D.5. *The habit of internal mobility reconciles us to each other, and makes it possible to maintain many paradoxes in society*—especially the reconciliation of equality with individual opportunity. How have we managed to believe in—and preserve—both these myths as operating ideas, in despite of unequal ability, luck, and achievement? On the one hand, by anti-monopolistic and regulatory legislation, abetted by redistributive taxation; on the other, by the freedom for the little fellows (as for everyone else) to move and to try again. So mobility has stepped in as our free lands gave out. And even though all spaces are now more or less occupied, a man can still get away from his boss and give himself a second or third or fourth or fifth chance. As was suggested in chapter 2, it has been the freedom to move which has made possible the symbiosis of equality and individualism in this country. Mobility has been our greatest single permit to be both free and equal.

From some of our earlier analyses of the social and institutional effects of migration, and from much of the immediately preceding discussion, we may deduce that mobility is not without psychological implications for the individual as well as for the group. This carries us again to the fourth Law, which states:

IV. *The process of moving alters the . . . temperament . . . of the movers, not only by an original selection but on the road as well and also at journey's end.* How?

IV. D. *Migration and Repeated Movement Will Subject the Personality to Severe Strains, bring changes of attitude and temper, and intensify certain migrant characteristics.* First of all, there is a process of atomization.

IV. D.1. *The individual is stripped of his protections and forced to go ahead on his own.* Detached from his old community, deprived of the care and support of the people he has known, no longer able to count on familiar customs and attitudes, in other words, stripped of his envelope, he must suddenly make face to a strange world and learn to draw strength from himself. With no authorities to guide or compel him, he must learn self-discipline. Not all survive that test, or in surviving make the same response:

(1) Some become remarkably independent, even rugged individualists in many ways.

(2) The moral weaklings may suffer a disintegration of character, a demoralization or further detachment from the social codes, or they may carry irresponsibility to the point of anti-social attitudes and crime.

(3) The rebel temperaments may become still more undisciplined and rebellious. Dissenter personalities may be strengthened in their egotistic defiance.

(4) Freed from restraints but insecure, a number may take refuge in action, physical violence, an increased destructiveness and intemperance. I suspect that the violence of American life owes more than a little to the fact that moving subjects people to a severe uprooting, confronts them with almost intolerable novelties and strangeness, and demands overt action. Having lost their identity, many can rediscover it only through some physical gesture. Violence tells us perhaps as much about moving as about injustice.[2]

(5) Other movers fall a prey to doubt. Uprooted, insecure, seeing their old verities questioned or denied on every hand yet unable to discover and learn a new set of protective commandments, they become uneasy, nervous, unstable, or mentally ill. Too rapid social changes seem to have like effects. With the decline of the old religious authorities, the comforts of confession, or the cleansing absolution of evangelical worship and conversion, our modern movers seem to be carrying their anxieties more and more to the psychiatrist's couch.[3]

(6) Then there are the guilty and the conscience-stricken: those who cannot forget, the hyphenated-movers, the migrants with divided loyalties. Established at their destination and proud of their new successes, they still harbor reservations about the new society, regrets for old ways, and a bad conscience for the country and the duties they left behind. When these guilt feelings become marked, one of two things seems to happen. Either the immigrant develops a longing for the fatherland and an unrealistically rosy memory of its perfections—and with that

an inferiority complex—or else, suppressing his doubts, he resorts to self-justification and almost deliberately exaggerates the ignorance, poverty, corruption, and injustice of the Old World on which he has turned his back. Europe as the graveyard of liberty and the sinkhole of iniquity becomes the image. And many Californians entertain like contradictory feelings about the Atlantic coast. The effete and dominating East, it seems to some; whereas others long for New England, with its more human scale. Unquestionably, migration can put a hyphen or an exclamation mark into one's loyalties.

(7) An even more marked effect of the uprooting, the social detachment, and the obvious accent on individualism is the loneliness that it brings. Americans, say our French observers, are lonely and bored. "Which of us is not forever a stranger and alone?" asked Thomas Wolfe. "Loneliness is stamped on the American face; it rises like an exhalation from the American landscape" (Van Wyck Brooks). The paradigmatic American, according to some critics, has been Ishmael the outcast, or Adam the lonely man. Detached from time and place, and insubmissive to circumstance, he comes alive, says Thornton Wilder, only in action. But being lonely and insecure, he feels the need for reassurance profoundly, and almost desperately wants to be liked. On voyages abroad, only the most parboiled tourists, or the sudden millionaires, don't care whether they are liked. Again, much of our foreign policy seems to reflect our loneliness and psychological insecurity. Typically, we help the backward and the disadvantaged to stand on their own feet, and to become democratic and prosperous like ourselves. In return for which we seem to have a great yearning not to be feared but to be loved.

(8) Mobility and loneliness have also, as noted in chapter 7, helped develop in our ever-changing society

our peculiar cordiality with strangers, the hail-fellow attitudes, the ready and somewhat shallow gregariousness,
the joiner personality.

(9) Americans are boastful? Yes. But one boasts
more easily to strangers or new acquaintances. Americans
are noisy and aggressive and assertive? So they say. But
does one throw one's weight around to impress lifelong
friends? Not too often. Rather, we have learned to move
among strangers, and expect to be accepted, but are just a
mite insecure about ourselves and the reception, and so
are tempted to overdo the performance.

Consideration of these last deficiencies and exaggerations carries us beyond the lonely individual to another
important theme:

IV. D.2. *Migration and repeated movement intensify
certain migrant characteristics, and ultimately alter the
balance of the society.* If the original uprooting means deprivation, exposure, and insecurity, later moves will come
easier and even strengthen or harden the mover in certain
ambitions and attitudes. Having learned what it takes to
be a self-supporting individual, and perhaps a "good guy"
or cooperative citizen, he is confirmed in the responses of
the ready traveler—and on his psyche the grooves of action and the scars of repeated displacements will begin to
show. Among many marks or signs of the mobile existence,
let us list some of the most obvious.

(1) *The habit of wandering.* The first step is truly
the hardest. And once on the road, quite a few movers
seem unable to stop. Is it the excitement of the adventure?
The love of novelty? An addiction to loneliness? The feeling of being hemmed in, tied down, almost imprisoned by
the growing attachments and responsibilities of membership in a settled community? Whatever the conscious or

unconscious motives, movement seems to be cumulative and habit-forming. Practice makes restless.

(2) *An optimistic faith.* Americans are notorious around the world for their lunk-headed optimism: an optimism that the Great Depression only temporarily diminished, a confidence that even Vietnam has only partially shaken, an assumption of progress that underlies and helps explain the very frustrations and protests of the younger generation. Of course much of this optimism stems from success: from the success of the American political experiment but especially our material success, from the lifting of the lower classes of Europe into the American middle class, from the conquest of nature and the creation of unprecedented affluence, no doubt also from our youthful and naïve nationalism. Yet it is worth noting that for most of those who came here, unless they were desperate or driven, it took optimism to move across the Atlantic—and such hopeful, future-minded characters kept coming and kept coming for three hundred years. Then for each generation of immigrants, when the first move succeeded and other moves became possible, they had more confidence, invested that confidence again, and again drew dividends. So there was a reinforcement of faith, a compounding of the capital of hope. Even today we believe—we almost have to believe—that each fresh move will be for the better (unless we are helplessly addicted, and have got the habit of moving so into our blood that we are sick and cannot stop). Which is to say that for even a moderately mobile and restless society, optimism is an indispensable ingredient.

(3)*Activism or accent on action.* Moving itself is an action, and at destination further action is required if the move is to succeed. So in theory, mobility must be the enemy of leisure. But for Americans this decision had been

indicated at the very start. For emigration did not appeal to aristocrats; so they and their arts of leisure were left behind; and instead came the swarms of young workers. As was pointed out by Chevalier and Tocqueville, and as has been noted by innumerable foreign observers since, ours has been and remains an almost feverishly active society.

(4) *Love of novelty, and the psychology of change.* Enough has already been said to suggest the close connections between mobility and change. Yet perhaps it is legitimate for an American to remark that we know of no other people so in love with change. Is that just possibly in part because other peoples are more aware of their inheritances, of good things from the past, hence also of the destructiveness of change and the losses that novelty for novelty's sake may bring? Is it that they don't want to have to live with too many such mistakes, with too many accusations of betrayal or abandonment? Whereas the American can and does leave his mistakes behind. There is a careless abandon in his style, not only with his landscapes but with his ancestors and with his past. For most of us change has become almost automatically good. And for our youth—compared to whom no other younger generation was ever so pampered—everything must now be "reformed," that is, changed. Only a special society, a society for whom innovation had become an almost casual habit and change an article of belief, could tolerate such suggestions.

(5) *A paradoxical conservatism.* I have made this argument before but it will stand repeating. Movers are *in some things* astonishingly conservative. Emigration means deprivations: one cannot take everything along on the ship, in the covered wagon, or by train or plane. So one chooses the possessions most needed, the heirlooms most

loved, the ideas and customs that are most precious. And one clings to these through every possible hardship. In the new home, with fewer rivals for attention and care, these saved possessions expand into the vacuum of the migrants' lives. Especially if they are ideas or beliefs, they become almost holy. So there comes to be a concentration of loyalty and devotion on a few selected values or rituals or possessions—and a great resistance to change in those particulars. Thus, quite a few Puritans became more, not less, Puritan in migrating;[4] and for them visibly the right religion, a proper government, and adequate Protestant education or a basic literacy continued to outweigh all the arts and sciences. By contrast a far larger number of men, who abandoned the tragic but colorful tapestries of their European heritage for the sake of economic goods, persisted in their pursuit of gain: they kept moving and moving again to better themselves, and finally concentrated so fanatically on production and consumption that the good life came to be defined for them almost exclusively in material terms, in disregard or even contempt of spiritual and intellectual values. Perhaps we must say therefore that migration promotes not only the simplification of culture but the exaggeration of certain of its elements. What one moves for, what one abandons other goods for, what one suffers so much for, may even rise to the plane of an absolute value: an eternal security in this insecure world.

So emotionally, as well as institutionally, mobility will promote changes of balance, and strong fibers of conservatism interlacing the patterns of change. It follows that (as Huntington once proposed),

(6) *New societies, formed by migration, will be narrower and more intense.* The loyalties will have been concentrated and deepened. The focus of a greater activity

will be on fewer goods. One can detect this in all the English colonies. One can see it spelled out plainly in the peopling of the Old Northwest territories, in the mixed but limited personnel of settlement—with pioneer farmers and cattle drovers, land speculators and town boosters, politicians and lawyers, all in quite unusual numbers on the National Road, balanced only by a few missionaries and teachers, some hell-fire preachers with their fundamentalist followers, or now and again a utopian prophet with his gathered band of communitarians. Later on, in the Middle West, it seemed enough to have a land office and a courthouse, several churches and a school, a steamboat landing and a depot, and behold! Civilization was established forever in the land. Without music and the fine arts, without literature or philosophy, without universities or professional schools, without museums or libraries (unless some dedicated and dauntless enthusiast, some Johnny Appleseed of learning and culture, insisted on bringing these in). The concentration on the material and the religiously emotional goods of life (the neglect of the intellectual and artistic) was there for all to see: it meant a narrower and more intense society, but plain and shallow, without cultural depth.

(7) *Long migrations also seem to appeal to the cranks and fanatics and to create extreme types.* Thus the society of early Texas was unbalanced by more than its desperadoes. Still later, on the West Coast, the intermingling of exploiters with zealots, of optimists with reactionaries, of men-on-the-make with fundamentalists, occult seers, and fanatics of many kinds would make California a byword in the nation. It should not have surprised us—for California was the end of the line.

Not to close this analysis on a note so macabre, let us recognize that,

(8) *The contacts and fresh mixtures will be stimulating,* even compelling, to many migrants, and will promote many awakenings or changes in the mover's value system. In addition to his learned responsiveness to novelty and change, his outward friendliness and affability with strangers, his desire to belong, and his acceptance of popular opinion, theoretical reflection will suggest many possible by-products from the great mix-master experience. I single out for emphasis, once more,

(9) *The leveling of status and of values,* or the promotion of egalitarianism, not only among men but among ideas. Here the peopling of the American West seems to have provided the illustration par excellence. In a society that was democratic first of all by circumstance—where the settlers were strangers to each other; where there were no pedigrees, no estates, and no family reputations to remember; where each arrival was on his own, but unknown and to be accepted as a fellow citizen; a society where first names were a sufficient identification—in our democracy of circumstance, the experience of equal treatment seems also to have generated or reinforced *a belief in equality* as a political and social good. In due course the town would have its rich men and its poor, its judges and its senators and its drunks. But the spirit of egalitarianism, the refusal to acknowledge superiority, the dislike of arrogance or condescension, would persist. "Who does he think he is?" we hear the American say.

The M-Factor
in American History—

The shaping of character and
the promotion of change

It is time now to return to the question with which we started. Is there any such thing as "national character"? In particular, is there, or has there ever been, an "American Character"? Many critics question, or even deny, the idea. Students of American civilization generally seem to start out by thinking there must be an American Character. But then they encounter great difficulties in defining this character—that is, they find too many different or contradictory types, none of the types unique, all of them appearing also in other cultures, a few of them perhaps unstable across the years. The result? Even conscientious scholars are driven to despair, and many decide that American society is neither consistent nor original nor completely different. On top of that we seem to be forever changing. Therefore, we have no distinctive character.

Now such a judgment, I submit, may be just a little foolish. For theoretically it isn't scientific, and practically it doesn't make sense. Theoretically, is it not a poor kind of science which says that, because you and I cannot wholly know a thing or exactly define it, it doesn't exist? Just because we cannot scientifically define Americanism would seem a quite insufficient reason for ignoring its existence. What has not existed, rather, may be that intuition of causes, that exact grasp of detail, that art of proportion, that science of social structure, which will enable us to say: this is, in a sum total way, different, *sui generis,* peculiar. After all, a combination does not have to be unique in all its elements, or even in a single one of these elements, to be different in sum total. I will assert that theoretically there may be an American Character, even though that character may have been composed of familiar elements, even though it is only the proportions which have been different, even though the resulting society may be mixed, contradictory, pluralistic, unjelled. The very indeterminism of a society may be a distinguishing mark. Theoretically, I see no barrier to believing that an American Character may exist.

On the contrary, on the grounds of common sense, I see many reasons to believe that there is and has been an American Character, for one thing because the most intelligent thinkers and observers have thought so, and have kept on thinking so, across the years. These observers may have differed in the labels they attached to us, they may have argued about the causes of our American peculiarities, but every one of them has thought that the Americans are a little odd in their psychology, and a little different in their social institutions. Crèvecoeur went so far as to call the American a "New Man." And he defined this new man as the Western Pilgrim: "He is an American who leaves behind his ancient prejudices and manners." But whatever the definition, from Crèvecoeur to Tocqueville to André Siegfried, from Dickens to Bryce to Denis Brogan, from Lieber to Keyserling or Robert Jungk, the most thoughtful commentators have asserted that there is and has been (and, alas, will continue to be) an American Character.

What caused this Americanism to emerge? Many things, no doubt; far too many even to list. And I mean to focus our attention on a single extraordinary peculiarity of our experience: the migration factor in our history, our excessive mobility. Yet before we return to The Moving American, let us recall some classic interpretations which have exercised a strong influence on the writing of American history, and on our thinking about America generally.

How are Americans different? In the beginning was the Word, and the Word had it that we were a Chosen People, a seed sifted out of the populations of Europe, a community of saints destined to create a better society on this earth. Like the Israelites of old, we were a people under divine command. As we sang in the old hymn: "O God, beneath Thy guiding hand our exiled fathers crossed the sea!"

After about 150 years, there succeeded to this biblical interpretation the thought that, if we were not always more holy, we were at least more free. As an independent nation, our destiny was to bring liberty, self-government, republicanism, the art of federal decentralization to the succor of oppressed mankind. So to the religious mission there succeeded a political mission—which was what Alexis de Tocqueville came to study.

From the beginning, also, there had always been an economic mission. America was El Dorado: the golden opportunity, the country of get-rich-quick, the land of the second chance, the asylum for the poverty-stricken. So, as foreign and native observers alike commented, America was (1) the land of goodness, (2) the land of liberty, and (3) the land of plenty.

For a long while these three national myths satisfied. Toward the end of the nineteenth century, however, there emerged a series of more sophisticated, or "scientific," explanations, and, in particular, one which has exercised enormous influence. What was it changed Europeans into Americans?

For historians of the past generation, the frontier hypothesis of Frederick Jackson Turner supplied the classic answer. It was the frontier experience which made us different. That is, it was our struggle with the wilderness—it was exploiting the vast free lands of the interior —it was freeing ourselves from the past, "breaking the cake of custom," leaving behind the fetters of settled society and the refinements of civilization to start over again in the woods—it was the lonely pioneers chopping out clearings on the road westward—it was getting together with other pioneers to rebuild a simpler, freer society—it was pulling up stakes and repeating the process—it was moving and moving again until in 1890 the free land and the West were all used up. On the frontier, said Turner, society became atomic, individualism flourished, democracy was generated, national legislation was encouraged. The opportunities of the West also opened a gate of escape for the oppressed of the East, and so contributed to the democratization and Americanization of the seaboard. And the frontier transformed personal character. As Turner phrased it:

> That coarseness and strength combined with acuteness and inquisitiveness; that practical, inventive turn of mind, quick to find expedients; that masterful grasp of material things, lacking in the artistic but powerful to effect great

ends; that restless, nervous energy; that dominant individualism, working for good and evil, and withal that
buoyancy and exuberance which comes with freedom—
these are traits of the frontier, or traits called out elsewhere because of the existence of the frontier.[1]

In effect, said Turner, it was primarily the molding
influence of the frontier which had transformed so many
European materials into a new American amalgam. In his
oft-quoted phrase, the frontier was "the line of most rapid
and effective Americanization."

For a long while this satisfied. But about forty years
ago, when Turner died, and his imaginative idea was making its way into popular speech, and Franklin Delano Roosevelt was using the disappearance of the frontier to
justify a welfare state, a number of people discovered political reasons for questioning the doctrine. Historians also
grew uneasy. For one thing, the hypothesis seemed too nationalistic, too provincial (and, as we now see, too anti-
intellectual). For a second, it produced too few novelties.
For a third, the frontier concept embraced too many over-
lapping or discordant influences. Again, the frontier cause
seemed to be credited with inconsistent results: it made
Americans both sectional and nationalistic, cooperative
and individualistic, repetitive yet original. Once again,
one wondered how many Americans could have been
affected. And how were we to stay American after 1890,
when the frontier disappeared? In the upshot, the frontier
theory seemed to explain far too much by far too little.[2]

Yet, for all this, it was a difficult theory to discard.
For if the frontier did not produce the effects ascribed to
it, what did?

I believe we now have at least a small part of the answer. It had been hinted at by many perceptive observers,
not least by Tocqueville or by Chevalier or by Lieber or

by Sarmiento. I will now call it the "M-Factor" in American history.

What made and kept us different was not just the wildness of the North American continent, nor its vast empty spaces, nor even its wealth of resources, powerful as must have been those influences. No. It was, first of all, the M-Factor: the factor of movement, migration, mobility. Colonization was one part of it; immigration, another; the westward movement itself was a fraction, but only a fraction, of the whole. This whole began with many Old World uprootings. It gathered force with the transatlantic passage. It flooded onto the farmlands of the mid-continent. But increasingly it meant movement also *away* from the frontier, from farm to town, from region to region, from city to city. Individuals, families, churches, villages, on occasion whole countrysides participated and continued to participate—some purposefully, some casually, and some almost feverishly—until movement had become a habit, and that habit was taken for granted. A full 140 years ago, Tocqueville was impressed by our *inquiétude du caractère,* or restless temper. To the German expatriate Francis Lieber, movement had become our "historical task." As we have also noted, Chevalier likened us to Tartars *"encamped* not established on the soil." And Sarmiento was so intrigued by our propensity for traveling around that he predicted that, if the trump of doom were suddenly to sound, it would surprise two-thirds of the Americans out on the roads like ants. (That was in the 1840's. Would it be otherwise tomorrow?)

Along this three hundred-year trail, in this unending experience of displacement, I will say again that the receding Western frontier played an important part. Yet that part was obviously limited. For if people moved to the frontier, they moved also before there was a frontier, and kept on moving even more enthusiastically when the frontier closed.

In retrospect, Frederick Jackson Turner may be seen as a great poet-historian, who more than half sensed the power that was in migration, but then imprisoned this giant in the rough homespun of the vanishing pioneers. So we of a later generation must once again return to the great question: What has made and still makes Europeans into restless Americans?

I believe it was and is primarily the M-Factor: the factor of movement, migration, mobility. And I propose now to restate, as briefly and cogently as I can, the argument of the preceding chapters.

Motion Means Change

My basic proposition is obvious, and is drawn straight from the "Laws of Migrability" or probabilities of motion: *Motion means change.* So the Europeans who moved would inevitably differ from those who stayed home.

Why should motion cause change? Theoretically, as we have seen, there are three chief reasons. First, because institutions do not move easily. Second, because migrants are not average people. And in the third place, because of the exposure to new circumstances: to the accidents and hardships and encounters of the journey, and to the new geography and the strange society at destination. Movement means exposure, and successive exposures lead to unexpected transformations. We should note as well that the addition or subtraction of the movers has noticeable consequences for the receiving and the parent societies.

At this point many interpreters will certainly wish to object, and it would be well to state and try to meet their objections. Each will have his preferred causes, either at point of origin or—more surely—at destination. The largest and most vocal group, one may anticipate, will be the environmentalists. Americans generally prefer the environmental explanations: man is everywhere much alike and only his circumstances differ. Crudely stated, the environment causes and can cure human ills—there is no such thing as an autonomous man—the ghetto makes the criminal—prosperity brings happiness—we are different because this land made us different—it was the North American continent that converted Europeans into a free, prosperous, democratic society. America made us into Americans.

Oddly enough, America didn't do that for the aborigines, or for the Spanish who preceded or the French who rivaled the English settlers. America also allowed (created?) chattel slavery on the same soil. In Turnerian terms, were all our frontiers alike, from New England to the Great Plains and from the bayou country to the deserts of Arizona? Yet if they weren't geographically alike, how could they have made and kept us so consistently different? Wasn't it perhaps a process rather than a place, and movement that counted rather than free land? In my judgment, the physical influence of the land has been grossly exaggerated. Geographic determinism is an old Greek idea which has led a precarious existence but survived because it contained some measures of truth; basically it recognized that nature is limiting, and that men are lazy, hence inclined to take the paths of least resistance. In modern terms, some continents offer more opportunities or more difficulties than others. But to claim that they make national character is to put too much pressure into that fatal balloon. Let us clearly acknowledge the importance of Atlantic distances and the savage wilderness in colonial days, then the invitations to dispersion and exploitative farming in the virgin spaces of the Mississippi Valley, and all the power and wealth we have managed to draw from our mineral discoveries in the last 120 years. Out of a combination of accidents, economic ambitions, cultural inventions, and physical resources we have indeed made ourselves into a "people of plenty." But, as Tocqueville asked long ago, why are Americans so uneasy and restless in their pursuit of gain, and so unsatisfied in their prosperity? Could they have overestimated their continent? Were they perhaps looking for something else?

A second major objection to the importance of the M-Factor will come from the opposite end of the spectrum: from the biological determinists or the historical geneticists who believe that the inheritance counts for more than Americans will admit. It may be argued, for example, that most of the American Character was made in Europe, or that migrations are often the result or the symptom of changes that have already taken place in the parent society. And with such suggestions I have considerable sympathy. On the one hand, some immigrants were so obstinate in their tribal ways that they were Americanized only long after they got here (have the Amish succumbed yet?). On the other, not a few American types, like the Puritan and the businessman, had already appeared in sixteenth-century Europe.[3] So migration served both as prologue and as epilogue; it has been the means of change and the effect of change, as well as the cause.

Yet no movement of people or institutions, however started or motivated, can take place without further alterations. For migration selects special types for moving; it subjects them to exceptional strains on the journey; and it then compels them to rebuild, with liberty to choose or refuse from the mail-order catalogue of western experience. On top of all that, repeated movements, such as we in our country have known, seem to have a cumulative or progressive effect.

The Breadth of Change

What parts of a civilization, what elements in a society, does the M-Factor attack? Apparently, all parts. Following Ellsworth Huntington, who came to see in migration a Darwinian selective force so strong that it affected the stock and temperament of a people as well as its culture, I am prepared to think that—for selective and for other reasons as well—movement changes the physical population, the institutions and group structures, the social habits and traditions, the personal character and attitudes of the migrants.

Argument has already been offered that movement has shaken or reshaped the American family, the American home, the transplanted English village and town, our cities with their slums and their suburbs, the laws and taxes and welfare programs of the states, the federal Constitution, and some of the operating principles of our national government. Again, the relation of mobility and dispersion to early religious toleration, disestablishment, and excessive sectarianism has been suggested (as has a possible connection between the later recirculation of believers and recent efforts at church reunion, or the ecumenical urge).

When we glanced at the American economy, what did we find? An economy in which transportation has loomed extraordinarily large—witness the railroads, the automobile age, and the airplane industry of today— witness also in our myths how prairie schooners and pony express, paddlewheelers and the long whistle of the trains,

Ford cars and the *Spirit of St. Louis* have entered into the folklore of our people.

> The wheels are singing to the railroad track
> If you go, you can't come back.
> Hear the whistle blow.[4]

For Americans, it has been said, the automobile restates a national principle, since, after all, the settler was the first auto-mobile. More soberly, without unusual mobility, one can see no economic United States; without uprooted farmers, no sweeping westward movement; without a very mobile labor supply, no rapid industrialization; without mobile consumers, finally, only a much delayed national market.

So perhaps enough evidence has already been given on the pervasive influence of our footloose condition? Notwithstanding, I will permit myself just a few additional reminders in the shape of some familiar and even commonplace facts about the American population.

The American population? It was formed and re-formed by migration. To begin with, we were all immigrants. Moreover, because the Atlantic was open, people from many lands and nations came to these shores, until we were the leading conglomerate of the West, a Rainbow Division of Europe. Political scientists have called us a pluralistic society. Sociologists find culture conflicts endemic. (And can we not almost feel the submerged ethnic culture flows now rising to the surface of our national life?)

Again, because the migrants did not all come at once but in intermittent surges, and because in free movements the later comers, as strangers, are handicapped and must enter the lower levels of their class and occupation, the natives or earlier comers have repeatedly found themselves pushed upstairs, to the more skilled jobs, to the managerial posts, to the position of employers and capitalists (see ch. 9). At the same time, moving upstairs was difficult, so difficult that the older stock felt it had to cut down on the number of its own children if it was to graduate them into the higher levels of living, so difficult that the next-to-last comers tended to resent the labor competition of the newcomers and tried to exclude them. Thus the Yankees industrialized with the aid of other peoples' children. Meanwhile these laboring generations, as they matured, tried to keep the jobs for themselves and, whether as skilled artisans or later trade union bosses, as Know-Nothings in the 1850's or McCarthyites a century later, became the strongest champions of immigration restriction, the most suspicious of new foreigners, the uncompromising 100 percenters. So from 1820 to 1920, what ought to have been for the Anglo-American population a series of European additions became instead a progressive physical substitution. And after 1920, the freedom to immigrate was shut off by the votes of the very groups which had benefited from it earlier. But why did not and has not this stepladder movement of infiltration produced a stratified, hierarchical, skyscraper society? The answer is again the M-Factor, but this time internal migration. Inside, the freedom to move remained, and a man could get out of his cellar in town by building a one-story cabin upcountry, or he could come off his eroded acres into Chicago, where the rising buildings and professions had elevators in them.

If we turn from questions of nationality and occupational opportunity to the age and sex characteristics of our population, we find that here, too, the M-Factor has left deep marks. For three hundred years, or at least until the Great Depression, we were a young country. We boasted

of it. Foreigners rarely failed to mention the childlike innocence, the boyish enthusiasm, the youthful drive and
bustle and activity-for-activity's sake of these strange
Americans. The youth of America, quipped Oscar Wilde,
is its oldest tradition. And perhaps we were guilty of a certain "shortage of adults." At least the demographers have
proved that our Constitution was made for adolescents—
as late as 1820 the median age of the population was only
sixteen years, and it was not until well into the twentieth
century that the median soared above twenty-five. That is,
it was only after preventive medicine had started to pro-
long the lives of the infirm, and immigration restriction
had cut down on the annual influx of young bachelors and
young marrieds, that we first really began to feel middle-
aged. How did the M-Factor figure in this? Quite simply
and powerfully. For students of migration have rediscovered the fact that it is overwhelmingly the young, between
the ages of fifteen and twenty-five, who move—and in the
first waves or pioneer phases, it is primarily the young
men. The frontiers, whether of farm or factory, start em-
phatically male ("Oh Susannah, oh don't you cry for me!").

Yet the men were not to have it all their own way, for
the M-Factor can give things a sardonic twist. Migration
has perennially represented rebellion against past tyrannies or authorities, against the father no less than against
the lord or priest, against the husband no less than against
the father. Thus, after the first settlements had been established, the open spaces and open opportunities of this
country just invited the younger generation to leave home
and strike out on their own, and the able young men accepted the invitation. Even today it is the rare son of ability who does not insist on leaving the town where he was
born to try to make his way in a larger world. Meanwhile
the pioneer women, being scarce as well as weak, found

that they had inadvertently acquired a scarcity value. For them, as well as for the children, migration meant progressive emancipation—an emancipation eventually crowned by woman suffrage, Mother's Day, and much symbolic statuary. Thus, as our lonely forefathers pushed relentlessly westward, and the idea of equality came galloping up behind, the Pioneer Mother replaced the Pilgrim Father on the sculptor's pedestal in the town square. (It may be argued that in some spheres, e.g., the universities and business corporations, the equalizations have not gone nearly far enough. Yet one may recall also the increasingly querulous complaints of our English and continental friends that we have turned into a woman-run and child-dominated subcivilization.)

But enough of such illustrations.

Let us now proceed to ask, on a more systematic basis, how, just how, have migration and movement acted to convert Europeans into something rich and strange? For answers we could go back to the "Laws of Migrability" and of "Move Effect." But I prefer to draw from both theory and experience a vision or condensed statement of the ten imperatives of motion.

The Systematic Promotion of Change

Considering the matter very broadly, I propose that the M-Factor has been (turn by turn or even all at once): (1) the great Eliminator; (2) the persistent Distorter; (3) an arch-Conservator; (4) an almost irresistible Disintegrator or Atomizer; (5) a heart stimulant or Energizer; and (6) the prime source of Optimism in the American atmosphere, a never-failing ozone of hope. Also (7) the Secularizer and Externalizer of our beliefs; (8) the indispensable Lubricator of our political economy; and (9) the Equalizer and

Democratizer and Homogenizer of social life. Finally (10) the M-Factor has put its brand on the American Character, and has been responsible to a degree not yet appreciated for many of the strengths and weaknesses, peculiarities and contradictions, irrationalities and emotionalisms that our writers have found and are still finding in the lonely American. No doubt, careful reflection will suggest still other ways in which migration has shaken its European ingredients into new patterns. But let us consider merely these ten, with just a hint or two of historical testimony by way of illumination.

Migration was the great *Eliminator?* Nothing could be plainer. In theory, you can't take everything with you when you move. Some goods are too bulky or delicate to be put on ship; some household possessions will fall out of the covered wagon. Again, in a free migration, not all elements in a society will wish to move; the dregs will be too spiritless and impoverished to emigrate unaided; the ruling classes entirely too successful and satisfied. Check this theory against our Anglo-American history and what do we find? In the early colonization there came out of England the rising middle classes, with some admixture of the lowest elements, but with only a few aristocratic leaders. Ours started, therefore, as a decapitated society,* virtually without nobles or bishops, judges or learned lawyers, artists, playwrights, or great poets. Taking a hopeful view, a student of mine once maintained that settlement transferred the accent from "nobility" to "ability." Considering the transfer culturally, however, one must recognize a tragic impoverishment.** Despite all our gains of good-

---

* The reader may want to refer again to ch. 1, where this point and the next two are developed.

** *"The Importance of the Absence of Things,"* according to C. Vann Woodward (C.V.W. to G.W.P., Feb. 19, 1960), has been "historically a favorite means of establishing national identity. The classic

ness or plenty or freedom, the men of the highest attainments and greatest skills have stayed home—and with them their arts and refinements, their leisure-class culture. The same process of abandonment, of flight from the élite and their standards, would be discernible later in the settlement of the West. Axiomatically, the fine arts, the theoretical sciences, the most advanced tools and machinery, are not found or produced on moving frontiers. Like war or fire or inflation, migration has been a great destroyer of inherited treasure.

At first glance such destruction may seem only temporary, to be replaced "when we have time." Yet meanwhile some elements are missing, the balance is changed, the old society has been distorted—and before long one may get reconciled to doing without. On top of this, the M-Factor has promoted *Distortion* in an even more drastic way. For moving forces the reclassification of values. Why? Because the land of destination attracts more strongly for one or two presumed goods than for the others (as for economic opportunity perhaps, or political freedom, or the right to worship in one's own way). So if a family is to go, they have to believe, or persuade themselves, that the particular goods to be realized are more

---

example, I suppose, and incidentally a turning point in American attitude toward 'the absences,' would probably be the passage from Henry James' *Hawthorne* . . .

> No State, in the European sense of the word, and indeed barely a specific national name. No sovereign, no court, no personal loyalty, no aristocracy, no church, no clergy, no army, no diplomatic service, no country gentlemen, no palaces, no castles, nor manors, nor old country houses, nor parsonages, nor thatched cottages, nor ivied ruins . . . no Oxford, nor Eton, nor Harrow . . . no Epsom, nor Ascot!

"And then the observation, 'if these things are left out, everything is left out.' James would make a slender basis for a turning point. And long after as well as before him 'the absences' constituted almost exclusively a national reservoir of complacency instead of a cause of lament."

important to them than all the other social goods, which may be diminished or even left behind altogether. If similar movements are made by later generations for like reasons, then these cherished values may rise almost to the status of holy commandments or natural rights, and in the nineteenth century become the polar magnets in a new value system. By elimination and wilful distortion, a moving people becomes a narrower society: thinner and shallower, yet in some things much more intense.

This calls attention to a third and almost paradoxical characteristic of migration: its *Conservatism*. People moved to save as well as to improve. But when they found they couldn't take everything with them, then a curious thing often happened. They came to value even more highly what they had succeeded in preserving. Having suffered such privations, having sacrificed so many other possessions, they clung to what was saved with a fiercer passion. Witness the Puritans with their Wilderness Zion, the Mormons under Brigham Young, or even Turner's leapfrogging pioneers. For these last, as for so many others, it had become easier to move than to change their vocation, their habits, their antiquated methods. To put this bluntly, for them the cheap lands of the West made it easier to keep on with their soil-mining and strip-farming, and possible to avoid such painful changes as learning a proper care of the land or the new crop rotation of the advanced parts of Europe and the East. So for the American farmer—or agriculturally speaking—the westward movement became the great postponement of American history. They profited personally, but it was a postponement nonetheless. Migration, I suggest, may be a way of promoting change—and of avoiding it, too. Flight can be an escape from the future as well as from the past.

The M-Factor, we must next realize, was an almost

irresistible *Disintegrator or Atomizer*. Few authoritarian institutions from Europe could stand the strain of Atlantic distances or the explosion of American space. So either they decentralized or they died. Thus, migration splintered the European university into a scattering of lonely colleges, and with continued movement we got the habit of college founding. So my own institution, through the efforts of its migrating graduates, became a mother of colleges a full century before it could accumulate enough substance in New Haven to rival the great foundations of Europe. Let me also illustrate, once again, by the early church. In Virginia the episcopal organization proved so little suited to the far-flung tobacco plantations that the Church of England almost withered away, whereas in New England the Puritan branch of the same church developed a localized or congregational organization, and flourished. Then two odd and rather contradictory things happened. Having abandoned their episcopal hierarchy and deference to central authority, the Protestant denominations splintered and splintered again. They exploded into empty space. They achieved mobility but, as religious institutions, at the cost of shrinking down to the sectarian or almost atomic level. By contrast, the Roman Catholics managed to resist disintegration. For when the Irish immigration poured life and vigor into American Catholicism, the hierarchy, intuitively recognizing that moving out on the lands might cripple the church as well as weaken the individual's faith, did their best to hold the new arrivals in the seaport towns, at least until some interior communities could be effectively churched. So the ecclesiastical structure was saved, but at a sacrifice of mobility. Ultimately, I believe, it will be found that our Catholics have moved less often, less widely, and less soon than their Protestant neighbors, hence have missed certain corrosive acids and opportunities in the M-Factor.

One of these opportunities, of course, was to stand on your own feet, to make your own way, and if need be to move again. In our expanding settlements the arm of the state (like the authority of the bishops) shriveled, and a kind of *physical individualism* sprouted. On the trail, society tended to break down into chance parties of moving families or individuals. And at the destination everything was to be reconstructed. It took energy and courage to move, and more energy to make the move succeed. Hence, *Migration was a great Stimulus to action*—and when such action repeatedly succeeded (or, as we may say, "worked"), then perhaps the beginnings of a habit of action had been established, both for oneself and for one's neighbor. The American reputation for self-help and neighborly helpfulness, for physical individualism and constructive energy, for restless activity and almost ceaseless activism, surely needs no underlining.

Migration was not only the Destroyer, Distorter, Conservator, Atomizer, and Energizer of western society, but its most effective *"Optimizer."* First of all, out of the welter of Old World classes and temperaments it selected the up-and-coming and the hopeful. Pessimists didn't bother; you had to be an optimist to move. Next, it required sacrifice and waiting, and so captured many believers, the men of faith. Finally, it rewarded the successful —and those who weren't lucky were given a second try. America the Golden was the land of the second chance. And from failure it offered a full timetable of escapes.[5]

I realize that it is customary at this point to do a ritualistic dance around the statue of the golden calf and credit our optimism or success primarily to the sheer wealth of the continent. But if we did become a "people of plenty," and if that plenty left its mark even on the size of our automobiles, let us not forget that the beginnings were almost invariably hard, and what the land long offered most of was tough places and violent weather. What kind of plenty was it converted the gravel patch of New England into smiling farms? Lots of hard work, I should say, and plenty of faith. Again, who but a lunk-headed optimist would grow wheat in western Kansas? Or who in his right mind would go settle in Dakota Territory? No. The Black Hills gold and the U.S. farm bounties, these bonanzas were later and almost accidental discoveries. In my book, optimism made more states than vice versa. Many a town existed first, or only, in the imagination. "Boost, don't knock" has been the slogan of new communities just abuilding, and the booster is Mr. Johnny-come-lately. We began as migrants, that is, wishful thinkers, and each wave of immigration, each boatload from abroad, brought us fresh injections of this heart stimulant. For Europe's poor, the freedom to come changed "tomorrow" from a threat into a promise. For its men of faith, the act of moving and moving again substituted "the future" for "the heavenly hereafter." And with time, the mission of American idealists came to be in and for this world. From infant damnation to the social gospel is but a long tramp?

As for the *Secularizing and Externalizing influence of Mobility*, which Pitirim A. Sorokin early explored, I hope I may be allowed to cite his judgments. But first let me refer back to what was said in chapter 8 about our transient and superficial relations with nature, and with things. There it was proposed that in our condition of spatial restlessness, in our economy of built-in obsolescence, in our culture of constant change, we Americans have learned to set a high value on what is new and different and spectacular. Things keep getting better. Change itself seems good. Yet since no change is final, necessarily our engagement with new things and places, our attachment to even the latest machine or labor-saving device or residential community will be limited in depth and duration. Meanwhile, our judgments of value will be pragmatic: what works for now will be acceptable for now. Ours is proverbially a society of spontaneity and improvisation, and many of our commitments turn out to be provisional, "for the time being." Again, it was proposed that in our restless society Americans have had to learn to adjust, to accommodate to repeated exposures—perhaps we have even become hardened by overexposure.

From his own studies and command of the European literature, Sorokin reached a series of even more decisive conclusions. Spatial mobility, he said, encourages more plastic and versatile behavior, decreases narrow-mindedness, and facilitates innovations. It also encourages superficiality and decreases sensitiveness (otherwise we would go crazy), makes for impatience and touch-and-go habits, generates skepticism and aversion to theory, drives the uneducated to sudden dogmas, diminishes intimacy with men and with things, increases loneliness, restlessness, sensual pleasures, and suicide. Among the broad social effects, Sorokin also found it to favor an increase of individualism followed by a vague cosmopolitanism and collectivism. Is it not time we took more account of such findings?

The M-Factor as the *Lubricator* of our political economy seems to me an almost self-evident proposition. Whether we think of it in terms of the liberty to leave home (to get an education, get married, or take that first job)—or as the opportunity to rise in society (by shifting jobs, or taking on new assignments)—or as an automatic safety device (the chance to escape or to start over)—or as our leading recreation and soul therapy (the joys of travel); or whether we think in terms of the total economy (the freedom to mobilize our resources of manpower and skill on a national scale), the M-Factor plays the role of lubricant, even fluid drive, in our economy. And psychologically it does something no less important: it keeps hope alive, and so reconciles our twin dogmas of freedom and equality. As has been remarked already, it is our permit to feel both more free and more equal than we otherwise could.

This brings us to the egalitarian effects: to the M-Factor's role as the *Equalizer, Democratizer, and Homogenizer* of our social life. And I hope I may be forgiven for some emphasis, because these democratic tendencies seem to me particularly important, and I have stumbled on some odd or even teasing illustrations.

Here the theoretical argument would be that the M-Factors are often democratic in their consequences, first because for the lower classes emigration means "getting out from under," the first step on the road up; secondly, because the hardships of the journey are no respecters of birth (witness the miserable failure of the early "Gentlemen" of the Jamestown Colony in Virginia). In the third place, and most significantly, the process of resettlement is a process of making new mixtures out of a gathering of strangers, each without authority, credentials, reputation, or other priority than that of arrival. In a new community (frontier or town), family and past performance hardly count. Everyone has to make his own mark, and stands equal with his fellow strangers. The social competition, as it were, starts over, with all the camaraderie and "gamesmanship" of a new catch-as-catch-can. Migration has been a great mix-master. And mixtures of anonymous elements are necessarily more democratic, at least at first.* So much for doctrine. Now for my illustrations.

My first illustration, if I may be allowed the personal reference, comes out of an effort to understand my own university. How explain Yale College of the 1890's, a college that prided itself on its democracy? It is true that there were occasional Whitneys, Vanderbilts, McCormicks, or Harknesses, with social pretensions and inordinate allowances. Yet evidently the game was wide open, and any self-help student from no matter how humble a background or obscure a school had a chance to show what he could do, rise to the top, and be the honor man in the Senior Society elections, if he had what it took. Now how was it possible that a college like Yale, with almost two hundred years of tradition and family attachments, could still offer so fair and square an opportunity to all comers? Because Yale was, in a sense, an annually renewed community, and because its constituents came, not just from around New Haven or New England but from all over the country, without prior knowledge of each other or claims to authority. It was a skeptical Harvard professor, European born, who first taught me this truth. Listen to George Santayana:

> The relations of one Yale student to another are completely simple and direct. They are like passengers in a ship. . . . They live in a sort of primitive brotherhood with a ready enthusiasm for every good or bad project, and a contagious good humor.
> . . . Nothing could be more American. . . . Here is sound, healthy principle, but no scrupulousness, love of life, trust in success, a ready jocoseness, a democratic

* The homogenization of the whole society, of course, comes later, from the circulation *and recirculation* of men, information, and goods, as mobility finally conquers empty space, so that there is created not only a national market but national media and an "American Way" of life.

amiability, and a radiant conviction that there is nothing better than oneself. It is a boyish type of character, earnest and quick in things practical, hasty and frivolous in things intellectual, but the boyishness is a healthy one, and in a young man, as in a young nation, it is perfection to have only the faults of youth.[6]

What Yale College and the frontier, and indeed much of the rest of America, had in common, Santayana suggests, was young Americans in a new mixture.

If this first illustration comes with a strange sound, let me hasten to propose my second. It concerns dogs. In France, on sabbatical a few years ago, I seemed to run into only two kinds of dogs. One was the pampered, pedigreed poodle, sitting with his mistress in the restaurants, even eating from her plate: the fine flower of canine aristocracy, and most grandly indifferent to strangers. The second type was nondescript and fierce, the savage watchdog at peasant doorway or chateau gate, guarding the family domain and inherited possessions, *les situations acquises*. This character disliked strangers on sight, and promptly tried to chew them up. After one or two close calls with such receptionists, I came back to the States—and found dogs of all sorts of ancestry, chiefly mixed. But what they showed mostly was curiosity, and a sort of friendly expectancy. Their tails said: "Howdy, stranger." For they were not guarding any particular place. They belonged to traveling men, and had been around.

My third illumination, if we can call it that, concerns money. Foreigners still accuse us of being excessively money-minded, of measuring everything by the almighty dollar. Our defenders answer: it's not the money, it's the power and the achievement. You make a million to prove you're a man; then, like as not, you give it away. After all, you can't take it with you.

Yet can't you? As I was once ruminating about this not altogether lovely aspect of our society, it suddenly came to me that on a journey, or in a new community, money was one of the few things that you could take along. Cash took the place of your pedigree or family letter of credit. It spoke with a certain authority, East or West. Money was power? Yes. But especially it was currency: the power that you could take with you.[7] Or, if you had none to bring, it was the authority you could most readily acquire; it was the demonstration of your manhood. So in our westward movement, behind the moving frontier, in the new towns of the Ohio and Mississippi valleys, and in our growing Great Lakes cities, money became the name of the game—and it was differentiation by dollars that first disturbed the democracy of the new mixtures.*

Having got diverted by some of the social consequences of the M-Factor, I must now turn to the most interesting effects of all: *the influence of migration on personal character and attitudes.* For if migration was the destroyer of cultural capital, the disintegrator of institutions, the simplifier and distorter of society, it was also the selector of people, the intensifier of the emotions, the breeder of an almost incurable loneliness. Let me briefly review the most striking signs of its influence.

Was it not the psychological imperatives of migration, even more than the empty continent, that helped make and keep us a nation of optimists? Was it not the physical demands of colonization and resettlement, as well as Calvinism and middle-class origins, that made us into

---

* If money, as personal power and authority, was easier to acquire and far more effective than family reputation or intellectual superiority, it could also be easy to lose: "From shirtsleeves to shirtsleeves in three generations," as the old saying had it.

such a nation of workers, activists, materialists, instrumentalists? The difference between what André Siegfried called "homo faber" or the American, and "homo sapiens" or the European, was it not perhaps that one of these characters had been sitting still?

Whereas we, poor pilgrims, had itching feet. Having moved to freedom, we proved unwilling to give up the freedom to move. Restless to start with, we became more so with repeated displacement. Did we not carry movement both visibly and audibly toward new extremes, a sort of folk obsession? *Here today and gone tomorrow.* The wandering mania has got into our blood, our houses, our attention, our very ways of speech. *Come on! Get going! Don't be a stick-in-the-mud! I don't know where I'm going, but I'm on my way. Anywhere I hang my hat is home, sweet home, to me.* In the revealing American vernacular it is impressive to observe how many "goods" are defined in terms of movement, and not least the *road to success.* Whereas to stop moving is to fail, to stop breathing, to expire.

Reinforcing the testimony of our vernacular are our social habits. Unable to stay put, thrown among fellow transients, having newcomers flood in about us, we have perforce become hospitable, and genial with strangers. Not knowing their ancestry, and caring less, first names have been all we needed. Lonely from disassociation we keep looking for lodges, or churches, or motor courts we can join. Frightened and not quite able to bear our independence, we oscillate between assertiveness and timidity, between an almost violent aggression and an almost cowardly conformity. Imaginative and suggestible, we are notorious for our fads and our instability. Insecure in our values, we have become adept at inventing dogmas to comfort ourselves. Not quite sure that our abandonment of the Old World and of the past was justified, we have long been haunted by ambivalent feelings: a mixed scorn-and-guilt complex about the older civilizations of Europe.

"It is a complex fate, being an American," said Henry James, "and one of the responsibilities it entails is fighting against a superstitious valuation of Europe." Ralph Waldo Emerson, the cheerful nationalist, felt the same way: "Can we never extract the tapeworm of Europe from the brain of our countrymen?"

Finally, because migration appealed for diverse reasons especially to extremists—to saints and real sinners, to fundamentalists and freethinkers, to dreamers and "tough bastards," to screwballs and hiders, to groupists and individualists side by side—our society has never received its fair share of balanced, equable, middle-of-the-road temperaments, but has been shot through with violent contradictions. Hence so many of our seeming inconsistencies, to this very day.

To me the migrant seems not a single or a simple character, but is he not recognizably different—and American?

Paradoxically, if we turn up the other side of the coin, there are the Europeans, fearful of becoming Americanized. Is this entirely out of weakness, or envy, or admiration? Hardly. Let us rather take note of a curious and somewhat unappreciated development. In the last generation mobility has swept the Continent. With their *vacances payées,* their *campings,* their folkwagons, our cousins have found a new freedom. So, if today there is Americanization in Europe, and if our ways of life seem to be coming closer together, may it not be in part because the Old World societies are as never before in movement, and because Siegfried's "homo sapiens," too, is taking to the roads?

I conclude that there may be—indeed there has been —such a thing as *Americanization by Motion.* Motion purges a society, marks the characters who have gone through its soul-surgery, shakes and thins the institutions, delays or accelerates their evolution, intensifies the feelings, and in these and many other ways unbalances or changes the proportions in the moving society. Looking backward, we can see that Americans started as Europeans with a special un-government stamp on them. Americans were the dissenter Europeans, the disappointed Europeans, the ambitious Europeans, the uprooted Europeans—the outcasts but also the workers and the wishful believers. Then on the road they became queerer still: the adventurous explorers and lonely pioneers, the shouting evangelists and the spreadeagle politicians, the democratic sojourners and the hospitable strangers. And if today we seem to have more than our share of ruthless operators and men-on-the-make, of crusaders and reformers and freedom riders, of men of violence and of libertarians, of zealots and of pragmatists—we should not be surprised.

It's been "a long, long trail a-winding into the land of our dreams." And we've been impatient. "Fly now and pay later" has always been our rule. For at the end of the trail which began at Liverpool or Bremen or some Mediterranean port, which poured through Ellis Island and the Erie Canal, which flowed on through Pittsburgh Landing and Council Bluffs to the Golden Gate: at the end of that trail, we would surely find release or at least a "Welcome Wagon"?

All of which is merely to remind us and to say again that the American society with its institutions and its culture, and the American personality with its generosities and shortcomings, its temperament and style, have been marked and shaped by the almost uninterrupted experience of migration. And our history, to a degree, has been that of Americanization by Motion.

Notes

1. "Americans Are Always Moving On . . ."
This essay was originally published under the title "The Moving American" in *The Yale Review* (Copyright 1954 Yale University Press), Autumn 1954. It has been modestly revised and is reproduced by the kind permission of the editor. The reader will find here an overview of the whole subject, with suggestion of the major themes and arguments to which body will be given in the chapters that follow.

1. W. Knox to Clerk of the Council, Historical Manuscripts Commission, Report on Manuscripts in Various Collections, VI (Dublin, 1909), as quoted in M. L. Hansen and J. B. Brebner, *The Mingling of the Canadian and American Peoples* (New Haven, 1940), p. 1.

2. Quoted by J. B. Brebner in *North Atlantic Triangle* (New Haven, 1945), p. 37.

3. Quoted from A. D. Richardson, *Beyond the Mississippi*, 1867, by James C. Malin, in "Mobility and History," *Agricultural History* (October 1943), 17:180.

4. I am indebted to Rosemary Carr Benét for original permission to quote these lines from the Prelude to *Western Star*, published by Rinehart and Company, Inc., Copyright 1943 by Stephen V. Benét. Copyright renewed 1971 by Rachel Benét Lewis, Thomas C. Benét, and Stephanie Benét Mahin; permission by Holt, Rinehart and Winston.

5. D. F. Sarmiento, "Travels in the United States in 1847," *A Sarmiento Anthology*, trans. by S. E. Grummon, ed. by A. W. Bunkley (Princeton, N. J., 1948), p. 207.

6. Fans of mobility may be edified and amused by Russell Baker's

"Observer: The National Motion Sickness," in *The New York Times,* Feb. 16, 1965.

7. For further statistics from the census and other sources, see below, especially chs. 2, 4, and 5.

8. Leacock's "Children's Poetry Revised," originally published in *Harper's Magazine* (July 1927), is reprinted from *Wet Wit and Dry Humor* (New York, 1931) by the kind permission of Dodd, Mead and Company.

9. *Oil Facts* (November–December 1966), quoting the Bureau of Public Roads; *1971 Automobile Facts and Figures,* p. 51. See also below, ch. 4 on travel.

10. In chs. 8, 9, and 10, I give these ideas systematic development.

11. "Pioneering may in part be described as the Romantic Movement in action," Lewis Mumford, *The Golden Day* (New York, 1926), p. 47. For the quotation by Marcus Lee Hansen, see his *The Atlantic Migration, 1607–1860* (Cambridge, Mass., 1940), p. 3.

12. A. M. Schlesinger, "What Then Is The American, This New Man?", *American Historical Review* (January 1943), XLVIII: 243. For a challenging interpretation of our "joining" instincts, see Rowland Berthoff, *An Unsettled People: Social Order and Disorder in American History* (New York, 1971)—and my comments in *Pacific Historical Review* (May 1972), XLI, no. 2, 236–8.

13. Charles Dickens, *American Notes,* last chapter.

2. Comparative Mobility

This essay originated as a broadcast on "Mobility" for the Forum Branch, Voice of America, U.S. Information Agency, in a 1967 series on "Comparative History" organized by C. Vann Woodward. The theme was given a preliminary airing at the annual meeting of the American Historical Association in December 1966. It was then rewritten, and published in C. Vann Woodward, ed., *The Comparative Approach to American History* (New York, 1968). I am indebted to the editor for permission to revise and integrate this background comparison into my larger study of The Moving American.

1. Eugene Gilbert, president of the Gilbert Youth Research, Inc.,

"Family Moving? Teeners would rather stay put," New Haven *Register,* Oct. 4, 1964.

2. Those interested in bringing these statistical estimates up to date should consult *1971 Automobile Facts and Figures,* of the Automobile Manufacturers Association, Inc., where total motor vehicle registrations for 1970 are stated at 90 million passenger vehicles and 19 million trucks and buses, with motor vehicle travel estimated at 1.125 trillion miles. For the same year, 1970, the Travelers Insurance Company's *Voice Behind the Wheel* (1971) listed 55,200 persons killed and more than 5 million persons injured.

3. Franklin D. Scott, "Migration in the Dynamics of History" (in *World Migration in Modern Times,* ed. by Scott, Englewood Cliffs, N.J., 1968). Another rather similar classification has been suggested by William Petersen, "A General Typology of Migration," in *The Politics of Population* (Garden City, N.Y., 1964). See also *Population* (Garden City, N.Y., 1969).

4. Petersen, *op. cit.,* makes an interesting distinction between "Forced" and "Impelled" migrations, as in the slave or coolie trades.

5. Frank Thistlethwaite, "Migration from Europe Overseas in the Nineteenth and Twentieth Centuries," *Rapports,* V, XIe Congrès International des Sciences historiques, Paris, 1960.

6. Michael Chevalier, *Society, Manners, and Politics in the United States* (New York, 1961), p. 60. See also pp. 130, 204–5, 270, and 297–9. I am indebted to John William Ward for calling my attention to Chevalier's observations.

3. *"Goin' Some"*

An abbreviated version of this speculative inquiry was originally published by the *South Atlantic Quarterly* (Autumn 1964), LXIII, No. 4; and I am indebted to the editor for permission to reprint. I should also like to acknowledge the many additions and embellishments contributed by friends. My colleague, the late distinguished historian David M. Potter, first called my attention to "Crossing the Divide" and other western euphemisms for dying. Professor Bernard N. Schilling of Rochester provided the quotations from Carlyle and President Kennedy. And my old classmate Arthur Milliken, retired headmaster of Westminster School, after teasing me about taking off "into the wild blue yonder," supplied Stephen

Vincent Benét's apostrophe to the American (in the Invocation to *John Brown's Body*):

> Stepchild of every exile from contempt
> And all the disavouched, hard-bitten pack
> Shipped overseas to steal a continent
> With neither shirts nor honor to their back.

1. In the *Encyclopedia Americana* (1956), as also in *Collier's Encyclopedia* (1955), the article on "Migration" followed immediately after one on "Migraine," and began by discussing animal migrations of a seasonal or a disaster sort—the *Americana* beginning with insects, crustacea, fishes, mammals, and birds, and *Collier's* treating birds, seals, bats, mule deer, wapiti, bison, and lemmings. Neither authority mentioned man. By contrast, Eugene Kulischer, in the *Encyclopaedia Britannica* (1957), was quite informative on the history and sociology of human (and especially European) migration, but passed over the psychological (and American) implications.

2. The late Basil Davenport gave me: "A rolling stone gathers no moss—but acquires a beautiful polish." He attributed this variant to George Ade, who is quoted in *The Permanent Ade*, ed. by Fred C. Kelly (Indianapolis, 1947): "A rolling stone gathers no moss and therefore will not be derided as a mossback. Roll as much as possible."

3. Pascal, *Pensées*, Sec. II, 139.

4. See *Past and Present*, Book IV, ch. 5, and J. A. Froude, *Thomas Carlyle, A History of the First Forty Years of His Life, 1795–1835* (1882), 1890 ed., II:26.

5. Max Sorre, *Les Migrations des Peuples* (Paris, 1955), p. 139.

4. *"Under a Wandering Star"*

This chapter has been revised and considerably expanded from an essay under the same title originally published in *The Virginia Quarterly Review* (Autumn 1963), XXXIX, No. 4 (material reprinted by permission).

1. Automobile Manufacturers Association, Inc., *1971 Automobile Facts and Figures,* p. 51.

2. Cf. the *Times Literary Supplement* review (Nov. 25, 1955) of G. D. H. Cole, *Studies in Class Structure,* and its conclusion that the leveling up of the working class had "deprived the middle class of two conditions which, perhaps more than any

others, conferred upon it a sense of belonging to a privileged section of the community. The first was its reliance on domestic servants. The second was its monopoly of long-distance travel." See also "The Lost Art of Travel," by Daniel Boorstin in his *The Image or What Happened to the American Dream?* (New York, 1962), and note 10, below.

3. *The New York Times Magazine,* May 3, 1964. See also *The New York Times,* Jan. 26, 1964, and *Look* (May 1964). For the recent developments and statistics from American Express, I am indebted to Mr. Thomas Hanrahan, manager—Public Relations, and to Mr. Jess Gregory, manager—Corporate Public Affairs. A convenient source for mobility statistics prior to 1960 is *Historical Statistics of the United States, Colonial Times to 1957,* 1960.

4. *Population Bulletin* (June 1964); *Oil Facts* (November–December 1966), (January–February 1968); Hal Boyle, "Place to Make Hay Is in the City," New Haven *Register,* Feb. 27, 1967. The 1970 estimates are from *1971 Automobile Facts and Figures.*

5. In the single year 1969 the number of visitors to our national parks, historical and recreation areas would be clocked at another 156 million (*1971 Automobile Facts and Figures,* p. 51).

6. F. R. Dulles, *Americans Abroad: Two Centuries of European Travel* (Ann Arbor, Mich., 1964). Dulles points out (p. 65) that though the flow in those days was a mere trickle, Americans going abroad were already complaining of a tourist flood.

7. I have not attempted to review the medical or fictional literature on "cures," spas, hot springs, mountain air, or wayside hospitals. A brief and interesting reminder is Lino Businco, "Travel as a Form of Therapy," (*loc?*), and "Il Riposo e lo Svago nel Turismo," Clinica Europea, *Attualità di Medicino* (September–October 1964), vol. III, no. 5. See also John Baur's "Health Seeker in the Westward Movement," *Miss. Valley Histl. Rev.* (June 1959). Baur quotes P. T. Barnum as saying of the Coloradans: "Two-thirds of them come here to die *and they can't do it!*" And another observer reported that "in some sections, it was so healthy that a man had to be killed to start a burying ground."

8. Carl L. Biemiller, "Our Wonderful Restlessness," *Holiday* (July 1952). By 1967 the Census Bureau estimated that 17% of whole-

sale and 24% of retail sales were automotive (*1971 Automobile Facts and Figures,* p. 42).

9. *Oil Facts* (May–June 1968). The same newsletter identified New Hampshire as the most dependent state, with 44.9% of all its tax revenues deriving from highway user taxes. For more recent tax estimates, see *1971 Automobile Facts and Figures.* On Vermont as a world crossroads for "transplanted New Yorkers and other foreigners on a native granite population base," see James Egan, "The Exotic Green Mountains," *Saturday Review,* July 6, 1968. For further discussion of the economics of mobility, see also below, ch. 6.

10. I acknowledge my indebtedness to the most informative and entertaining discussion by Daniel Boorstin of "The Lost Art of Travel," in his *The Image or What Happened to the American Dream?* (quotations from pp. 91–2 and 110), with its appended bibliographical guide. Boorstin suggests that the old independent and painful art of travel has been changed by democratic participation and capitalistic enterprise into a pre-packaged tourism: a spectator sport with adventure eliminated, with the attractions artificially presented, and encounters with historic places, museums, and monuments organized into so many predetermined "pseudo-events." Ultimately, the sightseer now merely verifies his own images: "Whether we seek models of greatness, or experience elsewhere on the earth, we look into a mirror, instead of out of a window, and we see only ourselves" (p. 117). The reader will be interested in Rembert W. Patrick, "The Mobile Frontier" (*Journal of Southern History* [February 1963], XXIX:3–18) with its illuminating analysis of our tourism to Florida. See also the travel articles in the *Saturday Review,* April 22, 1967, especially George Nelson, "Architecture for the New Itinerants." How deeply all of this would have offended Dr. Johnson, for whom "the use of travelling is to regulate imagination by reality, and instead of thinking how things may be, to see them as they are." Piozzi, *Johnsoniana,* p. 154.

11. "Frayn in America: On the Road," *The Observer* (London), Nov. 20, 1966.

12. I am indebted to Denis Brogan for gentle reminder on this point. The National Safety Council estimates that in twenty-five years, 1946–70, the U.S. death rate per hundred thousand vehicle miles dropped from 11 to 5.

13. The mobility ratios for the young range from 40% up to 80% and then down again. The Summary Volume of the 1960 Census calculated that 47% of the total population 5 five years or older had moved between April 1955 and April 1960, i.e., 55% of those aged 5–9 years, 46% of those 10–14, 47% of those 15–19, and 73% of those 20–29; but only 27% of the population aged 75 to 79. In early life the moving ratios tend to be higher for intermediate- and upper-income levels, but after age 35 mobility seems to shift toward the lower-income levels as failure or waning employability forces moves to cheaper neighborhoods. See the illuminating essays in Iowa State University Center for Agricultural and Economic Development, *Family Mobility in Our Dynamic Society* (Ames, Iowa, 1965). For corroboration, and statistics on the age, sex, occupation, education, and wealth of local and long-distance movers, see ch. 15, "Internal Migration and Residential Mobility," in Donald J. Bogue, *The Population of the United States* (Glencoe, Ill., 1959).

14. American Movers Conference, as reported in New Haven *Register*, April 18, 1963. I am indebted to John William Ward for this item. One of the larger moving companies now offers *How to Buy a Move*, a step-by-step moving guide.

15. See the U.S. Census 1960, *Characteristics of Population: Summary*. Also *Historical Statistics of U.S., Colonial Times to 1957*, 1960, and *Statistical Abstract of U.S.*, 1970. Valuable analyses of the census returns may be found in Population Reference Bureau, Inc., *Population Bulletin* (esp. March 1963, February 1964, February 1970).

16. We have not even listed the subways or the superhighway interests, or the billboard industry, or the giant oil companies, or the state motor vehicle departments, or the police cruisers, or the parking meters, or the suppliers of road metal and asphalt. In its report "U.S. Travel—Like 2 Million Trips to the Moon," *Oil Facts* (November–December 1966) estimated that "highway transportation accounts for one out of every six businesses and one out of every seven jobs in the nation." Cf. above, note 8.

17. Cf. U.S. Bureau of the Census, *Statistical Abstract of the United States*, 1970, pp. 667–83. The following estimates are from *The New York Times*, March 15, 1954; *Herald Tribune*, Oct. 12, 1955; New Haven *Register*, April 18, 1963.

18. See T. Lynn Smith, *The Sociology of Rural Life* (rev. ed., New York, 1947), p. 196. A 1940 Census estimated that the average American farm had been in the same hands only twelve years.

19. Siegfried, *op. cit.*, p. 222. See also pp. 136–7.

20. *The New York Times,* Jan. 5, 1971. The figures showed a cancerous growth from about 2500 derelicts in 1960 to 23,386 in 1964 and 72,961 in 1970.

21. About the American style(s) of movement, and motion as the heartbeat of our cities, there are epics to be composed. Years ago I cut out of some magazine a prose paean with photographs —"New York: City in Motion. A place that never stops going, going—going where?" by Harold B. Clark, which captured some of the poetry of that immobile yet ceaselessly mobile metropolis. In 1963, in his "Sunny Thoughts on the Icy Attitude," Marshall W. Fishwick wrote: "European history has been described as man's heroic but tragic search for a 'closed system.' America has followed another star. She has tried, in Walt Whitman's words, to 'take the hinges off the door.' American history is process more than product; the process of motion into and out of cities . . . going west and coming east . . . moving up and down the social ladder. In Old-World cities, buildings cluster like sheep, and protect one another against open space. But in New York, notes Jean Paul Sartre, 'Your streets are not sober little walks closed in between houses, but national highways. The moment you set foot in one of them, you understand that they go on to Boston or Chicago.' What is basically 'American' is the concern with process. . . ."

22. H. Gordon Sweet, from his experience with redevelopment in New Haven, has both illuminated and corrected my image of the slums.

23. After writing this I came upon: "Life consists in motion; and, as far as that goes, the United States presents certainly the most animated picture of universal bustle and activity of any country in the world." Francis J. Grund, *The Americans in Their Moral, Social and Political Relations* (1837), II:226 (quoted in G. E. Probst, *The Happy Republic* [New York, 1962], p. 154). And in 1836 Michael Chevalier penned the same thought: "If movement and the quick succession of sensations and ideas constitute life, here one lives a hundredfold more . . .", *Soci-*

ety, Manners, and Politics, ed. by J. William Ward (New York, 1961), p. 299.

24. Lyman Bryson, *The Drive Toward Reason, in the Service of a Free People* (New York, 1954), p. 75.

25. Steinbeck, *Travels with Charley,* Part I, pp. 3, 4, 10; Part II, p. 24. Copyright © 1961–62 John Steinbeck. All rights reserved. Reprinted by permission of The Viking Press, Inc.

26. I borrow this image from Marcus Lee Hansen, *The Immigrant in American History* (Cambridge, Mass., 1948), p. 61. Hansen saw both the migratory habit and the kind of agriculture as responsible: "Aversion to neighbors encouraged the impulse. Every local history tells of the pioneer who departed hastily when he learned that another family had settled in the vicinity. The distant sound of a rifle or the smoke of a camp fire—signs betokening the arrival of newcomers—caused him to hurry to his cabin, whistle to his dog and be off. Even the more sociable individual was easily set in motion. With so much land to choose from, one could never be content with what he happened to possess. Somewhere was a perfect hundred-and-sixty-acre tract: the right balance of meadow, arable and forest, a clearer spring, a more sheltered spot for his home, more wild game in the woods and fewer snakes and crows. He heard that conditions were better in Ohio, then in Illinois, then in Kansas—and he tried them all. For forty or sixty years he wandered in the wilderness in search of the Canaan that he believed existed."

27. Admirers of Tom Wolfe may be reminded of his account of the bus trip and his description of the "Beautiful People," in *The Electric Kool-Aid Acid Test* (New York, 1969).

28. Alan Jay Lerner, *Paint Your Wagon* (New York, 1952), copyrighted © 1951 by Alan Jay Lerner and Frederick Loewe, quoted by permission of Chappell and Co., Inc.

29. See Irving Brown, "The Gypsies in America," *Journal of the Gypsy Lore Society,* 1929, 3rd series, vol. VIII, no. 4, pp. 145–76.

30. I draw these portraits from an AP dispatch, with photographs, printed in the New Haven *Register,* Feb. 28, 1971 (dateline North Platte), and from a special dispatch to *The New York Times,* Aug. 16, 1971.

31. I am relying for this and other shrewd and informative comments on Barbara Carter, "The Jalopy Nomads," *The Reporter*, May 7, 1964. She quotes Travelers Aid people on the evident "erosion of resources, possessions, self assurance, and even the ability to plan. Some of our callers seem all but hypnotized. . . ." They move "in an endless trip to nowhere. Children grow up in the back seats of cars and never see the inside of a schoolroom."

32. Some investigators seem to find that, if the statistical samples are controlled for sex and age, the incidence of mental instability is as high or higher in the resident population (see Dunham H. Warren's review of Mildred B. Kantor's "Mobility and Mental Health" in *Milbank Memorial Fund Quarterly* [January 1966], vol. XLIV, no. 1, pp. 122–9). But B. Malzberg and E. S. Lee, in *Migration in Relation to Mental Disease* (Albany, N.Y., 1956), find higher insanity rates among immigrants. See also the 1958 dissertation abstract of J. P. Brantner, "Homeless Men: A Psychological and Mental Survey," in J. J. Mangalam, *Human Migration* (Lexington, Ky., 1968); also H. E. Blair, "Human Relations Problems of Migratory Students," National Association of Secondary School Principals *Bulletin* (March 1955), 39:63–70; and L. C. Robins and P. O'Neil, "Mortality, Mobility, and Crime: Problem Children Thirty Years Later," *American Sociological Review* (April 1958), XXIII:162–71.

33. This interpretation goes back at least to 1928, when Robert R. Park in his "Human Migration and the Marginal Man" (*American Journal of Sociology*, XXXIII, no. 6) called attention to the instability of the "marginal man" between two cultures. His emphasis, however, was perhaps more on the challenge to greatness inherent in wandering.

34. Frayn, "Frayn in America: On the Road."

35. For "permanent," see T. S. Matthews, "But Westward, Look!," *The American Scholar* (Autumn 1964), p. 515. For a French view of our contemporary nomadism, see P. and R. Gosset in *Réalités* (August 1953), esp. p. 52: "Personne n'hésite jamais dans ce pays—nous l'avons constaté cent fois et peut-être allons-nous radoter, excusez-nous-en—à déménager, pour un oui ou un non, famille et possessions dans une autre ville, dans un autre Etat, sur une terre où l'on n'est pas encore serré, où les 'opportunités' sont meilleures. Dans le même esprit, jamais un Américain bien constitué n'hésitera à abattre 2,000 kilomètres

pour aller respirer l'air de la mer si l'envie impérieuse lui en vient soudain. Pour cet homme perpetuellement en camp volant dans sa maison ultra confortable mais toujours sans fondations, on ne sait plus très bien si le nomadisme est un besoin, un moyen ou un but. . . .
"On a dit souvent qu'à la base, l'Américain est un pionnier. C'est commode pour l'interpréter mais bien simpliste. Il est surtout un émigrant perpétuel, un homme qui n'est définitivement chez lui ni ici ni ailleurs et encore moins dans les terres épuisées et dans les idées reçues. C'est un être disponible, toujours prêt à prendre la route."

36. Margaret Mead, *Male and Female, A Study of the Sexes in a Changing World* (New York, 1949), p. 353. Longfellow and Sandburg are quoted from D. Kin, *American Maxims;* and Crèvecoeur's definition is from his classic essay, "What, then, is the American: this new Man?", *Letters of an American Farmer.*

5. Be It Ever So Mobile . . .

This chapter owes much to our poets, our dictionaries, John Steinbeck, the contributions of friendly scholars, and some recent literature on mobile homes.

1. E. E. Hale to his son, aged 8, May 18, 1873, in E. E. Hale, Jr., *The Life and Letters of Edward Everett Hale* (Boston, 1917), I:5. I owe this quotation to Helen C. Boatfield, scholar of American biography, Benjamin Franklin, and the history of Yale.

2. Helen C. Boatfield found me this letter of Feb. 6, 1917, from Arthur T. Hadley to Charles B. Jennings of New London, in the Hadley Papers, Yale University, vol. 30, p. 453.

3. Paul Moor, "On Horseback to Heaven: Charles Ives," *Harper's* (September 1947), CXCVII:66.

4. Henry Seidel Canby, *The Age of Confidence: Life in the Nineties* (New York, 1934), p. 258. For a moving evocation of the American family of the 1890's, see his *American Memoir* (Boston, 1947), pp. 29–42.

5. Sir Edward Coke, *Third Institute*, p. 162.

6. I am greatly indebted to Earl Hilton, professor of English at Northern Michigan University, for calling my attention to *The House of the Seven Gables, a Romance* (see 1851 ed., pp. 194, 271–5). Hawthorne must have thought a good deal about mo-

bility. "This life of wandering," he wrote in *French and Italian Travels* (1872), vol. I, p. 51, "makes a three days residence in one place seem like home." But in *The Scarlet Letter*, he explored the psychology of sinners who stayed to face the music.

7. Thornton Wilder, "Toward an American Language," *The Atlantic* (July 1952), CXC:33.

8. This and the following quotations are from D. Kin, *Dictionary of American Maxims*, p. 237.

9. Arthur Milliken to G.W.P., Dec. 28, 1962.

10. "But Westward, Look!," *The American Scholar* (Autumn 1964), XXXIV:516–17. Matthews observed that "in England many people still stay put, and have for generations; Americans like to see that, although it's a way we will never be ourselves. . . ." Almost sixty years earlier, Colton Maynard in London had noted the same thing: the English "represent something definite— lands and responsibilities, an empire in the aggregate; and our American bloods don't represent anything beyond their own selfish desires. Besides, the grandchildren of these same English will be living in the same houses, talking in the same Parliament, playing cricket at the same Lord's; but it would puzzle Ezekiel to figure out where the grandchildren of twentieth century Wall Street and Riverside Drive may land." Colton Maynard, *Letters and Journals*, ed. by his mother (Baltimore, Md., 1914), p. 135.

11. I am obliged to Professor Mario S. DePillis of the University of Massachusetts for this and other sayings. The search for that "rest, refuge or satisfaction" which home was supposed to provide can lead to strange destinations, e.g., the Y.M.C.A. or Y.W.C.A. of past generations—or that ever-fluid refuge, the "commune," in ours.

12. The literature on the American family is too voluminous for citation (cf. Ernest W. Burgess and Harvey J. Locke, *The Family, from Institution to Companionship* [New York, 1960]). But from the point of view of mobility one should note: the greater ease of moving as the extended family has shrunk to nuclear size; the easier escape from moral controls and community censures that movement makes possible; the decline of neighborliness with commuting; the impersonality of apartment house living; the high rates of divorce among transients. Also the decline of parental authority—or the younger generation's search

for quick prestige among strangers, as opposed to the building of social respect among friends and neighbors in a stable community. With many of the immemorial functions of the family now taken over by schools, even younger children get out of the house and parents find themselves "reduced to inter-institutional chauffeurs." (I have drawn illumination from "The American Family: A Composite Picture," Pop. Ref. Bureau Population Profile, Dec. 30, 1963; Dr. R. Cancro, "Preserving the Species," *Saturday Review*, March 6, 1971; Bryan Wilson, "War of the Generations," *Daily Telegraph* [London], Aug., 1964, an essay since incorporated in *The Youth Culture and the Universities* [London, 1970].)

13. *The New Yorker*, March 9, 1963, p. 150.

14. Peter Blake, on *Yale Reports*, May 25, 1959.

15. André Maurois, "Contrastes de la Civilisation Américaine," *Le Figaro* (?), Feb. (?) 1964. Maurois's figure of 10% seems high. The phrase "gift of Home" I have taken from Joyce Kilmer, *The Snowman in the Yard*.

16. I shamelessly borrow these and many other facts and fancies from the outstanding article by Virginia Held, "Home Is Where You Park It," in *The Reporter* for Feb. 18, 1960. To her analysis I have added some of Steinbeck's wry commentaries in *Travels with Charley* and in *Saturday Evening Post*, July 2, 1966, plus some statistics and observations from Wiley Maloney, "Americans Crazy for Moving," Austin *American*, April 28, 1967, courtesy John D. Cofer.

17. Douglas E. Kneeland, "From 'Tin Can on Wheels' to 'The Mobile Home,' " *The New York Times Magazine*, May 9, 1971.

18. Irvin M. Horowitz, "Home Is Where You Park," *The New York Times*, April 4, 1971.

19. Maloney, Austin *American*, April 28, 1967.

20. By Mobile Home/Recreational Vehicle Dealers *Magazine* (April 1971).

21. Mobile Home Manufacturers Association, *Mobile Homes*, 1971.

22. With the California trailer courts now "lapping up the sides of hills, spilling into river beds," Steinbeck predicted that new ways of taxation would have to be provided to cope with schooling and other public costs.

23. I have not mentioned houseboats, or their parks called "ma-

rinas," or the resulting water pollution now coming under public regulation.

6. The Fifth Freedom

My interest in the connections between movement and novelty or change goes back a good many years, and has survived a considerable series of interruptions and discouragements. It was first aroused, I think, by Tocqueville's American letters and diaries, which I had the good fortune to encounter in 1928, and which made possible my *Tocqueville and Beaumont in America* (1938). The problem of novelty then figured, somewhat marginally, in the series of critical essays which I wrote on Turner's frontier theory in the years 1940–2. World War II, and preoccupation with the modern history of Yale, prevented further pursuit until the autumn of 1954, when the *Yale Review* printed my first general conspectus, entitled "The Moving American." A Guggenheim Fellowship to pursue this theme was then pretty well canceled out by a bad accident, and this was followed by six years of academic administration. Another sabbatical saw me back on the trail, then another six years of quasi-administrative responsibilities interrupted again. Meanwhile I had managed to attack the problem of mobility from a variety of angles and interpret my findings in a series of essays. In July 1964, the *American Historical Review* (LXIX:969–89) ventured to publish my summary view of the influence of mobility on our institutions and social character under the title "A Restless Temper . . ." The present chapter is a considerable expansion and deepening of the first half of that essay.

1. *Le Nouveau Monde et l'Europe* (Neuvièmes Rencontres Internationales de Genève: Premières Rencontres Intellectuelles de Saõ Paulo) (Neuchâtel, 1955), p. 173 *et passim*.

2. Thornton Wilder, "Toward an American Language," *The Atlantic* (July 1952), CXC:29 ff.

3. H.-J. Duteil, *La Grande Parade Américaine* (Paris, 1949), pp. 55 ff.

4. Philip Guedalla, *The Hundred Years* (London, 1936), p. 159.

5. See Melvin J. Lasky, "A Conversation with George Kennan," *Encounter* (March 1960), LXXVIII:50; Lewis Mumford, *The City in History* (New York, 1961), p. 408; Peter Blake, *God's Own Junkyard: The Planned Deterioration of America's Landscape* (New York, 1964); Ada Louise Huxtable, *The New York*

Times Book Review, Jan. 12, 1964. See also Dennis Hayes, "Can We Bust the Highway Trust?", *Saturday Review,* June 5, 1971.

6. Jerry M. Flint, "Crossroads for the Auto: A Time of Challenge," *The New York Times,* International Automobile Show, April 4, 1971. The "sitting in a perpetual traffic jam" is from Frank Donovan, *Wheels for a Nation* (New York, 1965), p. 261. Donovan also quotes Allan Nevins (pp. 158–60): "that it helped to change the national psychology and national manners and mores as well as the national economy cannot be questioned. No other single machine in all probability did so much to induce people of provincial mind to begin thinking in national terms; none did so much to knit together different parts of the country; none did more to create a sense of a freer and more spacious life."

7. In VW's *Think Small,* by Charles Addams *et al.* (VW publication, 1967). Recently a delayed echo sounded in *Le Monde* (July 9, 1970), which first spoke of "an inestimable gift of liberty," and then added: "Le désir de posséder un moyen de transport privé est violent et très largement répandu."

8. Simeon Strunsky, *The Living Tradition* (New York, 1939), p. 172.

9. The decline of regional dishes and medical nostrums under the assault of moving inhabitants has been noted in England: "Tradition Follows in a Tin—In the Kitchen by Syllabub," *The Observer* (London), Dec. 3, 1961.

10. In 1927, in his *Social Mobility* (p. 389), P. Sorokin noted that "if we have in present Western society an increase in territorial migration of individuals and circulation of social things and values, this means an increase of horizontal mobility in double proportion." In his *U.S. 40* (Boston, 1953), George R. Stewart called attention to what absence of circulation can mean: "A road has been called a 'symbol of flow'—not only of people and things, but also of ideas. Close the roads, and you block the flow of ideas. Thus the Iron Curtain went down across the roads of Europe, and all the modern devices of printing and radio have not been able to compensate."

11. In his 1899 classic, *The Growth of Cities in the Nineteenth Century* (p. 428), A. F. Weber declared that the migration to the city caused the substitution of personal income taxes for

general property taxes. Perhaps we should notice that income is a transportable property, while land is not.

12. For my understanding of the constitutional history of human mobility in America, I am much indebted to Robert H. Alsdorf (then candidate at Yale for the LL.B. and the M.A. in history), "The Right to Travel in the United States, 1787–1970"—a paper as yet unpublished, completed in my seminar Dec. 26, 1970. The reader may wish to consult Freund, Sutherland, Howe, and Brown, *Constitutional Law: Cases and Other Problems* (1961 ed.), I:390–7.

13. I am under obligations, as to both legal information and cultural interpretation, to Mark V. Tushnet (then candidate at Yale for the LL.B. and the M.A. in history) for his as yet unpublished seminar report of Dec. 18, 1970, "The History of Laws Regulating Entry to and Exit from the United States." The quotations that follow are from this paper. For a review of some of the pertinent background, see *Kent* v. *Dulles,* 357 U.S. 116 (1958).

14. An informative and entertaining account is Trevor L. Christie, "The Pedigree of the Passport," *Saturday Review,* March 9, 1968.

15. *Lynd* v. *Rusk,* 389 F.2d 940 (D.C. Cir. 1967). Now it appears that an oath of loyalty may be required to secure a passport or its renewal from the State Department.

16. In 1948, some fifty nations did endorse the Universal Declaration of Human Rights, which in Article XIII stated:

    1. Everyone has the right to freedom of movement and residence within the borders of each state.

    2. Everyone has the right to leave any country including his own and return to his country.

    Yet in the past two decades the practices of the nations have hardly conformed to this declaration. Nor is there an enforcing power.

7. "A Restless Temper . . ."

I have transposed and reworked the second half of the essay originally published, under the same title, in the July 1964 issue of the *American Historical Review.*

1. See Ann Hightower, "French Myths about America," in *The New York Times Magazine,* Feb. 27, 1949: "Take the mattress

story [that in the U.S. mattresses are thrown away every two years]. It only confirms what the Frenchman already 'knows' to be true—that the American home is a reverse assembly line to convert the products of whirring factories back to basic rubble. He still imagines a solid stream of gadgets, clothes and household materials being delivered to the front door to be tossed out the back when slightly used. If Americans admit that there was a widespread practice of buying a new car every year and turning in the old one, no other tale is too fabulous for belief."

2. Everett S. Lee, "The Turner Thesis Re-examined," *American Quarterly* (Spring 1961), vol. XIII, no. 1, p. 82.

3. On the American's relations with nature, I have drawn stimulus from: John Steinbeck, "America and the Americans," *Saturday Evening Post*, July 2, 1966; Robert C. Cook, "Outdoor Recreation Threatened by Excess Procreation," *Population Bulletin* (June 1964); A. L. Huxtable's review of Peter Blake's *God's Own Junkyard* in *The New York Times Book Review*, Jan. 12, 1964; Hans Huth, *Nature and the American* (Berkeley, 1957). The ingrained commercialism of American farming was noted among others by Richard Hofstadter in *The Age of Reform* (New York, 1955), p. 43. Now some of our conservationists have been trying to revive themes from the romantic poets, e.g., Wallace Stegner's "Geography of Hope" in *Population Bulletin* (June 1964), XX:104—"I can remember old fellows in my home town speaking feelingly of an evening spent on the big empty plains. It had taken the shrillness out of them. They had learned the trick of quiet."

4. See above, ch. 6, and Thornton Wilder, "Toward an American Language," *The Atlantic* (July 1952).

5. Thistlethwaite, *The Great Experiment*, p. 160. The basic idea clearly derives from F. J. Turner, *The Frontier in American History*.

6. The study by Seymour Lipset and R. Bendix, *Social Mobility in an Industrial Society* (Berkeley, 1959), seems to be incomplete and in need of a good deal of verification.

7. Richard Hofstadter, "The Pseudo-Conservative Revolt," *The American Scholar* (Winter 1954–5), vol. 24, no. 1, p. 17.

8. "Ce que les Français pensent des Américains," *Réalités* (August 1953), p. 32.

9. James Pope-Hennessy, *America Is an Atmosphere* (London, 1947), p. 95.

10. Denis de Rougemont, *Vivre en Amérique* (Paris, 1947), p. 181.

11. Alphonse de Calonne, "Maisons hautes en Angleterre et en Amérique," *La Revue des deux mondes*, 1894, XCII:859.

12. "The United States in 1847," *A Sarmiento Anthology*, trans. by S. E. Crummon and ed. by A. W. Bunkley (Princeton, N.J., 1948). See esp. pp. 209–17.

13. Chevalier, *Society, Manners, and Politics* . . . , ed. by J. William Ward, pp. 60, 130, 204, 270, 299. I am indebted to Professor Ward for calling my attention to these observations.

14. See, for example, Crèvecoeur, *Letters from an American Farmer*, or the colonial observers cited above in ch. 1, notes 1 and 2.

15. G. W. Pierson, *Tocqueville and Beaumont in America* (New York, 1938), pp. 189, 192–3, 239–40, 286, 573, 579, 589–92. For subsequent references, see pp. 370, 399, 420, 440, 567–9, 602.

16. Alexis de Tocqueville, *Democracy in America*, ed. by Phillips Bradley (New York, 1945), II:136–7.

17. Pierson, *Tocqueville and Beaumont in America*, pp. 118–19. The Pierson translation was made from a ms. copy of the Tocqueville diary, transcribed and forwarded in the 1920's by the local Tocqueville instituteur, Bonnel. The original text—which has now been established and printed by J. P. Mayer [and A. Jardin] in Alexis de Tocqueville, *Oeuvres Complètes* (Paris, 1957), V, *Voyages en Sicile et aux Etats-Unis*, pp. 208–9—shows additional paragraphing, one transposition of a sentence, and a few slight differences of wording; these do not produce any change of meaning. Cf. the new translation by George Lawrence in Alexis de Tocqueville, *Journey to America*, ed. J. P. Mayer (New Haven, 1960), pp. 182–3. For reasons that a comparison will make clear, I have preferred to read Tocqueville's message from my own (textually defective) translation.

8. Any "Laws of Migrability"?

1. E. G. Ravenstein, "The Laws of Migration," *Journal of the Royal Statistical Society* (June 1885), 48:167–235; and also "The Laws of Migration," *Journal of the Royal Statistical Society* (June 1889), 52:241–301 (see Reprints S-482, S-483

in Bobbs-Merrill reprint series in the Social Sciences). In these two papers Ravenstein summarized his conclusions, but not always in the same language or order; hence his "Laws" are only to be stated approximately. For a good analysis, see E. S. Lee, "A Theory of Migration," presented at the Mississippi Valley Historical Association meeting, April 23, 1965, and published in *Demography*, III, 1966. A capsule recapitulation might be:

I. Migration has many causes, but easily the greatest is the desire to "better" oneself.

II. The great majority proceed only a short distance—and females predominate.

III. Long-distance migrations go to great centers of commerce and industry—and are predominantly male.

IV. Inhabitants immediately around towns of rapid growth flood in; the gaps are filled by migrants from more remote districts, until the pull is felt a long way.

V. Each main current produces a compensating counter-current of feebler strength with similar features.

VI. The town-born are less migratory than the rural-born.

VII. "Migration means life and progress; a sedentary population stagnation"—and migration is increasing.

2. Ellsworth Huntington's interest in migration seems to have come about through a rather curious progression. He began with his great environmental hypothesis about climate and civilization, only to find that peoples in similar climates acted quite differently. This led him to insist on character also in race or kinship groups, a biological explanation, yet mysteriously groups of the same blood stock in the same climate belt still acted differently. So he was driven to recognize differences between moving and sedentary populations. He studied the Norse settlers of Iceland, the Parsees of India, the Jews, and the Puritan settlers of New England (the later movements of the Huntington family, and a number of occupational groups); and he emerged with file drawers of statistics and strong convictions about the selective influence of migration. His views may most readily be consulted in "Migration and Human Quality" (ch. 5 of *Mainsprings of Civilization* [New York, 1945]); but see also "The Selective Action of Migration," in *Zbiór Prac* (Lwów, 1934).

I had the pleasure of knowing Ellsworth Huntington at Yale,

and on March 4, 1942, recorded a long interview with him on "Laws of Migration." Reading through the four pages of dense pencilings, I am struck by how many of the ideas that have come to seem basic to me since appeared in that long interview. I should like here to record my indebtedness and gratitude.

3. In his *Social Mobility*, 1927, Pitirim A. Sorokin focused his attention on vertical mobility and based his findings quite largely on Russian materials and reports. But toward the end (pp. 508 ff.) he paid some attention to spatial mobility, and to its *effects* both for society and for the individual.

The social effects he saw as: (1) Under some conditions mobility facilitates a better distribution of individuals—there are fewer entrenched minorities; (2) it favors prosperity and social progress—up to a saturation point; (3) the continuity of the culture complex is shortened; (4) mobility favors atomization, and the diffusion of loyalties and antagonisms; (5) it favors increase of individualism, followed by a vague cosmopolitanism and collectivism[!].

As for the effects on individual behavior and psychology, he thought that: (1) Behavior becomes more plastic and versatile; (2) there is decrease of narrow-mindedness and occupational idiosyncrasies; (3) but increase of mental strain and nervousness; (4) mobility facilitates inventions and discoveries, through the greater chance of lucky combinations; (5) also intellectual life; (6) but also mental diseases; (7) mobility encourages superficiality, and decreases sensitiveness (otherwise we would go crazy), and it makes for impatience and touch-and-go habits; (8) it generates skepticism, cynicism, aversion to theory, and encourages anti-intellectualism, and drives the uneducated to sudden dogmas; (9) it diminishes intimacy with men or with things, increases loneliness, restlessness, sensual pleasures, and suicide; and (10) facilitates the disintegration of morals.

Sorokin's views, though neglecting causes, have exercised a quite discernible influence on my thinking about the psychological results of mobility.

4. Rudolf Heberle, *Über die Mobilität der Bevölkerung in den Vereinigten Staaten* (Jena, 1929). This study recognized many kinds of social movements and wide social effects; mobility's special appeal to dissenters, speculators, and romantics; the generation of moving habits, or mobility as a *Gewohnheit*, and the acceptance of impermanence as a norm. Heberle pointed

out that immigrants were less mobile than third- or fourth-generation Americans; that mobility discouraged spiritual and artistic life, decreased community spirit, made patriarchal family life almost nonexistent, and drove Americans into lodges, clubs, or associations instead. The atomization of society favored anonymity, conformity, intolerance, and an "incredible herd-spirit" (Huizinga). Heberle saw the Americans as Enlightenment individualists by inheritance—by practice turned into atomic men.

Once more I should like to acknowledge my obligations, and not least for the quotation from Leacock's poem, "I Wish I Could Remember" (see above, ch. 1).

5. See research memoranda by Thompson, Vance, and Thomas for the Social Science Research Council (*Bulletins* 30, 42, 43), 1937, 1938. A useful follow-up study—again revealingly inconclusive—was Albert Hoyt Hobbs, *Differentials in Internal Migration* (Philadelphia, 1942). See also the Scripps Foundation Studies by Donald J. Bogue and Margaret M. Hagood, *Subregional Migration in the United States, 1935–1940*, and *Differential Migration in the Corn and Cotton Belts* (Oxford, Ohio, 1953).

6. Among the more significant and rewarding studies have been: John R. Commons, *Races and Immigrants in America*, 1930; Carl Wittke, *We Who Built America*, 1939; Theodore C. Blegen, *Norwegian Migration to America*, 2 vols, 1931, 1940; Frank Thistlethwaite, *Migration from Europe Overseas in the Nineteenth and Twentieth Centuries*, XI, Congrès International des Sciences Historiques, 1960; Franklin D. Scott, *Emigration and Immigration*, A.H.A. Service Center, 1963; Maurice R. Davie, *World Immigration, With Special Reference to the U.S.*, 1936; Marcus Lee Hansen, *The Atlantic Migration, 1607–1860*, 1940; Oscar Handlin, *The Uprooted*, 1951; N. Glazer and D. C. Moynihan, *Beyond the Melting Pot*, 1963; Stephan Thernstrom, *Poverty and Progress: Social Mobility in a Nineteenth Century City*, 1964; Walter F. Willcox (ed.), *International Migration*, 2 vols., 1929, 1931; Everett S. Lee, "A Theory of Migration," *Demography*, III, 1966.

7. The work of C. C. Zimmerman, O. Klineberg, P. H. Landis, H. S. Shryock, Jr., R. Centers, and many others may be followed in the *American Sociological Review, American Journal of Sociology*, and *Social Forces*. See also D. J. Bogue, "Internal Migra-

tion," in *The Study of Population,* ed. by P. Hauser and O. D. Duncan (Chicago, 1959). J. J. Mangalam, *Human Migration: A Guide to Migration Literature in English, 1955–1962* (Lexington, Ky., 1968), is useful for its abstracts and quotations, but dispiriting in its revelation of the intellectual and interpretive vacuity of the great bulk of the sociological studies of our population movements. By contrast the reports in the *Population Bulletin* of the Population Reference Bureau, Inc., are not only informative but often pointed and revealing.

8. Everett S. Lee, formerly of the Population Studies Center at the University of Pennsylvania and more recently chairman of Sociology and Anthropology at the University of Massachusetts, has a number of significant publications to his credit, including: (with Benjamin Malzberg), *Migration and Mental Disease,* Soc. Sc. Research Council, 1956; "The Turner Thesis Re-examined," *American Quarterly* (Spring 1961); (with others) *Population Redistribution and Economic Growth, 1870–1950,* vol. II (Philadelphia, 1964); "A Theory of Migration," *Demography,* 1966, III, no. 1, pp. 47–57; and "America: A Nation of Migrants," *Vital Issues,* Center for Information on America (March 1967), 16: no. 7.

Coming into spatial mobility from demography and close study of the census schedules, with a special interest in economic groups and social categories—while I developed my historical interest, from a concern with Tocqueville, Turner, and culture transfer, toward a special curiosity about the psychology of mobility and what that psychology has meant for the American character—Lee and I have found our ideas converging, and our conclusions remarkably complementary. For a full appreciation of Lee's contributions, the reader should consult his Turner and *Vital Issues* articles and especially "A Theory of Migration." Yet perhaps, for purposes of comparison and accreditation, a condensed summary of the theory will be useful here.

Lee defines migration as "a permanent or semi-permanent change of residence" (thus excluding nomads, migratory workers, and vacationers). The factors in the decision to migrate are associated with the points of origin or of destination, the "intervening obstacles," and personal factors. Some elements are attractive, some repellent, on the average, to identifiable classes or groups; but individuals escape certain prediction;

"there is always an element of ignorance or even mystery about the area of destination"; it is the perception of the pluses and minuses that overcomes or reinforces the natural inertia; "the decision to migrate, therefore, is never completely rational"; and there will be many exceptions because of transient emotions, mental disorder, and accidents. There will also be times or ages when bonds are slackened suddenly—such as graduation, the first job, marriage, etc.—or sudden openings that overcome the negative prospects.

From these generalizations Lee proceeds to a series of hypotheses on the volume of migration. The volume will vary with the degree of diversity of the area of destination, and the diversity of the people involved; it will depend on the difficulty of the intervening obstacles, the expanding or contracting economy, and the progressiveness of the country; unless checks are imposed, both volume and rate will tend to increase.

Next, Lee develops one of Ravenstein's insights, the idea that migration proceeds in a well-defined stream, and generates a counter-stream—the efficiency of the migration (or net redistribution) being high if the major motives were dissatisfactions at home or if the intervening obstacles are great or if the economy is prosperous, low in depression, or if the points of origin and destination are similar.

Migrants, Lee states, "are not a random sample of the population at origin," but are selected because of differing responses. The selection will tend to be positive (for high quality) if the movers are responding to plus factors at the destination, negative (for low quality or failures) if to minus factors at origin, perhaps nonselective if the minus factors are "overwhelming." Taking all migrants together, selection tends to be bimodal; "that is, if their characteristics are plotted along a continuum ranging from poor to excellent, we often get a J-shaped or U-shaped curve." Intervening difficulties and distance increase the positive selection, whereas the less able tend simply to mill around in a restricted area. To which Lee adds an unexpected and challenging observation. Since migrants tend to have taken on already some of the characteristics of the population at destination, they will tend to be intermediate between the two populations, and may lower the quality of population, in terms of some characteristic, at both origin and destination (as, for example, in fertility or in education).

In Lee's other publications may be found further observations on the age-sex-occupation-education characteristics of migrants, on higher rates of mental illness, on other-directedness and pragmatism, gregariousness and superficiality, carelessness of surroundings, and change for change's sake. Among the social consequences will be the breakdown of the large family and of hereditary élites, the substitution of laws for customs, and the stimulation of nationalism (the convergence of Lee and Pierson is often worth remarking).

9. This three-part classification has been found useful by many analysts, though the precise titles may vary and the journey may be subordinated to the concept of "intervening obstacles" (cf. Lee).

10. I borrow emphasis and phrasing from William Carlson Smith's most useful *Americans in the Making: The Natural History of the Assimilation of Immigrants* (New York, 1939). For Wilder, see his *Atlantic* article.

11. Thistlethwaite, *Migration from Europe Overseas* . . . , p. 56; and *The Great Experiment*, pp. 106, 224, *et passim*.

12. Thistlethwaite, *Migration from Europe Overseas* . . . ; Mumford, *The Golden Day*, p. 11. I owe no inconsiderable debt to the first two, seminal chapters of Mumford's classic.

13. This range of questions was originally suggested to me by Ellsworth Huntington.

14. Huntington talked to me also about counter-selection by social events, e.g., the sudden drift of bums to Boston in the hope of loot during the police strike.

15. This idea has been disputed. And of course there must be varying susceptibilities, depending on the mental or psychological disturbance. But on the basic proposition I believe investigation will ultimately support Everett S. Lee.

16. Huntington told me that temperament was more important than education in promoting mobility.

17. For emphasis on the transfer points I am indebted to Lee, for distinction of occupation and distance and timing originally to Huntington.

18. Hobbs, *op. cit.*

19. Cf. Lee on volume, and on the intermediate character of the transfer population, with its averaging down of quality levels at both origin and destination (see above, note 8).

20. Theoretically, the economic determinists are open to the charge that they are deterministic, mutually contradictory, and inclined to reduce human beings to the status of robots in a crude materialistic game theory played by economic man. Specifically, the population studies of the 1930's and 1940's by C. Goodrich, F. Lorimer and F. Osborne, and Paul H. Landis were numerically interesting but psychologically simplistic and naïve. In 1926, H. Jerome made a useful contribution with his *Migration and the Business Cycles;* and J. Isaacs, *Economics of Migration,* 1947, still seems a broad and sensible survey of a long time span; but Brinley Thomas's acclaimed *Migration and Economic Growth,* 1954, strikes this reader as supersophisticated in its mathematical economics while almost totally disregarding the human elements in the equation: as if accident, or personality, or wide range of human emotions and motivations, or the extremely varied cultural and ethnic groups engaged in the process of immigration had nothing to do with the quantity and quality of the movement.

21. This runs counter to the assumptions of most historians and sociologists of American immigration, but will perhaps seem more reasonable to students of the long European experience. Lee's conclusions are more balanced but possibly lean my way.

22. At least in the past 140 years. Before that the smallness of the vessels, the dangers of the ocean, and the primitive state of navigation may have justified Dr. Johnson in his characteristic obiter dictum that "being in a ship is being in a jail, with the chance of being drowned" (Boswell's *Life*). Cf. also the judgment of Vere Gordon Childe, *What Happened in History* (Harmondsworth, Middlesex, 1946), p. 183, that "migration by sea owing to the slow, precarious and irregular voyages of ancient ships always involved a greater dislocation and disassociation of cultural elements than follows upon landwise migrations. By the voyage itself the component elements get jolted out of the rigid frame of custom in which they are embedded. . . ."

23. The reader will note my failure to list or assess what Lee and others describe as "intervening obstacles," e.g., wars or export laws or immigration quotas, etc. After some hesitation I incline to associate most such obstacles—when not really journey-connected—as belonging to the sending or the receiving societies, hence more appropriately studied within those categories; yet their very particularity makes it hard to generalize about them.

9. *"Move Effects"?*

1. In this chapter I take into consideration not all the effects of migration but some of the more inescapable consequences, first for the home country or community of origin, and next for the receiving country or society at destination. This leaves the impact of movement on the movers themselves for examination in the following chapter. But also, as the discerning reader will come to realize, it relegates the middle passage—or the effects of migration traffic on the pathways of movement—to a brief comment (see below, note 6). And it omits almost altogether the tremendously important prospects for cultural diffusion.

   This omission is regrettable but, as it seems to me, unavoidable. For the subject of culture contacts is too vast, too intricate, and too unexplored. It is true that certain anthropologists, from the days of Clarke Wissler and even earlier, became interested in the cultural as well as the demographic implications of diffusion for primitive or prehistoric man—and so initiated, a good half century ago, a discussion of culture centers and provinces, of culture carriers, of culture spread and modification, of culture contacts, repulsions, adjustments, assimilations, and survivals. Yet these pioneer efforts seem never to have been carried to fulfillment. And the cues they offered to historians, in command of a far fuller documentary evidence, failed to elicit any laws or schemes of probability. In a crude way no historian, dealing with a society's past or its neighborly relations, can avoid commenting, intentionally or unintentionally, on the spread of trade and of men and ideas. I have myself for many years tried deliberately to teach a course on the foreign contacts of American culture, and so could venture, from the American experience, some quasi-educated hypotheses for consideration. But that would have to be another book. So my cultural commentary in the second half of this chapter will be confined to some of the most obvious gross effects of our immigration and mobility.

2. Franklin D. Scott, in his "The Study of the Effects of Emigration," in *Scandinavian Economic History Review* ([1960], vol. VIII, no. 2, pp. 161–74), asks some important questions about the relation of emigration to social change, and suggests some of the probable answers.

3. So the Western frontier of the United States helped keep the East an open society, in part through the actual exploitation

of its abundance, but in large part as an idea of space and a reserve of free opportunity.

4. Cf. Halvdan Koht, *The American Spirit in Europe* (Philadelphia, 1949). This was an early, somewhat elementary survey of the eighteenth- and nineteenth-century repercussions, as seen by a distinguished Norse statesman from a north European point of view; but in its breadth, generosity, and imagination it sketched a panorama that has not yet been bettered, or filled in.

5. See the various studies (previously cited) by Franklin D. Scott; also his "The Causes and Consequences of Emigration in Sweden," *The Chronicle of the American Swedish Historical Fdn.* (Spring 1955); and "The Study of the Effects of Emigration," *Scandinavian Economic History Review,* vol. VIII, no. 2. For a variety of slants on emigration, see also Scott's edited *World Migration in Modern Times* (Englewood Cliffs, N.J., 1968).

6. At this point, an orderly analysis of move effects might take up the roads and ask about the impact of migration on man's systems for movement: on the overland journey, the transatlantic passage, the national or interurban transportation facilities, the commuters' rails and roads, or the rapid transit system within a city. But these are matters of great complexity. Because the movement of goods has often been the dominant force, the logistics of transportation and the economics of production and distribution have played a large role. Because journey lines so often crossed political boundaries, unnatural arrests or transfer points have been introduced. On top of that, the sociology of the highway is a considerable subject in itself; and as a humanist I am too ill-equipped for any attempt here to formulate a set of rules for the road. Yet certain long-range trends seem so evident as to deserve recognition, and further study by those interested in human mobility.

The first trend, historically, seems to have been the improvement of the means of transportation, as the growing movements of goods and of men created the demands and supplied the economic warranty, and as the technological conquest of space and time made a slow but accelerating progress. This improvement has been clearest in bulk, in speed, and in distance—but also in comfort and convenience.

The second great trend was then the emasculation of the journey. The dangers, hazards, and adventures have been minimized. Exposure was once one of the most powerful ingredients of the experience. No longer. We travel, strapped in, in glass and steel capsules, down steel or concrete grooves. Excitement? Even round-the-world flying takes place in standard containers. And much of the excitement has been drained off. Instead, the transportation systems have taken to substituting a set of commonplace and boring experiences: the car radio, the in-flight movie, etc. And Daniel Boorstin can claim that travel has been reduced to "pseudo-events."

A third long-range trend, and unmistakable, has been the clustering of production and sales and services and other businesses not only at the end but all along the arteries of transportation. A part of this was natural: the arteries were made for the exchange of goods. But a part was parasitical: the businessman came to feed on the traveler, immediately or by suggestion. Hence the roadside stands, shopping centers, and billboard industry. Indeed, the businesses of all sorts conducted along and with the traffic finally so impede that traffic—and the old artery becomes so clogged—that a new turnpike or interstate expressway has to be carved out of the countryside. Perhaps the parkways, restricted to passenger vehicles only, will testify not only to the seriousness of the arterial sclerosis but to the importance of the traveler in contemporary society? In any case, mobile societies seem ever to be adding new roads to old, and not just because the traffic has grown but because the old roads have become too encrusted with businesses trying to feed on the mobility. (How long will it be before satellite advertisements are sent into orbit to greet us air travelers at 35,000 feet? We have already planted a flag and a golf ball on the moon.)

Perhaps a fourth line of thought is more intriguing: Can one not describe a society by its roads, and its road signs?

10. And What Happens to Those Who Go?
This chapter, which analyzes the implications of the Fourth and Second Laws of Migration, is a summary of what, over a good many years of teaching, reading, and reflection, I think I have learned or can believe about the effects that movement is likely to have for the movers themselves and for their "household possessions."

1. This is a difficult and delicate point, and for several reasons. On the one hand, cultural historians will justifiably argue that toleration must have been already endemic in any parent society that would allow or generate such a diversity of enterprise

and competitive settlement in the first place. On the other hand, geographers and environmental historians will be inclined to give much of the credit to the lay of the land. In terms of comparative geography, the Spanish monarchs seem to have commanded New Spain through the single port of entry at Vera Cruz, the annual treasure fleets, and the prohibition of any commerce with outsiders—just as the kings of France ruled far-flung New France very conveniently through garrison towns commanding the great St. Lawrence entry to the continent. Whereas on the long indented Atlantic coastline between these two secure points of control, a man could go ashore almost anywhere.

Was it therefore geographic opportunity or the multiplicity and competitive character of private enterprise in old England or the quasi-social, quasi-psychological factor of mobility that generated the gradual but notable increase of toleration in the English settlements? The answer, I think, is all three. Let us envisage some speculative alternatives. Had the land claims been transposed, would their Spanish majesties—backed by their feudal bureaucracy and abetted on every hand by the autocratic and all-seeing Catholic Establishment—have allowed so many colonists and colonies in North America? Not if they could have helped it. But in the long run could they have prevented? Once again, how many garrisons would Louis XIV have needed to hold the river mouths and great bays and snug harbors all the way from Portsmouth to St. Augustine? One comes back to the thought that in fact both Spain and France tried to discourage free movement, along with other kinds of freedom and toleration; but these very discouragements proved long-range handicaps to their empires, since they meant far fewer men and far less enterprise and variety and strength. Meanwhile, and even despite the jugular controls, it was noticeable that the Atlantic distances and the opportunities of the New World interior brought evasion and evident corrosion of authority to the royal dependencies.

2. I have not seen this point made quite adequately, but André Maurois came close and John Steinbeck had hold of some of the elements. In "Contrastes de la Civilisation Américaine" (*Le Figaro* (?), Feb. (?) 1964), Maurois remarked on the absolutism and extremism and rebelliousness of Americans: "L'Américain voit tout en noir et blanc. En politique internationale, il cherche

des héros et des traîtres. Or, le plus souvent, il n'a devant lui que de pauvres hommes mêlés de fautes et de vertus. Le goût de l'Anglais pour le compromis parait souvent lâcheté ou cynicisme à l'Américain, cependant que l'intransigeance morale de l'Américain inquiète et choque l'Anglais. Ce goût américain des solutions extrêmes est d'ailleurs assez facile à comprendre. Qui a fait la civilisation américaine? Des Européens venus vers ce continent nouveau justement parce qu'ils voulaient une solution extrême. Ils étaient partis parce qu'ils ne pouvaient supporter certains formes de tyrannie, parce qu'ils étaient des rebelles. Et rebelles ils sont restés."

In his piece on "America and the Americans" in the *Saturday Evening Post* (July 2, 1966), Steinbeck focused rather on our extremism, our lack of restraint: "For the most part we are an intemperate people; we eat too much when we can, drink too much, indulge our senses too much. Even in our so-called virtues we are intemperate: a teetotaler is not content not to drink —he must stop all the drinking in the world; a vegetarian among us would outlaw the eating of meat. We work too hard, and many die under the strain; and then to make up for that we play with a violence just as suicidal."

3. If I seem to be substituting mobility for sex urges or parental fixations as the cause of at least some of the anxieties all about us, I hope I may be forgiven. Surely good sense will suggest that not all the ills and insecurities afflicting our rudderless generation should be blamed on a biological urge which has always been there, or on parents who used to be far more powerful for good or evil than they now are. Obviously, this is an oversimplification: I do not mean to caricature all modern psychiatry. But whether our soul doctors understand motion sickness remains a fair question.

4. Not all the Puritans, obviously. Witness the Puritans who migrated to the sugar islands of the West Indies. Yet their very choice of destination and company suggests that perhaps a Puritan devotion had not been the first and commanding reason for their moving? Or else they had not been able to pass on their vision; so their sons (like the descendants of the early Yankee missionaries in Hawaii) became sugar missionaries instead?

11. The M-Factor in American History

The challenge to summarize the influence of movement on the American Character, and to analyze mobility's systematic promotion of change, first presented itself in August 1957 when the American Studies Association held a joint session with the American Sociological Society in Washington on "Migration as a Force in American Civilization," with papers by Everett S. Lee and G. W. Pierson, and comments by Rupert B. Vance. A meeting of the New England American Studies Association at Brown University just a few weeks later provided a second chance to argue the question of an "American Character," and his relation to "The Moving American."

The next opportunity came in late June of 1961 when, by invitation, twelve professors from New Haven under the leadership of Hajo Holborn gave an "American Week" at the University of Munich—with some thirty-five sessions on the history, law, literature, art, philosophy, psychology, and economy of the American people. Under the title *Amerikanische Gelehrtenwoche,* and with a foreword by Rektor Julius Speer, a number of our addresses (including "The Migratory American") were printed by Ludwig-Maximilian-Universität in 1962. The same year saw the reproduction of my paper—with some slight textual amendments but now under the title, "The M-Factor in American History"—in the *American Quarterly* (summer supplement 1962), XIV:275–9 (Bobbs-Merrill reprint:H-314). I am indebted to Hennig Cohen for criticism and encouragement and to the Trustees of the University of Pennsylvania for permission to reproduce considerable parts of that revised essay and work them into the closing argument of this book.

1. Turner, *The Frontier in American History,* p. 37. See also pp. 3–4 *et passim.*

2. The "frontier" dispute generated a voluminous periodical literature, which deserves analysis and appraisal but which has been too variegated and complex for examination here. Suffice it to suggest that in the long run most of the defenses of the Turner hypothesis, or attempts at rehabilitation, will be found to be either emotional defenses of a beloved individual and his myth, or illustrations of small, fragmented, and quite inadequate segments of his hypothesis, presented as if such had been the kernel or even the whole of Turner's thought. The frontier as romantic memory and as mystique will survive. But the grand frontier hypothesis of renovation and Americanization, as origi-

nally presented in Turner's essays, can hardly be resuscitated and made to stand.

3. Cf. Mumford's declaration (*The Golden Day,* p. 74), that "the Protestant, the inventor, the politician, the explorer, the restless delocalized man—all these types appeared in Europe before they rallied together to form the composite American." See also M. L. Hansen's insistence that "Mass migration was the result of the breakup of something old and it was the preliminary of something new. It was a sign of change and it hastened change." *The Immigrant in American History* (Cambridge, Mass., 1948), p. 13.

4. From "Fast Freight" as rendered by the Kingston Trio in the late 1950's.

5. The alliance between movement and hope has been recognized by many. "The faith in the potentialities of Moving On springs from the optimism which is such an attractive and humanistic attribute of the American character, and nourishes the sense of liberty which Americans undoubtedly feel. Like the hope of heaven, it makes the shortcomings of the here and now endurable. . . ." Frayn, "Frayn in America, On the Road." Or again, "In a world of changing opportunities, the ability to move at will offers greater security to many persons than the most favored location." C. T. Little, *The Restless Americans* (New York, 1940), p. 32.

6. See George Santayana, "A Glimpse of Yale," *Harvard Monthly* (December 1892), XV:89–97.

7. Independently, and perhaps earlier, Frank Thistlethwaite reached the same conclusion. I would again refer the reader to the many perceptions in his *The Great Experiment.* And I again recommend Everett S. Lee's 1957 American Studies paper, as later printed under the title "The Turner Thesis Reexamined," *American Quarterly* (Spring 1961).

Index

Index

Index

Index

xi

Index

A Note About the Author

George Wilson Pierson was born in New York City in 1904 and received his B.A. (1926) and Ph.D. (1933) from Yale University. Since 1926 he has been a member of the Faculty of Yale, becoming Professor of History in 1944 and Larned Professor of History in 1946. He was Chairman of the Department of History from 1956 to 1962 and Director of the Division of Humanities from 1964 to 1970, and has been a Fellow of Davenport College since its founding.

Mr. Pierson has long been interested in the American character. His studies have ranged from Alexis de Tocqueville to the modern university, and from the frontier interpretation of American history to a pioneer course on the 400-year transit of culture across the Atlantic, as well as the more recent return impact of the American way of life around the world.

Aside from his influential critique of the frontier mystique, and a number of articles on the elective system, the rise of graduate education, the uses of history, and the role of the humanities in a liberal education, he is the author of: *Tocqueville and Beaumont in America* (1938); *Yale College: An Educational History, 1871–1921* (1952); and *Yale: The University College, 1921–1937* (1955); also *The Education of American Leaders: Comparative Contributions of U.S. Colleges and Universities* (1969).

The Moving American was conceived in the early 1950's, and was initially pursued as a Guggenheim Fellowship project, in France in 1955–56.

A Note About the Type

The text of this book is set in Caledonia, a type face designed by W(illiam) A(ddison) Dwiggins for the Mergenthaler Linotype Company in 1939. Dwiggins chose to call his new type face Caledonia, the Roman name for Scotland, because it was inspired by the Scotch types cast about 1833 by Alexander Wilson & Son, Glasgow type founders. However, there is a calligraphic quality about Caledonia that is totally lacking in the Wilson types. Dwiggins referred to an even earlier type face for this "liveliness of action"—one cut around 1790 by William Martin for the printer William Bulmer. Caledonia has more weight than the Martin letters, and the bottom finishing strokes (serifs) of the letters are cut straight across, without brackets, to make sharp angles with the upright stems, thus giving a "modern face" appearance.

W. A. Dwiggins (1880–1956) began an association with the Mergenthaler Linotype Company in 1929 and over the next twenty-seven years designed a number of book types, the most interesting of which are the Metro series, Electra, Caledonia, Eldorado, and Falcon.

This book was composed, printed and bound by H. Wolff Book Mfg. Co., New York, N.Y.

Typography and binding design are by Christine Aulicino.